There Is A Generation

WH Buzzard

ISBN: 1500385271
ISBN 13: 9781500385279
Library of Congress Control Number: 2014912531
CreateSpace Independent Publishing Platform
North Charleston, South Carolina

Cast of Characters

Timothy ("Tim"): an adventurous young mischief-maker
Hector ("Hect"): orphaned school dropout and Tim's best friend
Tim's mother: married but basically raising Tim as a single mom
Tim's father: an alcoholic who frequents posh "drying out" centers
Phantom: a hallucination that haunts Tim
Sheriff: a no-nonsense lawman with a desire to help troubled kids
Mauler: sheriff's dog, half chow, half Irish setter
Old man in '48 Chevy: murder mystery buff and reader of detective magazines
Eli: cowboy owner of The Pines Diner in Ruidoso, New Mexico
Snowball: married to Eli and a waitress at The Pines Diner
Zelda: girl who picks up Tim while hitchhiking
Sophia: bandleader and poetess
Lady and her son in Cadillac: rescues Tim off a New Mexico highway
T.J.: father of Becca, scam artist and trucker who reluctantly gives Hect a ride
Becca: T.J.'s beautiful but cunningly treacherous daughter
Rummy: homeless ex-prize fighter
Fast-One: work café owner known for her cruel practical jokes
Jake: arsonist and alcoholic bully
Blackie: a gigantic scorpion
Half Ear: one of three mules that befriend Tim
Bernardo and Maria: a farming couple in the desert of Mexico
Victor: a friend of Bernardo's
Juweel ("Ju"): a man without a country from somewhere in Africa

Contents

TO JOANIE, MY FIRST EDITOR,
AND TO LESLIE, MY MENTOR

There is a generation that curses its father,
And does not bless its mother.
                          Prv. 30:11

West Texas

Early 1950's

1

War Games

"SNATCH UP THAT rifle, goldbricker."

I lifted my head out of my hands. "I'm half-dead, you know?"

"Yeah, yeah, half-dead, I know, I know." Hect lay atop the fender of the truck's crushed headlight, positioned his rifle on the hood, and fired repeatedly. The shack he aimed at absorbed the shots to no greater effect than if they'd all missed, except for a tinkle of glass now and then when a bullet nicked a shard left in the window frame. Out of ammunition, he sat on the running board beside me. I could feel his disgust.

"It's a mighty sorry soldier what leaves a weapon in the dirt like that. It'd serve you right if they come yelling for blood out'a that bunker with guns blazing and your barrel's clogged up."

"I don't feel good, I told you."

"Humpteen jillion times, 's'all. That's humpteen jillion and one." He reloaded his rifle.

Damaged cars lay all around—some turned on one side, others upside down, still others demolished beyond recognition. Many had bullet holes that spider-webbed the glass of several windows.

The West Texas sun hammered our heads like nails. Heat off the metal truck body felt hot as off a stovetop. Worse than that, gasoline

— 1 —

fumes hung in the air, making me dizzy. A fuel tank on the truck dripped gas, leaving a dark, crusted stain on the dirt.

Hect squeegeed his brow with one finger and popped a line of drops in the dirt. He sweat a lot anyway, and the droplets ran down his face as if beads on a string. His buzzed haircut and almost perfectly round face, along with his being chunky, made him a target for kids at school. They taunted him with names like "Full Moon" or "Charlie Brown," after the cartoon strip. He'd dropped out of the seventh grade after failing it the year before, and I wished he hadn't, as his south-side accent needed improving badly. Because of it, I'd come under my own share of teasing, especially from my country-club pals. Instead of Hect or his real name, Hector, they called him "Hick."

"You hear me, Private? Snatch up that gun. What if them killers was to come squalling out of that hut? What're you to do about it—chunk dirt clods?"

"I'm not in the mood." Miserable, I dropped my head into my hands again. "No one's inside there anyway."

"Says you, no one's in there. If you don't think so, sashay out in the open and see if them murderers don't fill that ain't-in-the-mood noggin so full of pellets you'll be a walking maraca. At least then, you'd be useful as a decoy. Now get that weapon out of the dirt, soldier."

I picked up the end of the rifle, but only because the gun didn't belong to me, and I felt guilty treating his uncle's rifle like that. I brushed the barrel off.

"We're in a skirmish here, soldier. This ain't no child's play. Them cutthroats would die happy as eating pie if they could kill us, so you get serious."

"I'm not well, I told you. You wouldn't be either if you went through what I did last night. It was the worst of my li—"

"'Not well'? Is that what you said?" He shook his head as if he'd heard all he could stand and returned to loading his rifle clip. "You ain't half thought 'not well,' if them maniacs in that bunker get their blood-crusted hands on you. Now get up here and help out. I ain't able to finish them off alone."

"Gunfire hurts my headache."

"How'd I wind up with such a sissy partner? That's what I'd like to know. And don't tell me them skunks ain't in there again on account of they are so. I don't care what you say. Now, my plan is a frontal attack while you flank attack. We'll duck best we can, you left, me right."

"If I move, I'll throw up."

"You ain't got no say in this, Private. Which one of us is the officer here? Me, not you. These are my uncle's rifles, and we'll do as I say so." He snorted. "Shoot, your momma won't even let you own a cap pistol, so don't tell me I ain't in command. Now, we'll rush the enemy head-on. They won't be expecting that."

"Here goes!" I bent over and made a gagging noise. "Ugh, almost."

"I ought to shoot you for insubordination, is what. I'd be within my rights too. It's legal for a commanding officer to kill a coward who disobeys on the battlefield. If I didn't need you to help fight these scoundrels, I would too."

"Ack! For real, this time!" I bent over, my shoulders on my knees, my head between my thighs, and burped. Nothing else.

"My blamed luck," Hect muttered. "Here I am in desperate straits, facing fanatic killers, and I got a pansy for a sidekick. Come on now, won't you help?" His tone reduced to pleading. "Buck up and cover me, at least. I'll do the rest." He stood up and leaned around the fender and emptied his clip into the shanty. Pieces of glass shattered. "Wahoo! That'll show them killers. If only I had me a flamethrower," he said while peeking over the truck's hood. "I'd set that place ablaze with a flamethrower and cook them rascals."

A humming noise caught my attention and I forgot about being sick. "You hear that?" I cupped one ear. "That buzzing—where's it coming from?" With the barrel of the rifle, I pushed aside a branch of a large mesquite bush. "*Look at that!*"

A wasp nest big as a dinner plate had so many yellow jackets covering it that the branch bent under its weight. "You ever see one that big? Watch this." I picked up one of our beer bottle caps and tossed it at the swarm. The tiny tin disk glanced off a limb, ricocheted off another, and nicked the brown, paper-like wad. Wasps broke away like a hunk falling off a cake, dissolving all to crumbs and buzzing furiously. They flew every which way, zipping around, but then returned to their labors, droning softer as they worked.

"Here, soldier!" Hect cried. "Are you going to help me or no?"

"I told you already. I'm lucky to be alive after last night. I should be in a sickbed in the hospital, not out here with you. Now, for the last time, I don't feel well."

"You kidding me? You ever once thought what'd become of Iwo Jima if John Wayne had left off on account he *don't feel well?* We'd lost the Pacific, if not World War II, you nitwit."

"Look, if you want to fight Japs, go ahead. I'll fight who I want." I shook up my beer, put my thumb over the opening, and released a stream of suds over the nest. The wasps flew out in a screaming squadron. Some dipped close to our heads and dive-bombed all around us. After that, they flew back to the sopping nest, starting repairs.

"Will you leave off with them yeller jackets? You keep messing with them, and they'll be on us." He sat on the running board and blotted a sweaty forehead on his sleeve, and then wiped his lower face with the last dry spot on his shirt. "I know why it is you mess with them hot-tailed devils, on account of your yeller, just like them."

I flinched. Sometimes his teasing went too far. When the insults got out of hand, drastic measures only would make him take it back. "Yellow, am I? Is that so? You know, I heard once that if you hold your breath, wasps won't sting you."

"Oh, they'll sting you, all right. Don't think they won't. They'll sting you good. Don't believe them old wives tales, no siree. They ain't true. Not a bit of it. You can swell up like a blimp, and they'll poke them chili-hot stingers in you till you yodel Dixie."

"But, you just said I was 'yellow,' right? Isn't that what you said?"

"Hold on now. I know that tone. OK-OK, I didn't mean 'yeller' exactly. It's just a joke. Don't…"

I lurched forward, jabbed the wad with the rifle barrel, and knocked it swinging. A banzai charge hurtled out of the bush, RRRRRing like mini buzz saws, zinging around our heads fast as bullets, darting every which way. We both balled up and threw our arms over our necks. The loud buzzing went on for what seemed like minutes and then died away. I peeked out from under my arms. All the wasps had gathered in a ball around the dangling nest, swarming at the thread still attached to the branch.

"Whew!" Hect sighed, uncovering his head. "That was close."

"Not so yellow after all, huh?"

"Not yeller, I meant stupid." Hect stood up, and his rifle fell out of his hand and struck the truck's gas tank. "Man alive!" He snatched the weapon back away. "This baby's loaded and might'a shot that tank and set off the…" He stopped and gave a curious look. His eyes widened, and his round, sweaty face broke into a grin. "*Gas!* How come me not to think of it 'fore now? Why, the answer's right here." He patted the barrel. "Here's my flamethrower. We'll smoke them yeller buggers."

"Smoke them?" I looked at the mesquite bush, thinking he meant the wasps. "How?"

"This wreck's got fuel, ain't it? Has to on account of the leak. See?"

Sure enough, a glistening bead trembled at the bottom of the tank's welded seam and fell in a single drop. The dark, hard-packed sand quickly absorbed it.

I snorted. "At that rate, it'd take a month to fill a beer bottle."

"Not if we taken the cap off first. A beer bottle will fit down in the opening easy."

"Yeah, and one spark will blow us both to kingdom come."

His face fell. "It's on account you ain't never done any real work or fixed nothing on your own that you're so short on common sense. Everything's always been done for you." He held up his beer. "How's it to strike a spark? It's glass, moron."

"Aw, why don't you shut up? That's enough with the name-calling. I'm tired of playing stupid war games. Let's quit."

"You sure are touchy lately. Can't hardly tease you no more." He shrugged. "Anyhow, I ain't about to set off no explosion, but we are fixing to have us some fun. Watch this."

I stepped back, just in case, while Hect undid the cap and inserted an empty beer bottle, reaching down until his shoulder fit into the opening. After pulling the bottle back out, he took his handkerchief, stuffed one end in the neck, and turned it upside down until the rag dripped.

Then it hit me. "Molotov cocktail!"

"Not no smudge pot, Tim-boy."

"This ought to fix those little yellow buggers." I rubbed my hands excitedly, hoping the nest didn't fall before we got our chance to set it on fire. "Let's see how they like a bomb. Their little fried yellow bodies will be scattered all over the place."

"There's my old partner again." Hect produced a book of paper matches from his front jeans pocket. "Here, light me up."

I struck a flame. One touch and the rag burst into a bluish tongue. Rather than pitch the bomb under the bush, as I'd expected, Hect stepped away from the truck and, in a sidearm swing, hurled the fiery bottle. It arched in a sputtering, comet-like streak over the wrecked cars, fell as a smoking missile, and vanished behind the peak of the shanty's roof.

We both waited. I didn't dare draw a breath.

"Missed!" Hect clapped his hands in anger. "Durned, if I ain't throwed it too far."

"Have you lost your mind?" I jabbed a finger at the mesquite bush. "I thought…How come…I thought you'd put it under the wasp nest. Where'd you get the dumb idea of setting the shack on fire? You want the cops, the fire department, the whole town out here?"

"Don't nobody know about this place. It's been deserted for years."

"They'll know if it's on *fire*. Besides, I might have to sleep out here tonight. Where else can I go? Not home, for sure."

"You? Out here?" He snickered.

The way he said it, he thought that the dumbest idea ever. After thinking about it, I couldn't really disagree.

"You? Out here?" he said again. "Oh, that's a good one. Remember, there ain't no fridge out here and no fluffy bed neither. And no ironed sheets, no water cooler blowing cool air down on you, no maid to fix your meals and make your bed for you. All them comforts you've got used to—there ain't none out here."

"So?" I would've liked to sound more confident.

"And no sleeping all day neither. You know why? On account of there's creepy-crawlies out here. Scorpions! Lots of them. Ain't no one more scared of scorpions than you."

He had me there. Wasps at a distance I could handle, but scorpions were another matter. Hect knew it too. Once, we caught one in a jar, and he dared me to let the insect touch my palm. I tried, being careful to tilt the jar slowly in order to stay away from its stinger, but at the last moment, lost my nerve. He never let me live it down either, no matter how daring I might be in other ways. All in all, then, who knew where I'd end up staying tonight. Maybe I'd have to eat humble pie and return home after all. Besides, with no place to stay and no place to hide, they'd find me in time anyhow. A snapping noise made me look up. "*Hect!*"

A black cloud entwined with orange flame erupted out of the roof of the shack, scattering cinders in tracer-like arches. Dry, sun baked wood exploded in a ball of fire as the roof collapsed, gulping beams and shingles and spewing up sparks and embers. The heat made me turn my face and hike a shoulder for a shield. Peeking past my arm, boiling smoke towered above the shanty making an asphalt-colored road across a blue sky.

"Man alive!" Hect yelled. "I ain't never!"

"Everyone for miles saw that."

"Let's git!" Hect sprinted in the opposite direction from town, leaving his rifle.

I started to follow but stopped, looking toward home, wondering what to do. Behind me, Hect had already shrunk in size with the distance. I must decide. Once he reached the brush, he'd be gone, and I'd be left alone. Hearing the wail of sirens from the direction of town, only one thing came to mind—they're coming! Oh, they're coming! They'll be here! Still undecided, I looked at the burning shack.

The sight almost knocked me over. Within a fiery window, a figure stood like someone having a peek outside, except for being engulfed in flames. For a horrifying instant, we faced each other as two strangers meeting, except that one of us blazed in a ghastly torch. Fire leaped out the window, past the human shape, in petals of rosy flame. Glass shards blew out in what must've been a furnace-like rush of wind, shattering in the air. The tinkling noise jolted me. I took off after Hect. "Wait! Wait! Wait up!"

Hect stopped and put his hands on his waist rolls. He huffed and blew as his shoulders lifted and fell.

"Wait!" I ran with all my might, gasping for air. "Wait up! Someone… in…there!"

"What?"

"In shack…someone."

Hect bent over, huffing, his round face lifting, looking at me. "Can't be."

"Someone…I tell you." Running in the soft sand was more like falling forward and catching myself with each step. "In window."

"Naw."

"On fire. I saw him."

"Why ain't…he showed hisself…'fore now?" he said in between breaths.

"Shooting at him." I caught up to him. With my hands on the small of my back, I leaned backward, panting. "Or maybe…drunk."

We both turned and looked at the shanty. The smoke reached so far into a cloudless sky, it looked like a narrow thunderhead. Sirens wailed in the distance.

"Gotta go! Let's git!"

"Wait!" I couldn't think. Everything happened so fast. "Don't leave me…alone."

"Not alone…for long." He panted. "Firemen coming…sheriff, too."

"We run, we'll look guilty."

"We stay, we go to jail. Ever been?"

"No."

"Like to?"

"Well…"

"Meanest rascals on earth in jail." He took a breath. "A softy like you wouldn't last no time."

After one last look toward home, we ran into a broad, waterless desert.

2

Flight

RUNNING IN SOFT sand was as awkward as wearing galoshes, but I managed to keep Hect in sight. I'd lost all sense of direction, but the wailing sirens behind served as a compass. Each time one of us got winded, the other would stop, and we'd both wheeze and huff, but one look behind at black smoke staining a lake-blue sky, and we'd start running again. Finally, I fell to my knees, unable to get enough air, and couldn't get back up. "Asth…ma. Can't…breathe."

Hect trotted back. "A little more." He gulped air too. "Rest then."

He reached under my arm, and together, we stumbled on, at last coming to one of the rare hiding places on the flat, barren desert: a mesquite-crowded cow pond. Normally, mesquite won't hide anything. The shrub that covers West Texas is a sickly bush with thorns as long as ten-penny nails and leaves the size of peanut skins—that is, until its near water. Then the branches thicken up, the trunk expands to a hefty size and, before long, there's a full-grown tree.

Once we reached the brushy barrier, Hect and I hunted for the always-present but nearly invisible cow trail. Having found it, we bent over and wound our way through the thorny hedge, wincing and yelping at the inevitable scrapes and pricks, until we came to a brown pond—a West Texas version of a desert oasis. We collapsed together on a cow-patty-littered bank. Neither of us moved from that point on.

That night, I awoke on a hard shore, drew a breath rank with the aroma of baked algae, and stared up out of a ring of mesquite. The fragment of sky had a zillion stars, making me feel so small and sort of lost. Had it really been only yesterday morning when I awoke all snug and comfortable in my own bed? At that moment, paradise had nothing on my bedroom.

꧁꧂

HEAVY DRAPES BLOCKED an afternoon sun, creating an artificial night. Directly overhead, a damp wind blew down out of a ceiling vent from the water cooler on the roof. Fresh sheets still had the outdoorsy smell from drying on the clothesline as I sank into my mattress. On the other side of the bedroom walls broiled a West Texas scorcher, but inside my room, it felt winterish. A knock on the door shattered the mood.

"Timmy, are you in there?"

I pulled the comforter over my head.

More knocking. "Timmy, are you awake?"

I pressed the pillow to my ears.

More knocking. "Timmy, I'm coming in. One…"

She wasn't giving up. In that case, two can play this game. I jumped out of bed and threw back the covers.

"Two…"

Hurrying, I arranged my pillow and pulled the comforter over it, but inspired by an idea on how to increase the effect, I threw back the down quilt, grabbed my latest purchase from the joke shop off my nightstand, put it on the pillow just so, and covered it again.

"Two and a half…"

With no time to dress, I dashed in my underwear around the foot of my bed to the closet and slid the door closed, leaving just space enough to peek out.

"Three." The bedroom door opened.

Through the crack, I saw her start one direction, stop, start another direction, and stop again, as though unable to make up her mind. Heavy hipped with narrow shoulders, she looked like a vase rocking back and forth. She then crept past the bed to the windows and flung open quilted drapes. Sunlight tumbled over her, filling the room.

Now for the test. I silently cleared my throat. "Beat it!"

"Oh, my, such talk. I never heard the like of it before."

I covered my mouth, stifling a giggle. She'd spoken to the mound on the bed, which delighted me no end. If only they could see me now at the joke shop. "Beat it, I said!"

"It's the middle of the afternoon." She balled her fists on her hips with elbows stuck out like handles on a vase. "When I was a little girl, we weren't allowed to sleep the day away. And how often do I have to remind you to always say 'please'?"

"Beat it, *please!*"

She took a deep breath and let it out slowly. "So this is the thanks I get for not disturbing you. I wish sometimes I could stay in bed until afternoon. When I was a little girl, we were poor and had housework to do instead of sleep." She reached for the covers.

"Don't!"

Her hand stopped mid-reach. "What did I just this minute tell you to always say?"

"Don't, or else."

"No. I told you not two seconds ago. Don't, what?"

"Don't, or you'll regret it."

She grabbed the covers and flung them back. Instead of finding the boy she'd expected, a cockroach the size of a shoe sat on the pillow. With a scream, mother sprang backward, knocking the nightstand over, along with a lamp and seldom-used alarm clock, all crashing to the floor, but she managed to wheel around in time to keep her balance.

Meanwhile, I shoved open the closet, dashed for the bedroom door as she lunged for me, but I ducked under her grasp. Once out in the hallway, I ran to the bathroom and shut the door just in time.

More loud knocking. "Timmy Collins!" she called, sounding out of breath. She never used my last name except as the last straw. "You answer me this instant."

"What?"

"Our trip to the coast is off."

"What trip?"

"The one I planned to surprise you with."

"To Galveston? Aw, that's for little kids with pails and shovels building sand castles. I'm too old for that."

"OK. Forget going to Houston either."

"Not Houston. A bunch of tall buildings, crowds, and shopping—who cares?"

"Well, where would you like to go?"

After years of this same game, I knew better than to say. "Nowhere."

"Oh, there must be someplace." Her tone sweetened suspiciously. "Think about it. Of all the places we've traveled over the entire world, which is your favorite? Mexico?" she prompted. "Or South America? Or Europe? It can be anyplace you choose. Come on, pick one."

"Antarctica." I just said it for something to say.

"Forget it!" she lashed out. "No chance, young man. We're not going because your conduct lately does not warrant any fun trips."

She kept on, but the reflection in the medicine cabinet mirror interested me more. Why had I not had the good luck to be born with strong, rugged features instead of cursed with a face so thin it looked constructed out of bird bones? Why not square jawed, overhanging eyebrows and maybe even a broken nose that healed crooked? What adventurer had penciled eyebrows, a wishbone jaw, and a delicate nose? None that I ever read about. In the background, half-listening to mother talk, I heard something, or thought I did, but couldn't be sure. The only way to know was to make her repeat herself. "Mom, you forgot something."

She stopped talking.

"Think about it."

"Timmy Collins, you interrupted me right in the middle of what I was saying. This is one more example of your forgetting your manners lately."

"Yeah, but you forgot something—like, my ventriloquism, maybe?"

"Sorry, after your attitude lately, no compliments."

"Aw, come on. You thought I was still in bed. I watched from the closet. Go on, admit it, you thought my voice came from under the covers. Credit where credit's due. I'm good enough for the stage, right? A pro?"

"Not in the mood, too bad."

"Aw, gee." I purposely lowered my tone. "I guess I'm not any good then, after all."

"Not good!" she gasped. "Of course you're not good—*excellent* maybe or the best ever." A soft thud sounded as she leaned her head against the door, sighing. "Oh, Timmy, if only you'd apply those marvelous talents to something besides ventriloquism. You're so gifted. Everyone says so. Which one of your teachers hasn't complained, 'If only Timothy would apply himself'? And yet, you waste your time on gags and vaudeville hokum at that silly carnival store."

"Joke shop." I perked up. "The cockroach was a real hoot, huh?" But I didn't want to stray too far from what she originally said. "Now, what were you saying a while ago?"

"Oh, yes. Thanks for reminding me. I was saying, when you finish grooming, come out to the kitchen, please. I want help with some chores."

My reflection in the mirror squinted in agony. I knew it. That word. It had the same ugly sound as *homework*, *school*, or *time to wake up*, and it meant the ruin of a perfectly good summer afternoon. "Aw, now? Not today. What about later?"

"Don't give me that, please. It won't hurt you to do a little work around here."

"All right, all right, I shouldn't have pulled the cockroach gag, how's that? Is that what I have to say? I'm sorry we won't be going to...to...oh, wherever. Is that good enough? Only let me skip out this once."

"*This once*—you can't be serious. Why, I can't remember the last time you helped out around here. Besides, I'm only talking about washing dishes and cleaning restrooms."

"Gak! Scraping dried food off plates and handling leftovers, I'd as soon die. And I wouldn't dare stoop to touch a toilet with my bare hands. Get the maid to do it."

"She's sick. Oh, come on." She chuckled, but it sounded artificial. "It'll be good for you. You'll learn how to take care of yourself so one day when you're on your own, you'll know how. Anyway, let's not argue. I know, we'll make a game out of it. It'll be fun."

"She's faking it, trying to get the day off. Tell the maid to come in or she's fired."

"She's having surgery. And her name's Maude, not 'the maid.' She's been with us five years, and you can call her by name."

"'Surgery,' oh, sure. That's a good one."

"Never mind." She sighed. "It's more trouble to get you to work than it is to do it myself. You know, one of these days, you might end up needing to know how to do some of these things. What if one day you find yourself alone, and I'm not around? What'll you do then? Life's not all fun and games, you know? Sometimes things change. Sometimes things change real fast. You might find yourself with just you to depend on and having to make a living without anyone to help. It can happen."

❧

HULKING SHAPES SURROUNDED me, and nearby, what looked like glitter lay on top of a tar pit. Slowly, my mind oriented, and I realized the mesquite bushes were just shadowy figures, and the sparkly stuff on the pond's surface only reflected stars. A little past my feet, Hect's quiet form lay sleeping. Relieved, I sank back. Despite feeling as if any second a predator waited to pounce on me out of the brush, I couldn't stay awake.

3

The Phantom

BEFORE OPENING MY eyes, warmth crept along my body as the sun rose over the tops of mesquite, slowly shoving the shade off me. Considering what lay ahead, it seemed best to go back to sleep, but the crawling heat wouldn't permit it. The start of what promised to be the worst day of my life had begun. As if to prove it, the instant I opened my eyes, sunshine poked bright fingers in them, blinding me. I sat up and rubbed the balls of my fists into my eye sockets until sight returned.

Hect slept on, still in the shade, his round head resting on part of a dry cow patty. A lizard perched on his hip, its tail erect and tiny neck craned as if waiting for whoever on the food chain might show up next. Nearby, a brown pond the size of a wading pool took up most of the circle of mesquite, and visible above the top branches, a windmill propeller turned with a monotonous click-bang, click-bang, click-bang. Directly below the windmill, a full trough would be spilling over, sending a trickling stream through the brush to the pond. It seemed unfair for my friend to sleep, leaving me to face such a bad day alone. "Hect!"

The lizard on his hip sprang for its life and vanished into the underbrush.

"Wake up, Hect. We're stranded next to this scummy pond with no food, no water, nothing. I'm thirsty."

Hect rose like an exhumed body, and ruffled cow dung out of his hair with one hand and brushed sand off his cheeks with the other. He suddenly stopped mussing his hair, sat up ramrod straight, and looked wild-eyed. "Murderers! Killers! Oh, why'd you wake me? I was so happy asleep. Now I remember it all and wish't I was dead. We done it, all right. Burnt up a poor, old helpless bum. Ayee! Our lives are ruin't—ruin't, I say."

"Aw, not again." I didn't have the energy for this on top of everything else. "We went over and over this last night. Nothing we do is going to change anything, certainly not moaning and groaning all over again."

"Well, ain't you the satisfied one!" he said, sounding offended. "For a fella who just took a life and is on his way to death row, you hardly seem bothered at all."

"It's not that. It's that it doesn't get us anywhere to keep wailing over the same gloomy stuff. Every time I woke up last night, that's all I heard. Let's think about what to do from now on. Put that other stuff behind us."

"Judging from you, this ain't no difficulty at all. We may as well do a jig back to town and turn ourselves in and start our life sentences." His eyes narrowed. "You sure you seen somebody in that window yesterday?"

The question caught me off guard. "Why?" Something about his stare made me look away. "Of course. Sure, I did. Why tell a lie about something like that?"

"Who said you was lying? No one said you was lying."

"Why else would you ask such a question?"

"On account of you ain't never seemed too upset about all this. Even last night, you acted funny, like, well, like you was thinking of something else."

"Thinking of something else?" I wished that came out more sincere. "Look, I'm upset just like you—really, really upset. Only, I don't see what good it does to fall all to pieces. That doesn't mean I'm not upset."

Hect studied me. We'd been friends so long I worried he knew my thoughts. Could he read my mind? He had suspicions already, I knew, and might even have guessed my doubts. Things seemed so different this morning, less certain. With a brand-new day, even I couldn't be sure anymore—had there been a man on fire in that shack, or not? It seemed so. I'm sure I saw something, but what? It wouldn't be the first time I'd seen something unexplainable lately. The truth be known, I might even have confessed my uncertainty to him. No better friend existed in the world, but I wasn't ready. Not yet. To tell him about the visions yesterday that kept appearing and disappearing, there'd be too many questions afterward. Questions I didn't have answers to. No, before admitting anything, I had to find out for sure if the man on fire had been real, but I wished he'd quit staring at me.

"You're acting weird," Hect said, his eyes narrowing. "If I didn't know better, I'd say you was hiding something."

"Now I'm *hiding* something." I acted annoyed, hoping to throw him off. "Why don't you come right out and say it? OK, I made the whole thing up. I didn't see anyone in that shack and lied about it so we'd spend the night by this stinking pond with nothing to drink."

"Whoa, simmer down. No need to blow your stack. I ain't saying you storied, but the point is, we can't never go back to town. From here on out, we're criminals on the run. The onliest chance we got is to make it to Mexico."

"Mexico?" The word hit hard. I'd hoped things wouldn't get any worse, but to start life over in a strange land among foreigners whose language I couldn't speak seemed a fate worse than death. "But that's hundreds of miles away. With no money, no food, no water, how can we travel that far?"

"We got water, leastwise. Plenty out yonder in the cow trough under the windmill."

I made a face.

"OK, rich boy. Maybe it ain't bottled water delivered off a truck like you're used to, and maybe it'll turn your teeth brown as eating mud, but it's wet. You'll get used to the taste."

"What about money and food?"

"One thing at a time."

We both got to our feet. Hect said I looked breaded for frying with so much sand stuck to me. He was trying to cheer me up, I guess, but it didn't work. After stretching out the kinks and dusting off, I looked around. "Where can we wash up? And not in that mud hole either."

"Outside the mesquite. Good water too."

We ducked down and made our way back through the thorny hedgerow along the same cow trail. At the base of the windmill, a pipe dribbled water down an algae goatee into a brim-full cement trough.

I bathed in the trickle, cupping my hands and splashing myself, careful not to get my shirt wet. My less finicky friend, on the other hand, broke through the crust floating on the surface and practically swam laps. The hard water tasted bitter as sucking an orange rind.

After drinking all I could, I wiped my mouth on one corner of my shirt. "That made me hungry. How much longer can we go, you think?"

"Longer than what?"

"Before we starve."

Hect rolled his eyes. "It's only been since yesterday."

"Yeah, but I've never gone this long without food. I'm just asking a simple question. How long can you go before starvation? Three days?"

"Oh, lots longer than that. Five. Six, maybe, if you got meat on you, like me. Skinny as you are, I'd say buzzards already got an eye on you, licking their chops."

"Funny." Even though it'd been a joke, I had a mental image of the flesh-eating birds on top of me. "On second thought, maybe we should go back and give ourselves up. If we told them what happened, they might believe we didn't mean to harm anyone?"

"Oh, they'll believe us all right, yeah-sure. Here we shot the place to pieces and them lead bullets didn't burn up in that fire neither. Whoever you seen in that window didn't go nowhere's, you can count on that." He screwed up his face. "Could be we wounded the ole boy, and they'll find the bullets in him. That'll convict us of murder one right there. Not to mention us tossing a Molotov cocktail on the roof and setting the place ablaze. Now what part of all that you think a jury will buy we didn't mean no harm?"

I started to say something, changed my mind, and changed it back again. "I hate to bring this up, and don't take me wrong, but you just now said 'we' threw the fire bomb. Actually, to be correct, I had nothing to do with throwing it."

"Aha!" Hect cried, as if he had been waiting for just such a remark. "You mean, 'sides striking the match that lit the rag afire? Remember, he who lights the fuse gets sent upriver same as him who throws the bomb."

"OK, but I thought you meant to put it under the nest of yellow jackets."

"And you got it in mind a jury will swaller a line like that? You can't mean it."

"Forget it. Anyway..." At the sound of a motor, I shaded my eyes and turned in that direction. "Hect, take cover!"

We dove under a mesquite as a shadow passed overhead. The small airplane flew so low the bushes shook. Had we been beside the pond, we'd been spotted for sure. After a second pass, the plane flew off.

"What was that?" I plucked green goatheads carefully from my forearms from where I'd landed in a patch. Luckily, the stickers hadn't died yet and the sharp horns were relatively soft. "A crop duster—way out here?"

"No cotton to spray clear out this a'ways. Flying pipelines, reckon?"

"Pipelines?" I pulled out the last sticker. "There're no pump jacks or oil tanks around."

"Who else would be checking out waterho—?" He didn't finish. "The sheriff must'a hired a search plane. Nothing else makes sense. They're hunting two killers. Us, that's who."

"Yeah, well, maybe."

"*Maybe?* What else?"

I wanted to tell him. I wanted to say it was more likely my mother, not the sheriff. She'd be the one to hire a pipeline inspector from my dad's oil company to fly out here looking for us, but how could I say so without tipping him off to what happened last night? Which would then lead to questions like how come your mother hired an airplane? What've you done now? Why didn't you tell me before this about seeing weird stuff? And on and on. Oh, if only I knew for sure. Had there been someone on fire in that window, or not? The more I thought about it, the less certain it became. On the other hand, maybe the sheriff *did* hire the airplane. Who knew? One thing, though, until I found out what really happened, I couldn't let on to anyone, even my best friend.

We crawled out from beneath the mesquite.

"Look it!" Hect whispered. "That bird's checking out every waterhole, all right. We best hide out till night."

"But there're hundreds of cattle ponds out here. He can't inspect them all."

"Just the same, soon as it gets dark, we scram. With him flying around, we don't dare risk it in daylight."

"Scram? Where?"

"See them power lines over yonder?" Hect pointed to the horizon. "Them toothpick-size thingamajigs is really tall towers up close, big as oil derricks. That's Highway Eighty. Them power lines run a'side it. If we was to make it that far, we might could hitch a ride headed west to El Paso. From there, we cross into Juarez. The law can't touch us in Mexico."

"Oh, that. Again with Mexico." Even though the mention of that country made me want to curl up and die, I couldn't think of anyplace else to go. "Yeah, I suppose."

Waiting for the sun to go down turned into a misery I never imagined. For one thing, my empty stomach seemed to be digesting itself, but for another, a smothering heat lay atop me like a fat kid so that I couldn't breathe. Plus, my skin fried under a broiling sun, and the sweat and sand mixed together, making me itch like crazy, but worst of all, my mind couldn't rest. Had I really seen a person on fire in that shack? Everything depended on knowing. If not, then we'd committed no crime, at least not a serious one, but if so, then Hect and I would be on the run in Mexico from now on. How to tell for sure? Only one way I knew: to go over every detail of last night, taking one thing at a time, and piece together exactly what happened. Besides, what else was there to do while lying here suffering?

⚜

EVERYTHING WOULD'VE WORKED okay if Mother hadn't stayed up late. Any other night, she'd been in bed after the ten o'clock news so that by twelve there shouldn't have been a problem. I'd snuck in the house before in worse condition. A light in the den had been left on, which would've been a red flag if not for the stranger tailing me. That creep wasn't getting in the house on my watch. He was very clever, though, only appearing in glimpses before dodging behind a bush or ducking into an alley or hiding in back of a tree. Added to that, after the spiked punch at the pool party that afternoon, plus goofballs, I had a hard time focusing. It took all my effort just to walk without losing my balance on the spongy, unlevel ground.

Once inside the house, after quietly easing the door closed, sure enough the table lamp across the room had been left on. I considered turning it off, but the figurines, vases, and all the other breakables along the way seemed daring me to try. Good thing too, because not a second after that, the room tilted blurrily, and I had to put a hand on the wall, steadying it.

After the dizzy spell passed, I searched my pockets for the key to lock the front door but found nothing. Talk about creepy; how'd I get inside? Had Mother left the door unlocked? That'd be a first. Maybe the key dropped on the floor. Bad idea. In bending over, I lost my balance and head-butted the wall, raising a big ruckus.

As I struggled to regain my footing, I lost my grip and fell into the wall again, this time crumpling to the floor.

"Timmy!" Mother shrieked. "Sorry, I didn't mean to startle you like that. Are you all right?" She helped me to my feet. "I've been worried sick about you all day."

Now I'd done it. Trapped like a rat. With the door behind me closed and Mother blocking the hallway, escape was impossible.

"Where on earth have you been for the last, what, twelve hours or so? Not the pool party. Mrs. Blankenship called and said some boys snuck liquor in the punch, and she'd ended the party early and sent everyone home from the country club. What happened?"

Past her form, a row of picture windows looked like solid black mirrors. I didn't want to alert her, but the stranger could be standing out there, and we'd never know. The thing could be watching, waiting for just the right moment to make a move.

"Well, answer m—No, no, on second thought, I don't want to know. It'd only upset me anyway. Keep it to yourself, but where have you been all this time?"

What was there to say? Should I tell her the danger she was in? Should I let her know we weren't alone or leave her ignorant and hope nothing happened?

"I'm waiting to hear. Well? Or, no, come to think of it, I don't want to know that either. It's none of my business anyway. You can tell me some other time."

Yes, that's it—'some other time'. I'll tell her later, but for now, the less said, the better. If she knew about the stranger slinking around, she might fall to pieces. Time to be calm, pretend all was under control, change the subject. Like, for instance, who left the front door unlocked?

"May I have my change back?" she asked. "You know, from the ten dollars."

The amount had a familiar ring.

"Remember? I gave it to you as you were leaving." She huffed. "Don't tell me you spent it all? I very clearly told you to buy a snack but to bring me the change. So, I'm to take it, you splurged away the whole ten, did you?"

I went through my pockets, but just for show, as they'd already turned up empty when I'd searched for the deadbolt key. The effort threw off my balance, and I took a half-step sideways.

"Dear gussie!" she exclaimed. "What smells so horrid? Come out of this dark hallway into the l—*Timmy!* What in the name of—? Oh, my heavens, you're covered in…What's—?"

Before I could answer, she turned on the hall switch and the flash blinded me.

"Timmy! You look awful!" She caught my arm and pulled me toward her. "Oh, my stars, you must have rolled on the ground to be so covered in grass and mud. And the smell—have you thrown up too? What a mess—it's all down the front of you. Oh, I warned you, didn't I? Didn't I warn you? As heaven is my witness, I pleaded with you not to overdo on sweets. Malts, sodas, ice cream, candy—all such rich foods do nothing but make you deathly sick."

She let go of my arm, and I drifted backward.

"Well, there's no help for it, I suppose. Here, I'll go draw your bath. Leave your clothes, and I'll wash—no, they're beyond that. Throw them away. While you're undressing, I'll get a pair of clean Bermuda shorts."

I undressed in the laundry room, taking the shorts handed through a partially opened door and, with the help of the washing machine, put them on.

"Blame me," she said from outside the door. "Why'd I ever give you so much money? A dollar or two, maybe, but a ten was too much temptation. I hoped you'd have a good time at the party, but now, because of me, you've spent the whole amount and ended up terribly ill. There ought to be a law protecting children from villains peddling sweets."

I followed her through the house. Once we reached the bathroom, she turned the shower on. "I'll make some toast," she said in leaving. "It'll counteract the effects of all that sugar."

After cleaning up, I lay down on top of my bed. Toast and a glass of milk had been left on my nightstand, but the sight turned my stomach. Instead, I reviewed the day. It'd been a mixture of highs and lows, of feeling great and then sick, of rising to heights and tumbling into depths, of seeing incredible sights and then horrors. Despite feeling awful, I couldn't help but appreciate mother blaming sweets. She'd been close, closer than she'd ever imagined. It'd been sweets all right—candied peyote buttons, weed-laced fudge and whatever had been in the sugar cubes. Oh, brother, had I ever overdone sweets, but that wasn't the worst of it. Now what kind of shape would I be in tomorrow for our trip to the junkyard? Hect had already slipped his uncle's .22 rifles out of the house, plus swiping a couple of six packs, for which he'd pay dearly when the truth became known, so I had to show up, but at this point, it sure didn't sound fun to play war.

Something in the corner caught my attention. A figure, like a darker shade within a shade, stood in the shadow. Cold prickles ran over my skin. How'd the stranger get in here? Had I left the front door unlocked? Oh, yeah, the keys. Now I remember. They'd disappeared out of my pocket so I'd been unable to lock up. Only, somehow the figure seemed different from the one who'd dogged me all afternoon. For one thing, whenever I faced the shape straight on before, it vanished. But not this time. The longer I stared, the sharper the image got until a fully-formed silhouette. I kept opening and closing my eyes, but the shape remained.

Sick or not, I wasn't staying in a room with a stranger. I rolled off the bed and went hand over hand along the mattress to the bedpost, keeping as far from that corner as possible, across to the writing desk, next to the chest of drawers, and, after a breather, into my bathroom. With the door shut and the lights on, it felt safer, but not for long. An eerie sensation of someone close by came over me. On a hunch, I crawled to the door and pressed one eye to the crack at the bottom. Sure enough, two darker areas stood out from the rest of the shaded line, and, inching so close my eyelashes brushed the carpet, my blood ran cold at the sight of shoe toes like blunt snake heads.

A knock sent me recoiling. Up on my hands and knees, I crawled backward, searching the tiny room for a hiding place.

More thumping, louder.

The laundry hamper? No. Unlike the old days of hide-and-seek, I'd grown too big to fit the opening.

The door shivered as someone or something tried to open it. "Timmy, are you all right?"

I slumped forward, sighing.

"Timmy, answer me. Are you OK?"

"Yeah—OK."

"You left the front door unlocked. The keys were still in the outside lock. What're you thinking lately? Anyone could've walked in and taken me off."

So that's how the stranger got inside. It made sense now, but I had to calm her somehow. "I tried to be quiet and forgot." A lame excuse, but nothing else came to mind.

"Well, be more careful. Anyway, there's a snack on your nightstand. Good night."

"Before you go, do me a favor."

"What now—my goodness."

"Look in my bedroom and turn on the lights."

"Why?"

"Just look around."

"For what?"

"Nothing, anything."

"Oh, now I get it. I see what you're up to. No, it's too late for gags. The cockroach in your bed this morning was enough. Turn on your own lights and look around your own bedroom."

"It's no joke this time, honest, I swear. It's not a prank. Mom? Mom?"

No answer.

Not about to go back into the room with the stranger, but needing some clothes, I opened my bedroom door a crack, slipped a hand in and flipped the light switch. Gone! Thank goodness! But the visitor was sure to return with the dark so I hurriedly put on fresh jeans, a pull-over shirt, socks and tennis shoes; then scurried through the house. Once in the den, I plopped down on the couch in front of the picture windows. Restless and still with the nagging sense that the stranger was lurking around, I sat up and flipped on the wall switch, turning on the backyard floodlights.

The pale light illumed a colorless, empty lawn, except for two pecan saplings encased in a dome of night. Those pecan trees replaced the big old elms, which overlooked the neighbors' backyards. I used to love to climb up and sit in the branches. More than just trees, those elms had been family, always holding me no matter how high I climbed or when I jumped from limb to limb—my one haven to get away and daydream. Then the elm tree beetle plague hit, wiping out my hide-away. Now two puny, scrawny pecan trees remained that looked hardly stout enough to support a full-grown cat.

"*Timmy!*"

I jumped, almost rolling off the couch. My heart did cartwheels.

"What're you doing in here?"

Why scare me half to death like that? For what purpose? Who bursts into a room like a crazy person without warning?

"How come you turned on the outside lights?" she asked, obviously unaware she'd about given me a heart attack. "Did you hear something out there? Why're you staring at me like that?"

Should I tell her about the stranger? See if she thought that reason enough to turn on the lights. Might do her good to know someone crept about the house, but, no, that could cause even more problems. Better to keep things calm, at least outwardly. "I, um, can't sleep."

"Me either. OK, you might as well lay there while I open my present from your father. Maybe we'll get sleepy."

I rolled on my side and watched. While sitting cross-legged on the carpet, she ripped off wrappings from a box. Somehow her cheerfulness annoyed me. Never mind my shattered nerves. Never mind all I'd been through. Never mind my fighting off a nervous breakdown. Go ahead, have the time of your life.

"Oh, I can't stand the suspense!" She stroked the box like a pet. "Is it clothes to wear? No, it's too heavy. Shall I shake it? No, it might break. I guess it's true what they say: remorse is more thoughtful than romance. Look, a note." She opened the envelope. "A rhyme! How sweet." She giggled. "Here, let me read it."

> Forgive your hapless doofus, his tumble off the wagon,
> I'd like to say it'd be my last, but wouldn't that be braggin'?
> Sorry about our little tiff, and wish you were here.
> O, the mountains, the lakes, the herds of roaming deer.
> Massages, long strolls, we talk for hours and hours it seems
> Of problems, of fears, my memories, my dreams.
> Don't worry, having a ball, although I do miss the bubbly,

Still, life goes on and on, your ever loving hubby.

I eased up on one elbow and craned to look over the back of the couch, seeing my own image reflected in the picture window as vague, empty holes for eye sockets peered above a partly open mouth. What a difference from this morning in the medicine cabinet mirror when I wished for rugged, athletic features. Now anything would be an improvement over what looked like a death's head.

"*Timmy!*"

I jerked and spun around, bathed in cold chills. My face flushed warm. Again? A second time? Sneaking up and scaring me half to death once, I can forgive, but not twice. There wouldn't be a third time.

"Will you look at this?" She held up a sparkling crystal bowl with a diamond-like cut. "Isn't this magnificent? What a piece. You know, as much trouble as your father's been lately, there's one thing to admire about him—his good taste."

A movement in the backyard distracted me—a sort of flicker on the edge of my vision. I whipped around, looking past my reflection through the picture windows.

"Timmy!" mother cried from behind. "What is it? What's the matter?"

Behind me, the crystal bowl clattered atop the table. From the sounds, it'd either been dropped or knocked over, and more racket indicated she righted the bowl.

"What's wrong?" she gasped. "You look like you've seen a ghost! What is it?"

In the middle of the backyard, a man, or at least the form of a man, stood beside one of the pecan trees. Something about him reminded me of the stranger who'd been in the corner of my bedroom.

"Timmy! Tell me! You're deathly pale. What is it?"

Sweat drops tickled in my sideburns. So many things happened at once. Add to that, she kept calling my name over and over. I could see her reflection in the picture windows, arms out, reaching for me, but at the same time stopping and pulling back, as if thinking better of it.

"Timmy! Are you ill? You don't look well! You're sick, aren't you?"

I started to answer but lost the thought.

"Go back to bed, Timmy. OK? Let me put this crystal bowl up where it won't get broken, and I'll get one of my sleeping tablets. I promise, you won't know anything after that. Stay in bed all day, if you like. I won't bother you this time."

A ground fog curled around the stranger's legs like a slavish gray cat. He had on a scarf and overcoat—although who knows why in such hot weather—and a brimmed hat with the front slanted down in the style of the 1940s. With the collar of his overcoat up and his hat tipped to the front, his face remained a shadow, and with his hands tucked into his coat pockets and his feet covered by the fog, there appeared to be no person. Just clothes. Not a man at all.

"What's out the window, Timmy? You're white as death! What do you see?"

Wasn't it obvious? Did she still not see the danger? How blind. Would she never pull her head out of the sand? I craned my neck for a better view.

"Timmy! You're behaving crazy! Who're you talking to?"

'Talking'? Did she say talking? Who can talk with all the shrieking in the background?

"You've never acted like this! What's the matter with you? Oh, whenever I need your father, he's never around. Help! Oh, someone, help! Who are you shouting at, Timmy? Why're you yelling?"

Me yelling? What about her? And what did she have to be hysterical about anyway? Her problems hardly amounted to mine.

Beneath the stranger's hat and within the upturned collar, a smile appeared. That caught me off guard. I hadn't expected that. What's funny? The grin curved up at the ends and flashed like a cheap clown's trick.

"Timmy! Timmy! *Tim—meeey!*"

I pushed her away. The stranger darted across the yard on tiptoe and hid behind a pecan sapling. What could be more ridiculous? Such a skinny trunk could never hide a full-sized man. Realism didn't seem to matter anymore. The figure peered out from behind the pecan trunk and flashed a banana-size smile.

Behind me, the room went quiet. No more shrieking. I turned and searched for the reason, finally spying a form crouched beside the piano, pressed into a corner. Mother held the phone in one hand while covering the mouthpiece with the other.

Feeling a tickle on my neck as light as a breath, I whipped around and pitched backward. Not only had the stranger come forward, but he actually leaned through the picture window, and, by some twist of logic, managed somehow not to break the glass. More farfetched yet, the pane sliced through his middle, dividing his body into equal halves, yet without spilling even a drop of blood. So then, it'd not been a stranger at all—but a phantom.

From flat on my back, I sprang up, twisted in midair, and landed flat on my feet. On my way to the front door in full flight, I dodged Mother's attempted tackle and sprinted into the night. Unsure where the screaming came from, somehow the shrill sound kept pace with me.

4

Mauler

In West Texas, at the finish of the day, the brightness ends, not the heat. Now, when a breeze might have given some relief, the wind died. After all my hours under a scalding sun, listening to insects drone, gnats whine, and flies buzz, the desert got quiet and still as if all the wildlife took a break before the nighttime activities began. Even the chipper, perky peep of Bobwhite quails sounded more like exhausted cooing.

"Bingo!" Hect cried, crashing the silence. "The search plane's headed back to base to beat the dark, like as not. So take a last, long drink and fill your belly, Tim-boy, on account'a it'll be a spell 'fore another'n."

We started across the darkening desert, guided by the blinking red lights on the highline towers beside Highway 80. Just inhaling the dry air gave me cottonmouth.

"Can't work up enough juice to spit out a gnat," Hect panted. "Nor swaller it, hardly."

I stopped for a breather. "It seems to me the longer we walk, the farther away those towers get. Will we ever make it there?"

"Come on. No stopping. We only got tonight to get our business done. Come morning when the sun's up, if we ain't got water and cover by then, we're in a cooker. So, no stopping 'cept this desert floor opens up."

That was exactly what happened. We came to a wide gully as far across as a two-lane road. In the twilight, we could see that to go around would take too long, so we dropped to our knees and crawled to the edge, unsure of what might be at the bottom. On the way, we kept a sharp eye out for cast-off mesquite thorns, sticker burrs, goat-heads, or spiny cactus fragments, also being watchful for stinging ants, blister bugs, vinegarroons, tarantulas, and worst of all, scorpions. In the desert, as anyone knows who's grown up here, every living thing either stings, sticks, bites, burns, or is poisonous.

Once at the ravine, we peered over the rim. One look and we grabbed at one another. Below us, so close we could almost reach out and touch the roof, a car had parked, but not just any car. The white Ford had a red dome light. Everyone in town knew the sheriff's Ford.

No doubt the fire at the junkyard yesterday had brought him out, but why would he still be around? Why else, but he waited for two killers to show up. Then again, another option was just as likely. My mother probably had the whole town out searching for us. On a second look, I elbowed Hect. Just visible in the last rays before dark, a large thermos and lunch pail sat on the car's front seat.

As hungry and thirsty as I was, it took every last effort not to creep down there, grab the sheriff's meal, and try and get back up here without being noticed. As I stared longingly at the dinner, a hand grabbed the back of my head and shoved me face-first onto hot sand. I struggled, slipped the grasp, and shot Hect a scorching glare until seeing him point up the road as if he'd seen the Grim Reaper. Once faced around that way, I had to admit he just about had. A terror gripped me until I clutched the sand to keep from running away.

A dog squatted on heavy thighs, tethered by a long chain fastened to the Ford's bumper. More beast than dog, the animal looked every ounce of its rumored 150 pounds.

Hect mouthed the word "Mauler" and clutched his throat with teeth-like fingers, acting as if ripping it out.

I shuddered.

Part chow, part Irish setter, Mauler was the spitting image of a lion because of a reddish-brown mane surrounding a pug face. Our town had no need of an animal shelter for the reason that whenever the sheriff came across a stray, he simply let Mauler out. The dog catcher gathered the remains. A common joke around town had it that many local lawbreakers had been tattooed by Mauler's teeth for free.

Hect and I hunkered down and quietly crawled in reverse. We waited under a mesquite. If either one of us coughed or sneezed now, it'd be over. Just as I thought things couldn't get worse, they did. Over on the horizon, a pedestal of light moved along, which, combined with a distant moaning, indicated the airplane had come back with a spotlight.

"Mauler!" a gruff voice called out of the night.

Hect and I flattened. The voice could've come from anywhere with the way sounds play tricks in the desert, but there was no mistaking who it belonged to. The sheriff visited our class every school year and always ended his speech with the same warning that I could recite word for word: "None of you tender boys want to end up with the ornery skunks I keep penned behind bars on the top floor of my courthouse."

A gunshot rang out, echoing down the gulley. Hect and I balled up tight. Another shot exploded.

"Got him, Mauler!" the sheriff cried with obvious delight. "He's a whopper, too! Twenty rattles at least, just like I told you when I drove over him. Had a lump in his middle the size of a jackrabbit. OK, Mauler-boy, it's safe to untie you now. Here I come."

The dog whined, sounding excited.

"Ho, pal! No, don't jump on me. Down, boy. Down, I said. I wished you'd obey for once. Here, let's go find us a wolf to fight. Ready for a kill, boy?"

The animal whimpered, sounding eager.

I lay under the mesquite shivering, daring not to move despite gnats, horseflies, sweat bees, and every other irksome bug invading my ears, nose, and corners of my eyes. Hect and I didn't dare risk shooing them away either, even when they bit. Minutes passed like hours.

On the horizon, the plane approached ever closer with an unbroken drone. Mauler lapped at his water bowl, his teeth clicking along with the slurping.

"Let's go, Mauler!" the sheriff called. "Come on, boy."

I listened as hard as I could, trying to determine which direction the two headed, ready to sprint for it if I thought they came our way.

"No, boy. No, I said. What is it, Mauler? You smell something? Come on, there's nothing up that ridge. This way, boy. Come on."

A soft whistling along with the dog's panting grew fainter. For the first time since the pistol shots, I breathed, realizing the two had moved off in the opposite direction. The desert turned silent again.

Hect eased over closer. "Now's our chance. Go."

"Where?" I couldn't make out his face in the semi-dark. "Down there?"

"What choice we got? Ain't no going back, no going 'round, and can't stay here."

Unable to argue his reasoning, I crept to the rim warily, along with Hect, and peered over the edge. The road looked empty, but for how far? We couldn't see in the dark. If the sheriff had a flashlight, which he surely did, no light showed up anywhere, so that was hopeful. Hect went over first, and together, we skidded down on our backsides amid an avalanche of rock and dirt.

Abandoning all caution at the bottom, we went for the dog's water bowl first and, with hardly a qualm, shared it, saliva strands and all. Next, we dashed for the open windows of the Ford, Hect at the driver's side and me at the passenger window. He grabbed the thermos. I got the lunch pail, which turned out to contain the mother lode—sandwiches, apples, bananas, chips, and cookies. Hect, on the other hand, struck out with a thermos of hot coffee. We drank it anyway, but the dog's water tasted better. Gulping the last bites, we lost track of who might be nearby.

At a faint whine, we both froze. My mouth full and jaws clenched, daring not to swallow, and with ears attuned until they hummed, I heard the same noise again—a whimper like a dog puzzling over something. Time stood still. It was as if the whole desert stopped and listened.

A bark split the quiet—sharp yet restrained, calling out in the dark. We spit our mouthfuls and sprinted. More barks pierced the dark, now guttural and harsh, sounding like cloth ripping.

"Mauler! Come here! Heel! Come back here!"

We scrambled up the embankment opposite the one we came down, digging at the dirt with our hands, half crawling and half leaping. Once over the edge, the sandy soil slowed our running, but even worse, dark clumps of mesquite forced us to dodge this way and that. If we could've run in a straight line, we might've had a chance, but ducking in among the shadowy clumps took too much time.

Behind us, the barking turned to snarling coughs, growing louder, coming closer.

"Mauler! Mauler!" The sheriff sounded far behind. "Come back! No, Mauler!"

We zigzagged among the mounds. Hect, after his head start, took the lead. I stayed close behind but made a critical mistake. Worried the dog might be gaining ground, I looked back and ran flush into a mesquite. Thorns snagged my clothes, and branches tripped me so that I tumbled in the dirt. As soon as I hit, I rolled, sprang to my feet, and got back at full speed in short order, but Hect had gone.

A guttural huffing sounded at my heels. Worse yet, I'd lost stamina. From the nearness of the panting, I could tell the race was all but lost. Branches broke directly behind, along with the beast gasping. The thought occurred to me that once the monster caught up, no master would be there to pull him off. Adrenalin flooded my body, resulting in a final spurt.

The dark mesquite clumps vanished around me, and I had a sudden sense of flying. My feet left the ground and I soared into the wind, for a brief instant. Hard-packed ground slammed into me, and even as I rolled, it occurred to me I'd just left a short cliff. Out the corner of my eye, headlights passed at a terrific speed. A second set of beams flew by. Unaware which direction I'd been running, it took a second to realize I'd made it to Highway 80. One more roll, and I'd have ended up on asphalt.

"Mauler! Come back! Heel, boy! Mauler!"

The sheriff's distant cries cleared my mind. I jumped to my feet and, after a quick look both ways, hurried across the two-lane highway. An oncoming car sped past just as I arrived on the opposite side.

My hands on my knees, I gulped air. A sense of relief flooded me. The highway, at least in my mind, had become an impassable barrier that no creature in its right mind would dare risk crossing. I squatted on my heels, heaving and blowing as cars flew past, and even took time to worry about Hect. Would Mauler be after him now? Had my escape resulted in sacrificing my friend? Should I go back over and try to help?

The dark scene across the highway showed no sign of what might be happening on that side, but then, on the ledge, close to the same spot where I took my spill, a four-legged shadow appeared. I stopped breathing. The dark shape bore a striking resemblance to a lion. My worries about Hect, it now seemed, had been for nothing.

The dark, lion-like form turned one way and then the other, looking confused. Two cars whooshed by below, going opposite directions. After the car noise passed, a rapid panting could be heard. Unable to hold my breath longer, I covered my mouth and breathed quietly through my fingers. Even if it was possible to move without being seen, I couldn't run any farther.

"Mauler! Mauler!" the sheriff called from faraway. "Heel...boy... heel!"

Mauler disappeared back into the line of bushes. My legs gave way, and I fell to the sharp gravel, hoping with all my strength the brute dog had obeyed its master for once. Just in case, I scanned up and down the ridge. In the passing headlights, shadows played tricks with my eyes. One minute, a shape raced atop the crest—leaping and stretching, leaping and stretching—but with the next car, nothing.

Just as I began to think I'd outwitted Mauler, a familiar form burst out of the shadows, sprang off the embankment, sailed through the air like an arrow, and touched down beside the highway at almost the exact spot where I'd earlier crash-landed. In a single bound, the beast reached full speed again, leaped over the highway shoulder, cleared the first traffic lane with a growl, sprang to the middle of the road, coughed a snarl, and hurled itself into midair. I fell backward, staring up into grinning, wolfish jaws surrounded by a wild mane. Bracing for the landing, I saw a glint of eye, pointy teeth, and a coiled tongue as blinding lights flared. The animal vanished amid squalling brakes, a sickening crunch, and a "Yelp!" cut short.

Confusion followed after that. Out the corner of my eye, I saw a rag-like body land next to the road. There, in a mounded heap, lay a dark, unmoving figure. I shivered uncontrollably.

Even farther down the highway, a car pulled to the shoulder and a man stepped out. "You, sonny?" he called.

A truck roared by, followed by a motorcycle. In the passing lights, I saw an old man, short and slight, standing in the light of the opened car door. He called out again.

I couldn't hear him. "What?"

"Was that your dog, sonny?"

"Mine?" Why he'd asked didn't make sense. "No."

"Whose might it be, then? I feel terrible about what happened, and I'd like to make it up to them somehow."

"Belongs to yours truly, mister." Hect came out of the mesquite above the car. "Don't mean to give you no scare, old-timer, jumping out of the bushes like that, but I couldn't help overhearing. Yep, that'd be my dog. Loved him like a li'l brother, I did." He slid down the embankment and approached the driver, who backed away. "As you may figure, a fella can't hardly put it into words how he feels about his one and only dog. When I heard you'd kilt my pup, it plumb tore me up, it did, but when you said you wanted to make it up somehow, why, I taken heart. It's only right I give you the chance. A real sweetie, that dog. A little cranky at times, like we all are, but you couldn't hardly match him for a best bud. If you think I'm lying, ask my pal over yonder. Right, Tim-boy?"

I stared across the highway, trying to grasp what on earth he meant.

"Aw, ole Tim must be too tore up to say nothing half-sensible, I guess."

"Sonny, I'm heartbroken over this." The old man's voice shook. "I love animals, truly. Lost my own dog not too long ago. What can I do to make up for it, young fella?"

"The dog and me, we growed up together; did I mention that? Can't hardly put a price on a loss like that. How's it possible to put a dollar amount on a busted heart? Just think, I'll never get to tussle that fur nor feel that rough tongue on my cheek. But here now, my grief-struck pal over yonder and I could surely use a lift up the road. That would go a long way in making up for you slaughtering my pet. And maybe if you could spare, say, ten bucks."

"Ten!" the man gasped. "That's a mighty expensive dog, ain't it?"

"Not to be too hard on you, mister, but my lifelong buddy's tore up a'laying over yonder in that bar ditch like a wad of chew-bacca. Wasn't the dog's fault you come barreling along at a high rate of speed and so cruelly struck him lifeless."

"All right, all right, I get your point. Let's not overdo it."

One look at the man reaching for his back pocket and my confusion cleared. I trotted across the highway toward the parked car.

"My friend here and me," Hect said, "was on our way out west. What happened, I figure, was the dog being such a loving, friendly pet, run across to Tim's side of the highway when you come careening along and knocked him into the next kingdom."

The old man started crying. A smell of alcohol surrounded him. "Don't you boys think we should take time to bury the poor thing?" he blubbered.

"Naw. You can't beat buzzards for funerals. They're natural born at it."

A distant calling caught my ear. The voice was unmistakable. "Hurry, Hect!" I still couldn't think halfway straight. "Before the sheriff gets here."

"*Sheriff!*" the older man cried, sniveling. "What sheriff? Are you boys in trouble?"

"No, no." Hect laughed, grabbing my arm and giving me a meaningful shake. "He don't mean what you think. He meant something else."

"But I heard the boy say, 'sheriff.' What else could he mean?"

"Well…" Hect said, sounding at a loss. "Best ask him, I guess."

A strong whiff of booze on the old man's breath gave me an idea. "Drunks! The sheriff drives out this way looking for drunks."

"That's it!" Hect chimed in. "Like he said, the law's always out this way stopping drivers to see who's had one too many. They're real hard on sots around here too. But back to what I was saying—we sure do need a lift. That'd get a good start on making up for you murdering my dog."

"Drunk drivers?" the old man repeated, his tone indicating heightened concern. "You say the law's around here? I wasn't aware of that. I don't mind confiding in you boys that I've had a few toddies tonight my own self." After a pause, he spoke directly to Hect. "Young man, I'm a good judge of character, generally speaking, and I can tell you're sober as a Baptist preacher, so tell me the straight of it. Can you drive a column shift?"

"A column shift? Er...Let's see now...a column shift would be...?"

"A column shift, you know," the old man prodded. "This here forty-eight Chevy has a column shifter. They stopped making these in favor of newfangled automatic transmissions. A column shifter is where the lever is on the steering column—three gears forward and one in reverse."

"Oh, oh, *column shifter*—why didn't you say so, mister? Shoot, yeah, you bet I'm able to operate one. I thought you meant something else. Sure, a column shifter would be just pie to me. Why, there ain't a machine living what can outthink me."

I stared at Hect. Except for cars at the junkyard that we pretended to race, I never heard of him actually driving.

"Mauler!" a voice called from somewhere over the embankment. "Mauler!"

"You two hear that?" the old man asked, clearly alarmed.

"Coyotes," Hect said. "Desert wolves, we call them. Sound human, don't they? Most got the rabies. Let's scoot out'a here 'fore we get bit and end up foaming and snapping at what'all."

"I'll get in back," the older man said, opening the rear door.

5

The '48 Chevy

INSIDE THE '48 Chevy, an odor hit me so hard that, had it not been for the sheriff outside the car looking for us, I'd have jumped right back out. Every bad stink I'd ever smelled—stale cigarette butts, sour wine, body sweat, moldy food, and no telling what else, all mixed together into one overpowering, dizzying, gut-turning stench. After the urge to pass out went by, I rolled down my window and put my head near the door frame.

During the time the overhead dome light had been on, I glanced at the old fellow in back. He had a drawn, threadbare face with yellowish skin. The bill of his baseball cap bent straight up, as though he'd walked into a glass door and liked the effect.

Hect had gotten behind the steering wheel. I started to rib him about driving when I caught sight of a movement in his side mirror. Oncoming car lights showed a man's shape walking up the road behind us. Turning quickly to my own side mirror, the image wearing a cowboy hat had gotten closer. The headlights passed. "Go! Go! Go!"

"Hold your horses," Hect grumbled.

"No, now! Hurry! We got company! Go!"

Hect stomped the clutch, pulled the lever down on the steering column, and hit the gas, all without so much as a grinding noise. In the midst of everything, I had to admit I may have misjudged his driving ability. The car leaped forward as the engine revved to a high-pitched whine that lasted until the motor screamed for relief.

"Shift it! Shift it!" the old man in back yelled.

The attempt turned out not as lucky as his first try. Amid sharp grating noises, the car rolled slower and slower until, after a loud chunk, we frog-hopped and frog-hopped some more. As the car bucked down the road, I steadied myself, bracing one hand against the dashboard and grabbing the seat back. Finally, the engine died, and we rolled to a stop.

Before starting the car this time, Hect first shoved the lever into gear.

"Hurry, let's go!" I looked behind but saw only black. We'd gained some ground from the sheriff, but I couldn't be sure how far. "Go!"

When he let the clutch out, the shifting lever jumped back out as it hadn't been pushed in gear deep enough. More grinding noises followed. Hitting a slot at last, the car began rolling as the engine wound tighter and tighter while the interior filled with a choking, burning odor that actually improved the car's smell. Smoke rose up from the floorboard, and the engine died once again.

"Dadblamedit!" the old man cried in back. "If ain't no machine never out-thunk you, this here's not no Chevy. It's a Einstein."

"T'ain't my fault, mister," Hect said, restarting the car. "Something's wrong with your transmission."

"Likely gummed up with metal shavings, is my take."

The engine raced once more. The car lunged forward, lunged again, lunged a third time, and then we picked up speed. Hect pulled it out of that gear and, amid a series of ear-wrenching, metal-against-metal scrapes, thrust the shifter lever over and over. We rolled to a stop.

"Hot dang!" the old man squealed. "I ain't been this shook up since the last time I downed wine fizzes, two at a time. Speaking of, my nerves need calmed."

Hect grumbled, revving the engine until the car body trembled. After hopping a number of times, we slowly increased speed. All the while, the clutch smelled like the front tires were on fire, but our forward motion actually smoothed out, no longer interrupted by jerks and leaps. We cruised along at last. This time, Hect didn't shift at all, as he must've started in the last gear.

"Well, well, well," the old-timer sang in back. "Off we go. I'm grati-fied, too, I must say. This calls for a little some'n special. Here go, young'un."

I smelled the wine coming and expected a normal-sized bottle. As a result, the gallon jug almost slipped through my hands. Too thirsty to care what was inside it, I gulped until I couldn't stand anymore of the syrupy grape flavor. With a shiver, I passed the jug to Hect who cradled it in a crooked arm and chug-a-lugged his share. He passed it back.

"Whew-wee," the elderly gent cried. "I never seen such a thirsty pair, but not to worry. I got another bottle." From there on, the old man chatted nonstop, quoting one detective magazine after another until it became apparent we were riding with a murder-mystery buff.

I had trouble listening, though, because the wine had hit my empty stomach in a molten ball, bounced straight up, and burst inside my brain. Everything around me went swimmy and I worried even more about Hect, who'd drunk as much as me at least. "You driving OK?"

"Wished this dang highway would stay together. I ain't sure which one to follow."

The countryside passed in a dark smear. This time of night, few cars shared the highway with us. Our headlights showed empty pave-ment mostly, except for once in a while, when a pair of blinding head-light beams sped straight at us, filling the car in a dazzling glare, and with a whoosh, went past.

"Listen up, boys, and I'll tell you the strangest killing that ever has been solved." A cork popped in back, followed by a fresh wine scent. "This ain't out'a no cheap detect rag, neither. I seen it with my own two eyes. Being a bus driver a'fore retiring, we was driving through, let's see, Arizoner, if memory serves, when we come upon this wreck. A circus truck had laid over to its side. First on the scene was a Hitler-made Volkswagen, the littlest car you ever seed and with New York plates too. Well, I'll be dipped, if a elephant big as Tucson didn't come romping right up to the windshield of that car. Later on, after he was arrested, the driver told a reporter all he seen was part of a trunk, one eyeball, and half an ear. 'Big dumb hunk of gray idiot' is what the article said the driver called the animal. But wait—I've got in front of myself—when that little VW, the Germans call them, stopped with that mountain of mammal standing eyeball to eyeball, the traffic backs up a mile or better, including my bus." The old-timer paused for a few gulps. "Hot'che'mama!" He cleared his throat. "Like I was saying, we all parked in a long line at that packet'derm like we was waiting to get into a outdoor movie. Well, sir, the elephant hooks her trunk tow-truck-like under that tiny bumper and lifts the front end clean off the ground, front wheels and all, and gives it a shake. Out tumbles two dead bodies. It's the truth!" More gulping noises. "Ahhhh. Now then, here come all these newspaper articles and magazines telling about how smart elephants are, how they outthink humans, how they can solve murders, and such like. Warn't till later on that the animal trainer from the circus got the chance to tell a reporter what really went on. Shoot-fire, that elephant had delivered a stillborn calf earlier in the week, and she warn't but trying to get her dead baby to its feet. *But here!*" he shouted, jabbing a bony finger in between Hect and I that grazed my cheek. "Take this turnoff! Take it, I say!"

Hect yelped, jolted from a daze evidently, and wrenched the steering wheel to the right, overshooting the turnoff. The car barreled off the highway and bounced down a hill until finally leveling off. With us still traveling at a fast clip, the ride got bumpier and rocks knocked under the floorboard as dust filled the headlights. Finally, the car stopped, but at such a tilt, it felt just short of rolling over onto its side. I pulled myself up by the door handle.

"My head's spinning," Hect murmured. "Can't hardly keep my eyes open."

I worried we'd flipped. "Did we turn over?"

No one answered.

The sound of snoring came from the back of the car.

I thought I'd try again. "Did we turn over?"

Still no answer.

I didn't mind being ignored, though, mainly because, try as I might to keep awake, my blinks lasted longer each time. I shook my head and tried to focus. Through the windshield, the sky looked like the hemline of a ball gown covered in sequins. Fighting sleep, I stuck my head outside, hoping some air might help, but it only reminded me of a window I hadn't thought of lately—that burning window that framed a man covered in flames. Oh, if only I knew for sure. If only...

A blaring noise as loud as a horn against my ear trumpeted over the desert, along with a light of incredible brightness sweeping back and forth through the car. Dust flew in the opened window, filling the interior and choking me wide awake. The whole car body shook like the earth opened up and was swallowing us, followed by a booming, rumbling metallic clacking thudding outside. I clutched wildly for something to hang onto as grit exploded into the car in a hail of flying particles. Terrified, I could only think of one thing. "Tornado! Take cover! A tornado!"

"No, UFO!" Hect screamed. "UFO, I say! UFO, look!"

Sure enough, outside in the dense, swirling dust, sparks shot off giant wheels as a huge, rocket-shaped object soared past. The missile-like machine left as quickly as it arrived, leaving behind a silence as disorienting as the racket had been.

I turned in my seat. Out the back window, the hurling contraption became a diminishing red speck, shrank to ruby size, and melded into the stars on the horizon. Dazed, unable to speak, I got out, but in order to stand, it became necessary to put both hands on the car hood because of the steep embankment leading up to railroad tracks.

I looked across at my heavy-breathing friend. "UFO, huh? Some UFO."

6

The Cowboy

A HUMMING NOISE in between heavy thumps woke me. I peeked out one eyelid; then both eyes flew open. Buzzing mightily, a thumb-size, black and yellow bumblebee bumped the inside of the windshield in an effort to reach the wildflowers along the highway. Despite the open side windows, the bee stubbornly hurled itself over and over, head-butting the invisible barrier.

Hect and I left the car in a hurry. From a safe distance, we called warnings to the old man, who grunted angrily and resumed snoring. The battered bee, meanwhile, fell to the dash, walked in a circle as if considering what to do, and then resumed the same senseless head-banging. The bee's behavior seemed oddly human somehow.

With the sun still well below the desert floor, the partial daylight looked gray and bleak. Since I never got out of bed this early, except for school when in too big of a rush to notice, the morning seemed strange and unfamiliar. Summer days always began when the sun stood directly overhead, so to see it actually rise, especially to begin a day that'd probably turn out the worst of my life, filled me with dread. I leaned against the car fender and rubbed my temples. "Man, my head's killing me."

"Cheap wine," Hect said, unsympathetically as usual. "You'll get over it. But, say, that old-timer's liable to snooze all day. If a state trooper drives by and sees us parked down here, he'll check us out, sure."

Startled, I lifted my head out of my hands. "That reminds me. The sheriff was behind the car last night. He watched us drive off and probably read our tags."

"In that case, he reported us soon as he got back to his Ford. More'n likely, the law's been driving by all night. If we'd kept on going, they'd nabbed us, sure. It's dumb luck we parked off the road. That changes everything. Ain't no going on with these plates." He patted the '48 Chevy. "It's thumb-taxi time."

"Thumb-what?"

He hiked a thumb over his shoulder like a referee calling a runner out.

"You mean hitchhike?" I wilted inside and looked off down the road. The black ribbon stretched from one flat horizon all the way back to the other. Mother's warning repeated in my mind to never, ever get in a car with a stranger.

"Ain't never done it, have you?" Hect could always read my mind.

"No."

"Aw, ain't nothing to it. You stand aside the road and look like a teacher just told you you've been held back a grade. After a while, Joe Blow comes along, feels sorry for you, and stops. That's it."

"Do you have to pay?"

"Oh, that reminds me." He dug in his pocket. "Unless you get lucky, they'll want you to buy your own supper. So just in case, here's half." He handed me one of the fives the old man had given him last night. "But here now, it's way more harder for two to catch a ride than one. Most folks won't pick up a pair, so we best split up."

I kicked rocks, hoping he couldn't read my face. At that moment, I wanted to cry out, "No! Don't leave me. I can't—not alone. Let's stay together, OK?" But I felt too ashamed, so I shrugged. "Suit yourself."

"Aw, you fret too much," Hect said. "You'll do good."

"Yeah, sure."

"We got to get out'a here fast as we can. After breakfast, troopers are likely to start patrolling."

A knot came up in my throat. Close to tears, I turned and walked away. "See you." I didn't wipe at my eyes on purpose, but I couldn't help asking one parting request. "At El Paso, you wait for me—promise?"

"At the border crossing, I'll wait. If I don't, let me die slow 'n' painful."

While walking down the highway, I wondered how I ever got myself into such a mess—alone in the desert, no water, no food, maybe prey to some hungry coyote hiding behind a bush, about to get in a car with no telling what sort of weirdo. Could this be some type of payback? Had my time come to even the score for the wrongs I'd done? Was this the start of the same suffering I caused the man in the shack?

To make matters worse, Hect soon passed by in a Thunderbird convertible, waving like he'd just hit the jackpot. A Saint Bernard dog had its furry head above the two in the sleek red car. Forcing myself, I waved back and managed a half smile, barely keeping from running after them, shouting, "Wait!" Hect had always been the lucky one. What I wouldn't give to catch such a great ride.

After the Thunderbird disappeared, the highway seemed emptier than ever. Would a car come along, or would I stand here until dooms-day? Then again, if a car did come by, what if it turned out to be a highway patrol? So many things to worry about, I had to block them out or else be a nervous wreck.

More cars did come along. Lots of them as the morning got later, but none so much as slowed down, no matter how pitiful I looked. My hopes sank lower with each one, especially after I noticed the first buzzard circling overhead. Had the scavenger spotted a possible meal standing down here? Would others join, forming a circling buffet line above me? I watched the graceful bird float so high, riding the wind, looking free and beautiful, but once back on land, the drooling meat eater turned hideous, with a beak like two carving knives, happy to slice up those unable to resist.

Tires crushed in the gravel, causing me to look down. A pickup truck had pulled to the shoulder. Ignoring that part of me that wanted to take off the other direction, I ran to the window. A rancher type sat behind the steering wheel. "Where to, bucko?"

I thought about his question—name the wrong place, and he might drive off. It seemed best to generalize. "West."

With his thumb, he pushed back the brim of a cowboy hat with bird feathers, toothpicks, and wood matches tucked in the band. It struck me as odd that he wore a long-sleeved, flowered shirt rolled up to the shoulders and a padded vest as though, despite it being a summer scorcher, he expected winter. "West, you say?" he asked. "Where 'bouts?"

I still worried about being left behind. "Just west."

"There's lots of *west* out there, bucko. Which one?"

"Any one. May I get in?"

"Japan? How's that for west. You going to Japan?"

I feared my answer had been taken as smart-aleck, so I grinned to show no harm had been meant. "Not that far. Can I ride?"

"S'pose so. Get in, bucko."

I picked up an edge of irritation in his voice. "I'll go wherever you want to take me—that'll be fine."

Ignoring a twinge of uncertainty, I climbed in, and we got back on the highway. With the wind blowing in both windows and the pickup rumbling like the muffler had fallen off down the road, neither of us could hear the other. This worked out just fine with me, as I felt too tired to try and make conversation anyway.

The sun had risen above the horizon and shone brightly through the windshield, forcing my eyes shut. A warm wind blew in my face, and my head soon drifted over and vibrated against the window frame. For the first time in days, I felt almost worry free.

❦

GRAVEL KNOCKED UNDERNEATH the floorboard as cold, damp air blew in my face. I sat up, bewildered. What happened to the hot, dry wind? The pickup stopped, but the surroundings no longer looked even close to the same—no desert, no sand, no wide-open space. Now pine trees lined a steep road going uphill. I touched my face and felt water.

"End of the trail, bucko," the cowboy said.

A heavy mist hung in the tops of a forest beneath a low, dark sky. I couldn't make sense of anything. Where'd the sun go? What happened to the heat? What's with these mountains? I looked at the cowboy. "Where are we?"

"West." The cowboy winked, took a toothpick from his hatband, and picked his teeth. "You said let you off where I wanted. Well, here's where I want."

"Yeah, but..." I touched the dashboard. The leather felt real enough, so it couldn't be a dream. "Everything's changed."

"That's 'cause we're three hundred miles from where I picked you up. You been asleep nigh onto six hours. Now, I aim to turn off this highway and head down that dirt road yonder to my ranch. So, adios, bucko."

"But...How do I get to El Paso?"

"El Paso!" He took the toothpick out of his mouth and jabbed it like a lecturer's pointer. "To start with, bucko, I asked where it was you was headed. El Paso's south. We turned off north right after you conked out. We're halfway up the state of New Mexico."

"Which way do I go to El Paso?"

He leaned over the steering wheel and looked upward. "Judging from that sky, there's fixin' to come up a gulley-washer. If I was you, I'd head that way." He aimed his toothpick over the steering wheel. "If you're lucky, someone will come along and give you a ride, only this road ain't well-traveled. Straight west, you'll run onto a spank-new highway just built to Las Cruces, so head south. Hook a left and head, oh, about forty mile back east to El Paso. Now I've got to skedaddle, or this rain will have my road too muddy for travel."

I stepped out the door about as unwillingly as if we'd parked on a cliff edge. The pickup U-turned and drove across to the opposite shoulder and then disappeared over the edge. I ran to that side of the mountain and caught glimpses of the truck going in and out of the trees down a winding road. The truck vanished from sight for a long while but finally showed up far down at the bottom where the road flattened out and wound along the valley floor. The whole time, I silently pleaded with the cowboy to change his mind, to come back, to not leave me like this. How could he drive off and abandon me? For the first time, I noticed the cold—really noticed it.

With no jacket, I shivered and hugged myself. Now it made sense why the cowboy had worn long sleeves and a padded vest. Considering the change in elevation from the desert, it felt more like winter in the mountains. To make matters worse, the mist turned to a chilly rain. In no time, my clothes were soaked through, but that didn't concern me as much as who'd pick me up now? Who'd want someone sopping wet in their car? The answer, of course, was no one.

7

Abandoned

THE RAIN GOT heavier. Along a corridor of pines, gray clouds snagged in the tree tops. I tried to imagine what someone calm would do, someone not on the verge of an all-out panic, someone like Hect. Would he build a shelter of tree limbs and wait out the storm? Would he keep going even though no cars had come by? Other worries pressed in. Should I turn around and go back down the hill toward the desert or keep going up the hill in the direction the cowboy said? So many decisions to make that seemed like life and death that I couldn't even make one.

I missed Hect. Together, we always knew what to do. The reason I never knew without him, he told me, was that I'd grown up with too much. While he'd been forced to make it on his own in foster homes and living with relatives, I'd had maids and babysitters. A picture came to mind of him riding in that Thunderbird convertible, one arm around the St. Bernard, a hot wind in his face, sweating like always and happy as a king. I found out later that was hardly the case.

My situation, on the other hand, didn't seem like it could get any worse until, that is, dirty, gray-white patches appeared underneath the pine trees. My stomach dropped. I'd seen drifts like those before—on winter ski trips. No weatherman needed to tell me about it being colder in the mountains. It made sense that something far worse than just getting wet could happen. Rain at higher elevations turned to snow by evening and maybe flurries after nightfall. Catching a ride now became a matter of staying alive.

I re-crossed the highway and started walking uphill even though that meant an increase in altitude and drop in temperature, but who'd be crazy enough to ignore what the cowboy told me? The question was how to force cars to stop and give me a ride. Maybe jump in front of the first one to come along? Only, on this rain-slick highway no one could stop in time. Well then, what about lying on the side of the road and acting injured? Except, who'd see me in the rain? Added to that, the highway shoulders had turned into flowing creeks of runoff, no doubt icy-cold. No, barring a miracle, my chances seemed grim at best.

I pulled my wet shirt tight around me for warmth, but it didn't help. From my day's snow skiing, I'd learned the warning signs of hypothermia—sluggishness, disoriented, and most of all, sleepiness. Come to think of it, as far as sluggish went, putting one foot in front of the other took way too much effort already; and then, as far as being disoriented, who could've felt more lost? But the last one cinched it. Oh, to be tucked in my own bed, under my own quilt, with my head propped on a soft, cushy pillow, fast asleep. Hypothermia couldn't be far off.

Heavy, cold raindrops beat my hopes ever lower. I thought of nothing except that with each step, the elevation got higher and the temperature lower. The runoff along the shoulder had increased to a rushing stream as warmth-stealing water ran over my numb feet inside sopping tennis shoes.

A car splashed past me from behind, casting such a wave in its wake, it might as well have been off a speedboat. Not a brake light blinked. No sooner had it gone under a curtain of rain, than a truck appeared, barreling downhill and flinging a hail of stinging droplets. The tailwind knocked me back a step. I never had a chance to signal for a ride.

Bowing my head and trudging on, my thoughts turned solely dismal. Why? What was the point? Why go on? Who wanted someone dripping water inside their car? No one cared anyway. If only the end would come and get it over with.

A car whooshed past, hugging the shoulder, barely missing me. The driver had the nerve to honk. As if things weren't bad enough: a jerk. To leave me out here soaking wet—wasn't that enough? Must insult be added to injury? And yet, what if this turned out to be my just due? After what I'd done to the hobo at that shack in West Texas, didn't I have this coming? After all, what'd he done to deserve being burned alive? Did he have time to wonder who'd done this to him and why? And if he had his way, wouldn't he wish the same fate on me? How else to explain such a string of bad luck?

The next few cars flew by, but I didn't even try to flag them down. Why bother? What's the use? As I slogged along in a half-trance, my foot landed on a bottle that rolled, pitching me forward onto sharp gravel. Laying there in the cold runoff, I clutched a sore ankle as rain beat atop me like a small-fisted bully.

No longer having the will to get up, I thought of an old movie. In one particular scene, the explorer-hero got trapped in a snow bank after an avalanche. With his last few breaths, he moaned something about never feeling so warm and snug. Freezing to death for him amounted to little more than drifting off to sleep. For a way to go, it didn't seem all that bad. Already drowsy, I almost looked forward to it. Only a little while longer and…

A puffing noise intruded and I smelled exhaust. Aw, rats! *Now?* Why now? When the hard part was over, why'd they have to stop now? I almost wished they'd drive on.

"You there?" a female voice called nasally.

Should I answer or play dead? Maybe she'll leave.

"Hey, you there. Don't jump up all of a sudden, OK? That would scare the heebie-jeebies out of me. I'm only trying to help."

She prodded me with the toe of her shoe. I didn't react the first time, but then she nudged me above the hip in a ticklish spot, making me flinch.

"You're alive! Oh, good. Here, let me help you up. Oof! You're heavy. Why're you lying here? Did a car hit you? Are you sick? Here, stand up."

"F-f-freezing." Though wobbly, I got to my feet. "I-I-I'm f-f-freezing."

"I'll help you to the car, but you're too big. I can't support you. Come on, at least try."

"N-n-numb f-f-feet." I put one foot out and dragged the other up. "F-frost-bite."

"Oh, come on. You can do better than that. Try a little."

Once inside the small car, she turned the heater up all the way and steered back onto the highway. After a while, I thawed out enough to talk without my teeth chattering, telling her how no one would stop; how they left me to freeze; how close I came to death; how if she'd stopped any later, she'd have found a corpse, but the whole time, she kept the radio blaring so loud I had to shout above it. "Could we turn the radio down, please?"

"Turn it off," she said. "No music anyhow, just this freaky weather report."

"Because of the cold snap, you mean?"

"What cold snap?"

"Is it always this cold up here?"

"You're still cold? I'm burning up."

Something in the way she said it made me defensive. "It's freezing out there, you know?"

"Not hardly. The weatherman's told the temperature over and over. Seventy-two."

"Sev...?" I looked out my window in time to catch sight of a gray mound under a pine. "What about the snow under those trees?"

"Hail, you mean." She giggled. "It's summertime, silly. We had a horrid hailstorm this morning. Lots of wind, ice-balls the size of quarters, that's what made those drifts."

I didn't say what I thought. Seventy-two, my hind foot. Although it did seem odd, now that I thought about it, that wildflowers bloomed along the road. Anyhow, I knew better than to argue with her. After all, she'd rescued me.

The girl, meanwhile, talked enough for both of us. She had a habit of switching subjects before bothering to finish the last one. Her name was Zelda; she hated the rain; divorce in this country had become all too common; she'd turned seventeen last weekend; she was on the way to Albuquerque; she was going to a free concert tonight.

"Albuquerque!" It just hit me. "You said, Albuquerque. That's not on the way to El Paso, is it?"

"Heavens, no. I had a friend from El Paso once. She died tragically. Albuquerque's north. If you're going to El Paso, should I let you off?"

"*No!* Oh, sorry, I didn't mean to shout. I meant, no, thanks. I've had enough rain."

"We'll stop up ahead then and dry your clothes at a coin laundry. I'll bet you're hungry too. Take a guess at what the population for the state of New Mexico is."

"No idea."

"Seven hundred thousand. Can you imagine that? Some cities are bigger than that."

No longer listening, I noticed, even though she sat on a cushion, her head barely cleared the steering wheel. She had a ponytail on top that rose straight up like a water hydrant. Just then, she glanced over, catching me staring. From her frown, I guessed she awaited an answer. "Uh, sorry, what'd you ask?"

"I said, 'Why were you lying out in the rain like that beside the road?'"

How could I answer? Should I say something like, 'Oh, freezing to death in seventy-two degree weather'? Not likely. The problem was, no other half-believable excuses came to mind. Fortunately, we drove up behind a bread truck struggling to make it uphill, slowing our speed to a crawl. Backwash from the rear tires splashed our front windshield until the wipers couldn't clear the water off fast enough.

The girl leaned her head against the side glass while steering partway into the oncoming lane. "I can't see. That bread truck needs mud flaps, if you ask me."

I grunted, hoping once we got past the truck, she'd forget about asking any more personal questions, but, just in case, I ran through possible answers in my mind. Had a car hit me? No, in that case, where're the injuries? How about I hadn't eaten and fainted? Possible, but then how to explain all that stuff about freezing? Unable to come up with a worthwhile reason, I decided my only hope would be to get her off onto another subject.

She edged the car farther into the opposing lane but ducked back in time to avoid an oncoming tanker. No sooner had the big truck gone by than she wrenched the steering wheel, hurling the car into the left-hand lane as the tiny motor strained. We crept by the backwash off the truck, but the road curved to the right into a blind corner. Stiffening, I clutched my thighs in talon-like grips. The bread truck and our car sped neck and neck into the bend as we gradually built up speed. Edging up even with the truck's front end, we crept past at an agonizing pace. An oncoming car appeared out of the rain as we cut back into our lane in the nick of time.

"Ride 'em cowgirl!" she hollered. "Not bad for being blinded by all that dirty spray."

I breathed for the first time. "Whew, that's the first good luck I've had."

"Maybe it *is* good luck," she said. "Or maybe up till now you've made bad choices."

Caught off guard, I looked at her while wondering what kind of choice she'd call passing on a blind curve in the rain, but I held my tongue. "Yeah, could be." On the other hand, this had the potential to lead to a topic other than personal questions. "We all make bad choices, don't we?"

"We do, but the difference is where you put your trust. Luck's not much help when it's running against you, is it? A wanderer like you, what you need is God."

Caught off guard a second time, I hardly knew how to react. "You're talking like going to church and all that?"

"What's wrong with that?"

"Nothing—nothing at all, I guess." Despite being uncomfortable with the subject, it was better than personal questions. Even so, I couldn't resist teasing her. "So then, the key to making good choices is to stop believing in Santa Claus and start believing the Christmas story?"

"I wouldn't make fun, if I were you."

But who could resist such a lead in? "I'm not making fun. I just want to be clear. You're saying, if I believe in a baby born over a thousand years ago on Christmas Day—"

"God's Son," she interrupted.

"—in a manger with these wise men on camels from afar—"

"To die on a cross," she put in, "for your sins."

"—bearing gifts of gold, jewels and perfume after following this star, I'll make better choices?"

"You know the Christmas story, kind of, but not the meaning," she said. "God sent His Son to earth to rescue us. Sure, we make bad choices, some worse than others, but Jesus turns them around and makes the bad choices back to good ones. I'll start praying that you find that out for yourself one day."

It was too easy to poke fun. Besides, after she'd shown such concern, anymore jokes seemed out of place. "OK, you win."

"Anyway, you never told me why you were out there on the side of the road."

I winced. Cornered again. Here I'd done the very thing I intended not to do: end our talk and return to personal stuff. My only choice was to backtrack. "There is one thing along the lines of what we've been talking about, though, and maybe you could help me understand better, if you don't mind."

"Sure," she said. "Have at it."

"What about punishment?"

"And by that you mean…?"

"Punishment, you know." Somehow just mentioning the subject made me want to unload, but I had to be careful not to reveal too much. "Take me, for example. Was being left out in the rain like that and no one giving me a ride, my punishment?"

"I picked you up, didn't I?"

"Then you don't believe in punishment?"

"You didn't much like being out in the rain, did you?"

Frustrated, I decided to ask straight out. "Say, I did something wrong, so wrong it bothers me all the time. Everything reminds me of it and—what I'd like to know is—how to get back to normal, to being carefree. Not feeling guilty so much."

A semi blew past going the opposite way. Our car shuddered.

"Ask to be forgiven."

"That's all? That's it?" I studied the girl and noticed she'd be a lot prettier minus the spigot of hair. "Can't be. What about if a person got injured? Or died? Who pays for that?"

"That's the Christmas story."

"You don't understand." To keep from scaring her, it seemed best to change to the third person. "Say some guy—this is only for the sake of our discussion, remember—but say some guy did wrong and hurt someone—killed them—and got away clean. What then?"

"Lucky, I guess."

"Oh, no, not lucky, I promise you that. But, anyway, you see what I mean, don't you? If a person does wrong—steals, destroys property, kills, whatever—and gets away free, and there's no penalty ever, then people might as well do all the meanness they like. Who's to stop them? No one. I grew up in a house where there was no punishment and nothing made sense."

"God is love."

"So is my mother, but our family's a wreck. Something's missing. What scares me is that, if we went around that corner a minute ago and had a head-on and got killed, I'd have to pay for the wrongs I've done somehow."

"You mean, other than being scattered in a million pieces?"

"Yes, other than that. If not, then life's a whole lot like growing up in my house."

"How's that?"

"Chaos."

8

Sophia's Band

On the trip down the backside of the mountain, the rain remained at the higher elevations. Night arrived early because of the storm clouds. Below us and spread over a valley, Albuquerque lay at the base of foothills like a star that had crashed to earth, scattering sparkling particles in all directions. The highways ran with rivers of headlights.

Pine-scented wind blew in the windows and, for the first time in days, I inhaled a lungful of air without it being the result of running for my life. Earlier, the girl stopped at a coin-operated laundry, not only drying my clothes while I hid in the restroom, but also buying us burgers, fries, and malts at a drive-in across the street. Afterward, I felt bad as, even though I had the five bucks that Hect gave me, I hadn't offered to pay. Despite hating a skinflint, parting with any of my nest egg, my last security, proved impossible. Added to that, I'd forgotten the girl's name already and hadn't the nerve to ask for it after all her kindnesses.

With a full stomach and dry clothes, I had no intention of hitchhiking at night to El Paso, especially as thunder rumbled distantly and seemed to be growing louder. Instead, I agreed to go with her to the free concert in Albuquerque that night in spite of having no interest and really only waited for the storm clouds to pass. Then too, if they offered snacks, I might snag a few for later.

Our mountain road straightened into a sharp decline, like a ski slope ending at the city. We wound through a suburb and came at last to a stucco building with log ends along the roof line. A crowd had gathered outside. Next to the building was parked an old school bus, or so it looked, judging by its faded yellow color and partly scraped-off markings on the side, with a banner that read: SOPHIA'S BAND, EL PASO, TEXAS.

I perked up. Had my luck turned, finally? And yet, would the band allow a rider back to El Paso? Maybe so, but maybe not. As I discovered on the highway, some people wouldn't pick up a stranger no matter what. Then how to get aboard? As we drove through the parking lot, an idea started to form that completely changed my attitude. "At first, I wasn't so sure about this concert, now I'm glad to be here."

"Good," she said, stopping at the end of a line of cars. It wasn't a parking spot. She'd stopped in a driving lane, but something far more interesting caught my eye. "Do you suppose they leave the door on that bus open all the time?"

"Why not?" she said. "It's just a wore-out, rusty pile of junk. Who'd steal it?"

"Yeah, I guess."

Once out of the car, we shuffled in a crowd that packed tighter the closer we got to the gates. I kept my eye on her bobbing spigot until a puffy hairdo cut in between us. Once I got by Big Hair, the girl had disappeared. I couldn't even call out to her for having forgotten her name. After the gate, the confusion worsened as everyone dashed in different directions for the empty seats. I stayed behind by the back wall and, rising to my tiptoes now and then, tried to find her hair spigot.

The auditorium darkened except for stage lights. Applause erupted as a girl in a full skirt, puffy blouse, and rolled-over white socks, Sophia evidently, walked out, leading her band. She began a lively song backed up by guitars and a strong drumbeat that echoed throughout the large hall. Before I knew it, I got caught up with the cheering and began clapping and foot stomping as well, right up until the moment the room went dark. A silence spread over the crowd as a single beam of light shot through the dark, leaving a slanted spot on the stage surrounding Sophia. I moved up closer to the last row of seats, anticipating what would come next.

"This song was inspired by a news story that broke my heart," Sophia said in a singsong, her voice quaking. "It's a tale of a tragic young man. Although he never graduated high school, his parents enrolled him in college through connections, but after several years, he quit without finishing. He went from one job to another, never finding one that fulfilled his talents. Along the way, he fathered children by different women, although never staying long enough to enjoy the benefits of being a family man. Middle-aged and divorced several times, he moved back to his parents' home. In the bedroom where he'd grown up, among all his boyhood posters of sports heroes, he drank bottle after bottle of liquor, finally dying far too young." In a voice clear and resolute, Sophia sang a cappella:

> Americans have gobs of learning,
> but not a lick of common discerning.
> They jabber unending of raisin' their young;
> Prattling expertly with a knowing tongue.
> Discipline's too harsh, they proudly say;
> So their young treasures sleep and play.
> > That's how to raise a spoiled brat;
> > Yee-gads, not another spoiled brat.

> Work, the darlings, they never learned:
> Money, the sweethearts, they horde unearned;
> Wisdom, the dear ones, is forever spurned.
> So anxiety becomes their closest friend.
> Having nothing but fate to trust in;
> Boredom's the sole avoided sin.
> > That's how to raise a spoiled brat;
> > Yee-gads, not another spoiled brat.

Though their troubles go from bad to worse;
Though they're unaccountable until the hearse;
Though their wasted lives become a curse;
Still from problems, they do ardently run.
Penalties from poor choices is their outcome.
Decadence and perversion's the only fun.
> That's how to raise a spoiled brat;
> Yee-gads, not another spoiled brat.

At this point, the audience erupted in jeers and catcalls and concert programs filled the air. As individual hecklers joined in, the unhappy crowd seemed on the verge of losing control. Worried the concert might end early, I hurried from the building.

Outside, the air felt muggy. The rain from the mountains had finally caught up as drops polka-dotted the sidewalk. I dashed through the parking lot, ducked into the opened door of the bus, and made my way past scuffed-up instrument cases littering the aisle. At the back of the bus, I climbed over the last bench and wedged behind it.

Despite being cramped and bent at the waist in a V shape, I couldn't have been more pleased. Good luck at last. On my way to El Paso and in style, that is, compared to hitchhiking. My only regret was not being able to say good-bye and a proper thank you to the girl after she rescued me, dried my clothes, and bought hamburgers, especially as I never took time to learn her name. Then again, at least Hect and I would soon be together again. That made up for a lot, that is, if nothing else went wrong.

The bus motor started, putting me on edge. After idling forever, the bulky body moved as a whining engine wound tight, lifted a tone higher, lifted another tone, and lifted yet another until leveling off at a high-pitched hum. The unwieldy vehicle swayed with a gentle rocking motion. After several brief stops—traffic lights, I assumed—the engine remained at an unbroken purr.

Before long, my neck got a crick and the metal floor hurt my ankle and knee, but, I kept telling myself, it sure beats being out in the rain. Water ran down the bus windows and brought back memories of home. Would I ever get back? What would mother be doing? Probably on the phone with her sister, as usual. One thing, though, at least my father would have come home by this time.

Hot tears rose up as I realized that'd be the last we'd ever see each other again, or, that is, without steel bars separating us. The day Hect and I threw the fire bomb at the shack had ended any hope of ever having a normal life. I grit my teeth and clenched my fists, fighting against an overwhelming sadness. From here on, life would consist of hiding from the law and living in the shadows, so better get used to it.

Unable to hold back the tears, I managed to stifle any sobs or sniffles, using my shoulders to mop under my eyes and runny nose. Oh, how I missed home and how easy life used to be. Things hadn't been perfect, far from it, but so what? It beat not knowing what would come next or where I'd end up. Phooey on the life of an adventurer. If I could go back to a safe home, things would be different. I'd change. No more trouble, no more smart-mouth. I'd do my chores and not complain. I'd learned my lesson. Oh, but too late, too late. *Too late.*

The melody from that song kept going over and over in the back of my mind:

That's how to raise a spoiled brat;
Yee-gads, not another spoiled brat.

9

Hect and the Con Artists

BACK WHEN I'D been hitchhiking on Highway 80 in West Texas and saw Hect pass by in the red Thunderbird convertible, I'd thought him the luckiest guy in the whole wide world, but it turned out not to be true. The ride ended only a few miles down the road, and he then had his thumb out again. He told me later that riding with that "no-count, slobbering, tongue-wagging mutt over his head had been worser 'n losing a spit fight," plus the hound's breath smelt so like it'd eaten a bowl of stink bugs. Unable to bear the ride longer and thinking he'd hitch another one as easy as the first, he'd asked to be let out where two highways crossed. Big mistake.

This time, car after car went by, the same ones that'd passed me farther up the road. He stood there so long that he'd seen me go by in the pickup with my head against the doorframe, and then watched us turn north toward New Mexico. He had no idea what'd gotten into me to take such a detour and couldn't know I slept through it all. One thing he did know, though, was our planned meeting at the El Paso-Juarez border wouldn't happen anytime soon.

Hect stood there all morning. The temperature soared, he had nothing to drink, and the only shade around happened to be underneath the highway overpass I'd taken north. He crawled to the top of the cement incline, removed his boots to use for a pillow, and stretched out on a ledge, waiting for the hottest part of the day to end.

He awoke that afternoon with a throat so parched he told me, "Wasn't hardly no use to swaller," but then he saw something that made him dry gulp—a truck and trailer parked in the shade under the overpass. Judging by its blunt front end and the outline of a star on the door, it was an old Mack truck that'd come out of World War II. The exhaust pipe puffed black clouds, indicating the driver didn't intend to stay long. Hect slid down the cement ramp and not until he reached the bottom did he realize he'd been so excited that he'd left his boots.

The flatbed trailer in back of the cab had wood stakes as warped as a dinosaur skeleton. On the front of the trailer, a tarpaulin partially covered a pile of fireplace-size logs. Though the rocks hurt his feet, he dared not take time to go back up the incline after his boots for fear the trucker might drive off. So he tiptoed along a rocky shoulder but then stopped short, took an even bigger dry-gulp than before, blinked, and rubbed his eyes. Instead of the burly trucker that he'd expected, a young girl wrestled with ropes that tied down the tarpaulin. About his age, she filled out her jeans and T-shirt like no trucker he'd ever seen.

"Here! Let me!" He hopped toward her. "Give me the rope. I'll tie it for you."

The girl looked him up and down like she'd also seen something beyond belief, only of a more disappointing sort perhaps. Her red hair cut short reflected the sun like spun glass. "Where your shoes, fool?"

Uncertain whether or not she meant the name as a joke, he decided it really didn't matter. Considering his situation, he could hardly afford to get insulted. "What you need to tighten them straps," he said with a grin, "is a fella to get on t'other end of them ropes to back you up. I'll do it." He rounded the back of the trailer but pulled up short again.

A bald-headed man with a potbelly beat him to it. The man's stomach hung out his shirt at the bottom like a fat lip, and his trousers appeared in danger of losing their grip. He let go of the rope with one hand and hiked his britches up. "No hitchhikers, hillbilly."

Hect looked down at his stocking feet and wondered if the man and girl might not be kin, as they seemed to have a common trait for name calling.

"Hey, Poppa!" the girl cried from the other side of the truck. "That fool ain't got no shoes. Tell him to help me with these ropes. I ain't able."

"No," the fat man shouted back. "No hitchhikers, and I means it. Don't you cross my word, Daughter, you hear?"

The rope suddenly slackened, and the fat man nearly fell on his ample cushions.

"I ain't doing it, T.J. It's too hard for me."

Hect noticed she changed from calling him "Poppa" to "T.J." and suspected the name change had something to do with her getting her way.

"'T'ain't too hard, nuther." The man popped the loose rope angrily. "Don't go play-acting on me, Daughter. 'T'ain't no way I can do both sides at once't, you know that. Now pick up your end. You're not too old for an old-fashioned strapping, you know?"

The sound of weeping could be heard on the other side of the truck.

"Thunder 'n' lightning! Hogtie that malarkey, gal." The overweight man kicked gravel, hitched up his pants angrily, and glared at the youth. "Oh, go on, help the crybaby then, hillbilly, but don't be getting it in your head I'm your sugar pappy. You'll earn your keep, or we'll get shed of you quick-like, hear?"

Delighted, Hect bounded on tiptoe over the sharp rocks to the other side of the flatbed where, instead of crying, the girl smiled with sparkling eyes. She had about the prettiest face he'd ever seen as she handed him the rope and took a step back. He pulled the strap tight and started to tie a simple knot when she leaned in close against his shoulder. The smell was like sticking his nose in a rose, and it threw his body all out of kilter. He felt he was falling backward, sideways, and frontward all at the same time. Plus, his fingers hardly worked right.

"That ain't the way you tie a knot, hillbilly," she said.

He tried again.

"That ain't the way, neither. You're unhandy at knots, ain't you?"

His fingers got all tangled up.

"You tie a half hitch like a baboon."

The more she talked, the more he wondered if his first impression had been hasty. Pretty enough on the outside, she seemed a tad homely beneath the skin, but so what? As far as he was concerned, like most young men, "beauty" trumped everything.

"Looking at you," she said, "reminds me of a fella who spent his whole life with one foot atop the other hollering, 'Get out the way!' Oh, here, let me do it."

His face blushing, he stepped aside and watched her tightened the ropes expertly into knot after knot. Just as she finished, her father waddled around the back of the trailer.

"Look, T.J.," she said. "I'm checking his ropes, and see how good he done."

Her father inspected the knots and nodded. Afterward, he crooked a finger at the girl and the two moved off toward the back of the truck. As they talked, or rather argued, Hect spotted his boots at the ramp and debated whether to go for them.

A rock hit his shoulder. The stone hadn't been big enough to hurt anything except his feelings. The girl waved at him to hurry. Even though stung at heart, he shook it off, watching instead her curvy figure as she walked around and took the few steps up the passenger side into the cab. Sock-footed, he climbed in after her, too afraid to ask if they'd wait for him to get his boots.

The girl sat on the edge of the sleeper mattress, her feet dangling between the seats. Her father barely fit behind the steering wheel that'd rubbed a black stain on his T-shirt. Inside the cab lay crumpled snack sacks, empty soda bottles, and candy wrappers. Dust covered the dash thick enough to write in. After putting the truck in gear, the trucker guided the big rig out onto the highway. The girl handed Hect a two-quart thermos. He hastily unscrewed the cup cap, laid it aside and chugged straight from the container.

"What's your real name, hillbilly?" she asked.

He wiped his mouth on his forearm and handed the empty thermos back. "Hect."

"Hect? Sounds like a noise you make when throwing a fit. You know, gagging, jerking, stiff, foaming at the mouth, and gargling like, 'Hect, Hect, Hect, Hect!'" She laughed. "Oh, don't take it so serious. You look like no one ever teased you before. I'm always going on like that, but I don't mean nothing by it, do I, Poppa?"

The driver grunted.

"So, tell us where your from, Hecty."

Wincing, he almost preferred "hillbilly," but he didn't dare say so for fear of being put out on the side of the road. He made up his mind to say no more than necessary in an effort to save a little pride at least. "Back that a'way." He jerked a thumb over his shoulder.

"Tell us where you headed to."

"Up that a'way," he said, pointing ahead.

"Tell us where your home's at."

"Back that a'way," jerking a thumb over his shoulder again.

"Whew," she said. "You sure don't talk much. Same as T.J. here. How come you men don't never ask us gals questions like we ask you? Don't you care to know my name?"

"S'pect."

"It's Becca. That's short for Rebecca. Want to know where I'm going?"

"S'pose."

"To be a movie star."

"Hmph."

"Well, I'll declare. If someone told me they wanted to be a movie star, I'd sidle up aside them and jabber like a auctioneer. Don't you want to know what movie I'm about to hire out to and be a big star in?"

Hect had a new reason for giving curt answers. A black and white car with a flashing red light on top passed by. He'd been so startled, he couldn't think straight.

"Well, I'll tell you," she said, evidently not needing a response. "It's one they're filming across the border from El Paso over to Juarez,

Mexico. I seen it advertised in a movie mag about a prison, and they're hiring extras right about now. I've made up my mind to get me a part and end up a star in Hollywood someday."

Up ahead, the Highway Patrol stopped behind a pickup towing a horse trailer. As the gap closed between the Mack and those parked on the shoulder, the car's side door opened. A heavy-jawed officer glanced up as the truck passed. For a brief instant, Hect looked eye to eye with the man. He slid down in his seat.

"So, what's you think?" she asked. "Am I pretty enough to be a movie star?"

"Huh?" He scooted back upright and took a glance behind to make sure. "Oh, maybe so."

"My, my, it's flattery like that a girl just lives for. You sure know how to make a gal feel special."

The near miss, or what felt like it, reminded Hect that he better not get too huffy with the girl. He decided to forego their petty tit-for-tat. "Yeah, you're way pretty enough for the movies. Them other starlets today, why, they're dogs compared to you."

"Poppa?" the girl said. "I want Hecty here for my brother."

"No! You ain't getting him for no brother. You and me is family enough. Ain't no need for a brother. Forget it."

"But I want him, I said. I've made up my mind. You know yourself you always wished for a son. Why not him?"

"No. Now, I'm driving, so leave off pestering me."

"You're being contrary, T.J. Stop acting mule-headed for a second and think. He'll make a fine brother, except for having no shoes, but I'll loan him your galoshes. 'Sides, I'm worn out. Hecty can spell me from working so hard."

"You can't have him for no brother, Daughter. That's final. Don't mention it no more."

"Say trouble comes up," she persisted. "Like, say, you run onto someone who acts ornery. Why, me and Hecty here can start a scuffle, like brothers and sisters do. You'll get mad and say you got to go lick these two hammerheads, meaning us, and we'll jump in the truck and run for it. Anyhow, Hecty here can haul wood a whole lots faster than me."

"All you want, Daughter, is to get out of working. You ain't fooling me. You can't have him for no brother, and that's the finish of it."

"So, Hecty," she said, turning to him, "listen up, on account from now on you're my little brother. Me and T.J. work a con we call the 'poison log routine.' It works best in places like West Texas where there're no trees for firewood come winter. Truckers have to haul it in from faraway places like East Texas or New Mexico, and the cost is so high, folks are forever looking to hitch a deal come summertime."

Hect saw a town up ahead.

"Ut-oh," Becca said, her tone turning serious. "I ain't got time to explain more now."

"Pecos, Texas," her father crowed and for the first time showing some life. "Home to cantaloupes sweet as syrup and meat crispy as a honeycomb. Tastiest melons on this troubled planet, youngsters, let me tell you."

10

The Poison Log Routine

FLAT, BARREN, SANDY, sun-baked, and windblown, the land around Pecos, Texas couldn't have looked a more unlikely spot to farm, yet even-rowed furrows stretched as far as the eye could see. Between those plowed rows, tan globes a little smaller than basketballs lay by the multiple thousands in lines to the horizons. According to T.J., "'T'warn't no soil on earth could match that sun-dried sand for raising juicy cantaloupes."

At a roadside stand, T.J. bought a grocery sack full of melons and then filled the thermos at an irrigation canal. As he put it, "Hillbilly done drunk up all our water and left us not a'nuff to fill a teacup."

The three then cruised an upscale neighborhood in the Mack truck while pitching rinds out the windows. At a red brick house, T.J. slowed down and stopped. "This'd be it," he said, nodding at the other two. "My eye don't never deceive me."

Hect looked at the house, expecting to see something unusual, but other than the place being run-down compared to the rest of the neighborhood, saw nothing special. The lawn hadn't been cut in so long that weeds bloomed, the bushes in the beds had all died, and enough toys littered the yard as if an army of children abandoned a siege.

"Hillbilly," T.J. said, "time you learnt some'n. You see that cord of firewood in the carport yonder? It was cut no more'n two months ago, judging by its pale-green color. It's oak from down near Brady, is my guess, but it'll sell easy enough."

Hect nodded, pretending he'd been thinking the same thing.

"Now, listen up, hillbilly. Don't you never forget what I'm about to tell you. The poison log routine has to start off right. Start wrong, and you might as well pack it in on account of these here folks is upper-crusters, not like you. So, don't say nothing, or else they'll spot you as a hayseed 'fore you get two words out. Fact of the matter, we'll make you deef and dumb to be safe. Every now and then, give hand signals to your sister here."

Hect twiddled his fingers.

"That'll do." TJ opened his door but didn't turn off the motor. "Battery's low," he said on the way to the front door. "Rich folks gener-ally ain't of a mind to lend a working stiff no jumper cables."

Just before they reached the once-stately house, T.J. took hold of Hect by the nape of the neck. "Look it, hillbilly, if I get in a tight fix—and you'll know what I mean when it happens—then you and Daughter here start a squabble. I'll take it from there."

Becca stepped up next and got in *little brother's* face. "And I'm Big Sister, remember that. So, you got to do like I say."

Hect shrugged. So many people had been warning him all his life that he better do like they say that he hardly paid the threat any mind anymore. Besides, as always the case, what choice did he have? He climbed the steps to the front porch beside Becca. T.J., after giving the couple a last sizing-up look, pushed the doorbell. Chimes went off inside the house.

A well-dressed woman appeared in the doorway. Like her house, she'd seen better days. She had the typical West-Texas face: thin eyes, as though she'd spent her life squinting against sun and wind, leathery skin, and a complexion that looked permanently chapped. A clump of hair had escaped a tight bun and dangled in front of one eye. Three children peeked out from behind her skirt.

"Morning, little mother," T.J. began, grinning and tipping a finger to his bald head in a sort of salute. "I'm proud to see your flock clinging at your knees. You've a mighty fine litter."

Hect gawked. In the short walk up to the house, the grouchy old trucker changed from a coveralls personality to one more suited to a tuxedo. Not only that, but his voice took on such a cheerfulness and energy that, if Hect hadn't been riding with him and seen the man who spoke in grunts and threats only, he never would've believed two such opposite characters could exist in the same skin.

"What's on your mind, buster?" the woman snapped, her initial smile dropped off in favor of a wary pucker. She put one hand on the doorframe and one on a cocked hip. "If you're selling, cut it short. I'm in a hurry."

"Might fine day today, ain't it, little mother?"

She didn't answer.

T.J. cleared his throat. "Yes, ma'am, it's a real pleasure to see such smart-looking tykes." He moved to pat a little girl's blond head, but she clawed at him and pulled behind her mother.

"Look you," the woman said tiredly, "my old man left me a month ago with these three to raise, and I been searching for a job ever since. If you call me 'little mother' once more, I'll drive my knee so far in your backside you'll walk like a camel."

T.J. elbowed his daughter, who wheeled and backhanded Hect, who clutched a stinging cheek. The trucker then grabbed the boy by the neck and shook him so hard he saw double.

"Here, rascal," the fat man snarled. "You leave your sister be. I'll box your head so full of echoes till you think you live in a canyon." He turned back to the woman. "I'm sorry you had to witness that, little mo...er, ma'am. It's hard to raise young'uns without no woman to lend a hand."

Hect witnessed another remarkable personality change as the woman's features suddenly softened and her eyes lit up. "So, you're single, are you?" She tucked the loose strand back into her bun. "Why didn't you say so?" Her original smile returned.

"Yes, ma'am. She's been gone ten years now. Left me this here pride and joy." He patted Becca's head. "And this ornery half-wit," he added, indicating Hect, who busily rubbed a sore cheek. "The boy ain't never been able to speak nor hear much beyond a loud shout, but I do the best I can to keep them both with me."

"That's admirable of you to take on raising such a burden. You must have a trait or two that's worthwhile underneath all that Crisco. Would you three like some cake?"

"Like nothing better, only we got a job to get done."

"That so," she said, her curt tone returning. "Why're you bothering me then?"

"I stopped on account of that firewood you got stacked over yonder. You see, I been a firewood man for thirty years now and that stack is central Texas oak, ain't it?"

"How'm I to know? A truck like yours drives down the street and that nickel-hugging ex-old man of mine bought it. I got no idea where it comes from."

"I'm fixing to tell you where it's from. Brady, Texas, that's where, and the water wells around there have all come up radioactive. That firewood you got stacked yonder would make a Geiger counter chatter like a box full of false teeth."

"Radioactive, you say?"

"Yes, ma'am. I was on my way to your next-door neighbor to deliver my last load of wood you see on my flatbed yonder, when I seen your cord. I thought it best to warn you."

"Well, how dangerous is it?"

"No one knows for sure. If you burnt it reg'lar, it might won't make you or the kids too sick, but it'll sure do in a dog or a cat over time."

"I don't have a dog or cat."

"Still, I'd keep them kids out from in front of the fireplace this winter. A' course, you could always haul that wood back to Brady and ask for a refund, if you could find who owns the property where they cut the trees down."

"Is your head full of pickles, buster? Can a woman like me haul all that wood in the trunk of her car?"

"Just thought I'd warn you, ma'am." T.J. made a move as if to usher Hect and Becca off the woman's porch, but he really held them back. "I'll be on my way to deliver this last load to your neighbor."

"Hold on! You sure are in a rush. Say, is that wood on your truck OK?"

"It's mulberry, not oak. The roots stay near the surface. Besides, I don't get my wood from anywhere's near central Texas. It's from East Texas."

"Well then, why don't you trade that wood you got on your truck for mine? Then you can deliver my cord to my neighbor. She don't have kids, only a cat, but the critter's so sorry a little radiation might do it some good. That way, you can save me the trouble of hauling it back to Brady. How's that?"

T.J. pushed the two young people behind him protectively. "T'ain't legal, for one thing. I got a reputation to uphold, you know."

"Oh, don't get so high 'n' mighty." Her tone sweetened. "After you get done, I'll have us a chicken roasted and some mashed sweet-taters and cornbread for you and your youngsters."

The fat man appeared to squirm. "Ain't but one way I could make such a switch and not risk being seen. That's to pick up your wood and drive off. Then later, I'll come back and deliver to both of you and make the exchange. Maybe then we can all have supper, like you say."

After shaking the woman's hand to seal the deal, T.J. untied a wheelbarrow from the back of the truck. Hect loaded the so-called "contaminated" logs on the flatbed, and they drove a street over. The trucker sold it on the second try.

"It's mentioning the pets what does it, hillbilly," T.J. said instructively as they prowled another street. "There ain't a neighbor alive who wouldn't give to see the next-door dog or cat radiated."

11

A Close Call

AFTER WORKING THE poison log routine for the third time, Hect realized he liked being part of a winning team for a change. Neither T.J. nor Becca had actually invited him to join them, but he hoped they would. He'd never had such feelings on account of not staying in one place long enough to join anything like a sports team or some other school activity. Not only so, but having grown up in foster homes or else with relatives, he always had the sense of being *allowed* to be part of them, like a favor. For the first time ever, he saw a chance to earn a place without charity. Because of it, he wanted to get the little-brother role down pat, but just as he got ready to give it his best, T.J. quit. The trucker had a hard-and-fast rule never to go past time for husbands to get home from work. Men, he told the two, differed from gals on account of they were more likely to want to either ramrod or else lend a hand. He told of one old boy so eager to help he followed on his scooter all the way to the Oklahoma border.

On the way out of town, the trucker hit the brakes so suddenly the trailer wheels locked up as blue smoke blew past smelling of burnt rubber. He'd stopped next to a pile of red-colored firewood stacked at the curb. T.J. maneuvered the shifter and backed the big rig up. Neat rows of logs to a height of about four feet ran the length of a grand house with three chimneys. "Bless my soul, look it that. So nice'n evenly stacked just like gold bars."

"It's after five," Becca warned.

"Daughter, you'll not see nothing like that again in your lifetime. Them's two cords of prime cherry wood, and, judging by the split ends, they've been weathered from last fall. If you put them quarter cuts together, the trunks got to be forty-two inches 'round, anyhow. Wood like that burns so hot it'll make a cast-iron furnace blush rosy as a gal's cheeks, but it's wasteful. Many a barbeque rib joint will pay plenty for that tasty smoke."

Hect already had his door open and beat everyone up the walk. The doorbell sounded like a sledgehammer on an empty barrel.

A lady dressed in an outfit tight as a swimsuit answered. Her face dripped sweat, and a band held back wet hair. Female in every other way, she had a pair of mannish arms that looked to belong on a rough-neck in the oilfield. After one look, Hect's eagerness faded.

"Afternoon, lady," T.J. began, taking on his salesman personality. "Mighty fine day for a good ole, grunting exercise, ain't it?"

"What're you peddling?" The woman blotted her face with the end of a towel that hung off one shoulder. "I'm busy, pops."

The trucker flinched. "P...?" He seemed taken aback. "Oh, no, I—I ain't selling nothing today." To start, he sounded off his game. "I'm delivering that wood out yonder to your next-door neighbor, and I seen—"

"Hoa-up, pops! Back up. Which next-door neighbor?"

T.J. hitched up his pants and stepped backward off the porch. The fat man looked to either side. "That one, to the right. With the offset chimney."

"Harriet?" the woman called into the house.

A second woman appeared, also lathered up and even burlier than the first. Not as trim, her waist went straight up to ham-size shoulders. Hect's uneasiness worsened.

"Harriet," said the first woman. "How come you to order firewood from pops here when you don't burn none?"

"Here!" T.J. put in. "Beg pardon, ma'am, but either my two eyes have got the better of me or that's a brick smokestack at the back of the house?"

"Not for wood, it ain't," the second lady added. "It's for venting gas logs."

"Gas logs?" T.J. gasped as if he'd never heard of such. "Come again?"

"It's the latest thing." The lady drew herself up taller. "Out of Dallas. We don't burn wood anymore. Our fake logs look real and last forever, but the flame's gas."

Hect had never seen T.J. so off his stride. Because of it, he pretended to be overcome by a coughing spell, but really glanced behind for an escape route. Regrettably, a semicircle of thorny rose bushes hedged him in.

T.J., meanwhile, took a step farther back from the porch while at the same time, using his index finger to saw the back of his neck as if gaining time to think. A look of relief came over his face. "Blame my dogs, if I ain't got it backwards." He shook his head in disgust. "Now I see it. The house ain't on the right, neither, and I come within a hair of delivering to the wrong address. It's on the *left*, the one with the limestone chimney."

"Janice?" the first lady called, half turning but keeping an eye on the trucker.

A third woman appeared in the doorway, crowding the first two aside. She curled a barbell with globes of iron on each end big enough to chain a convict's ankle. Each time she lifted the weight, the skin stretched so tight it seemed the muscle might rip through.

"Pops here says you ordered firewood."

"It's him!" the third woman cried, dropping the weight with a crash. "On the radio just now, they said someone who hates pets is on the loose and stealing firewood."

Becca swung at Hect but missed, as he'd already leaped off the porch, trying to clear the rose hedge. Landing in the middle of the thorn bushes instead, he howled as the three women set upon T.J. They caught the fleeing trucker in the yard and wrestled him to the

— 77 —

ground. Hect struggled to break out of the clutching hedge, yelling his head off. Becca screamed and ran in circles as angry shouts from the women filled the air.

"Police!" one woman shrieked. "Call the cops!"

"I'll call," another wailed. "Hold him, you two." A door slammed.

T.J. bellowed. Becca bawled. The women cursed. Hect, however, at hearing the police mentioned, stopped fighting the hedge. The thorns lost importance as he realized in short order he'd be under arrest. Even worse, whatever warrants might be out on him—like for murder one, for example—would soon be discovered. Unless an idea came soon, he'd be in a cell on his way to prison or death row. The house door slammed, interrupting his thoughts.

"Where's your phone book, Maggie? I can't find the number."

"Forget it!" one of the women barked. "We don't need the cops. You two load him into my car, and we'll deliver Porky Pig to them ourselves."

"Hect!" Becca's voice lifted. "Help! Oh, help us! Hect! Hect! Hect! Hect!"

Hect's mind cleared like he'd heard an oracle. He knew exactly what to do and gingerly peeled the rose limbs off one at a time. Once free enough to climb onto the porch, he hurried down the steps, skirted the commotion with the adults, and stood erect in the middle of the front yard. So far none of the adults in the free-for-all noticed him as he un-tucked his shirt, reached up into the air, and began a clawing motion as if climbing an invisible ladder. A gulping noise arose in his throat as he fell onto his back, flung all fours out wide, kicked his feet, and flapped his arms, all the while holding his breath until the neck veins bulged. Spittle squeezed out the corners of compressed lips as he arched his back, shivering violently.

"Look!" cried one of the women, losing her angry tone.

"What's wrong with him?" another chimed in, sounding as frightened.

Hect looked over sort of walleyed, his face twisted. He saw, with hidden delight, the grown-ups had quit fighting. They gathered around him, staring down perplexed.

"He's purple!" a third woman exclaimed. "And covered in blood."

Thankful for the added effect of rosebush thorns, Hect rolled his eyes cow like, but he really searched the group for Becca. Once they made eye contact, he stared at her fixedly and started making a gurgling noise, something like, "Hect! Hect! Hect! Hect!"

"T.J.!" Becca leaped into the air and then grabbed her father's arm. "Hurry! Get help! Brother's having a *fit*! Hear him! It's a fit! A fit, I say!"

Hect redoubled his efforts at this, bowing from heels to head and going at it with all the vigor he could muster. "Hect! Hect! Hect! Hect!"

"Li'l brother's in a spasm!" she cried. "He'll croak this time. Oh, help!"

"Time's short!" T.J. wept. He ran toward the truck, stopped, turned about as if a thought occurred to him, and ran back to the group. "Hurry, Daughter! Where's the doc? No, ain't time! Hospital! Or he's a goner!"

"Oof!" Becca cried. "I can't lift him."

"I would, Daughter, but my back—"

"Out of my way!" The brawniest of the women pushed past the others and picked up the stiff body with the ease of a barbell. As she carried him, he flopped in her arms, kicking, gagging and drooling. Once she had him loaded into the cab, the worried-looking trucker and daughter hurriedly got in on the opposite side.

"Call a doc, missies!" T.J. hollered out his window. "Tell him to get medicine ready, on the hurry too." He shoved the shifter into gear, and they roared off down the street as he leaned out his window once more. "Not no ordinary medicine neither."

As they went, the three laughed until the tears flowed.

"'T'ain't calling you hillbilly no more," T.J. sang out. "From here on, it's boy genius. Man-o-man alive, I just thought I'd seen talent a'fore, but you, son—and from here on out, you *are* my son—you got a uncommon gift. Quick thinking, why that don't half a'scribe you."

"What about me?" the girl giggled. "After all, I'm the one who said his name sounds like having a fit."

❧

AFTER PECOS, HECT felt differently toward the father and daughter. His earlier desire to be part of a team had changed. For the first time, he found people he actually wanted to be around. He liked hearing them say his name, especially when bragging on him, and he also liked feeling as though someone special. Could that be what it felt like to be part of a family? He wasn't sure. One thing, though, he thought he might stay on with T.J. and Becca at El Paso. When they found Tim, maybe he'd want to join up and be a little brother too? This blissful state lasted all the way to Van Horn, Texas, where T.J. bought his first half pint of cherry vodka.

They stopped next at a truck stop diner in Sierra Blanca. T.J. bought two jugs of gin at the backdoor of the kitchen. About the size of canning jars, he drank the first one and flung the jug out the window before they reached halfway to El Paso. The more the trucker drank, the more he ranted about fuel costs rising to an unheard-of quarter a gallon, how the price of a new car had shot past a whopping nineteen hundred dollars, how going to a movie these days had risen from twenty to twenty-five cents, and who could afford that? After listening for hours, Hect thought again about being in a family. Maybe it was overrated after all. He looked forward instead to finding Tim and going on just the two of them, hoping only that Becca might want to join them.

El Paso arose out of the sand dunes like a hidden city. Mountains stood all around but so barren, the stubble of brush looked bristly as a five o'clock shadow on brown cheeks. Across the Rio Grande in Juarez, tiny huts filled the mountainside, seemingly stacked on top of each other. Mule-drawn or human-powered carts traveled on dirt roads while over on the El Paso side, busy highways of speeding cars wound among grand, shiny skyscrapers.

Once inside the city limits, T.J. stopped at one liquor store after another. The longer he drank, the better he drove, oddly enough, on account of he kept going slower. Before long, the truck crawled at about the same pace as people strolling on the sidewalk. Clouds of black smoke trailed behind, causing shoppers to gag and wave their arms in the air. Bored with staring at the passing storefronts, Hect glanced into the side mirror out his window, and sat bolt upright. "Law! It's the law!"

Becca leaned forward and looked into the same mirror. "Behind us!" she cried and backhanded the driver's shoulder. "Pick up speed, T.J. They're following us."

"Shet up, you li'l snip," the fat man slurred. "Leave off with your nagging and go play at your Raggedy Ann dolls." He stopped the big rig at a red light, but too late as the bumper stuck out into the intersection. The front wheels ended up so far past the crosswalk, people detoured around it into traffic and more than one shook a fist up at the driver in passing.

Hect lost sight of the patrol car in his side mirror, but by half standing, he spotted a red dome pull alongside T.J.'s window. The traffic light changed to green. Behind them, horns tooted politely. Becca punched her father's arm, and the fat man jerked as if startled from a trance. The truck lurched forward and stalled, halfway into the intersection. T.J. jerked the shifter out of gear and turned the ignition key. On what sounded like the last crank, the motor started. The engine roared, but the Mack didn't move because the trucker hadn't put the shifter back in gear. Behind them, horns blared, no longer politely. The traffic light turned red.

Hect noticed the red dome beside them hadn't moved on the green light either.

T.J. poked his head out his window and jerked erratically. "Shet up them horns!" he hollered out his window. "Honkin' devils!"

When the light turned green, the trucker rammed the shifter into gear, gunned the engine, and lifted his foot off the clutch. The truck shot backward with such force, Hect and Becca hit the windshield, knocking the glass out and shattering it in the street. A strong jolt from behind, along with the racket of crumpling metal, stopped the truck. Becca wound up out the window opening, clinging to the dashboard. Hect pulled her back into the cab, kicked his door open, dropped to the street, and helped Becca down. Across the cab, cops wrestled the potbellied driver out of his seat.

"I'm sick!" T.J. wept. "Diseased! Take me to a AA meeting! On the hurry too!"

Hect pulled Becca to the sidewalk. Once among the crowd, the two stopped and looked back. The truck's trailer sat atop a crushed car with a sign on the door that read *El Paso Gazette*. Helpful onlookers pulled people from the near-flattened car, one of whom had a camera around his neck. He began snapping pictures.

At the sight of the trailer, with all four back wheels off the ground, Hect realized the truck had not been rear-ended like he first thought, but that the trucker must've taken off in reverse.

A bright light popped in Hect's face that left a spot on his vision. He barely made out a man with a flash camera not ten feet away. With his luck, he figured he'd end up on the front page of tomorrow's paper for every cop in Texas to know exactly where to find him. Grabbing Becca's wrist, he pulled her through the crowd of onlookers. At one point, she jerked her hand free and started back, but Hect caught up to her. "He'll be OK, don't worry. They'll give him a nice iron bench to sleep it off and, come morn, he'll be fine."

"Who?" she fired back. "T.J.?"

"Yeah. He'll be all right."

"Who gives a hoot about him? It's my movie magazines, I want. I left them in the truck, along with directions to the place in Juarez where they're filming. We're going back."

"Back? No!"

"Are to. It's my dream, you hear? Nothing's going to stop me, nothing."

Judging by the determination on her face, he knew he better find a good reason to stop her and fast. "They've likely hitched the truck up by now to tow to the impound yard."

"I'm going back," she said fiercely, "with or without you. Now let go my arm, or I'll clock you a good one."

He released her, but only because he had an idea. "Stop flying off half-cocked for once and listen. You reckon movie big-shots are likely to hire a gal hauled to jail for having part in a drunken accident and running away? Think they'll want you for a star then? I'd say, no chance. We'd be way smarter to head for Old Mexico till things cool down around here and get your stuff later."

12

The Call of Doom

"WHAT'S THAT?" A voice called out, breaking the silence that'd lasted on the bus ever since Albuquerque. "See it? Sticking out in the aisle, see?"

After a long night of quiet humming, the man's question out of the blue scared the tar out of me. I'd been dreading those words, or ones similar, and had been waiting to hear them like the call of doom. My hiding place could hardly go undiscovered after a newly risen sun filled the bus with brilliant sunlight.

"Is that a foot?" a female voice asked, the same one that'd recited the poem.

My worst fears confirmed, I slowly drew my leg underneath the seat. To tell the truth, I almost felt relieved. In the cramped position I'd been in ever since climbing over the backseat, I didn't know how I'd last much longer anyhow.

"It's alive!" the man gasped. "Come out from behind there, you."

Since Albuquerque, I knew, sooner or later, there'd come a time when I'd have to step into the open, but it sure didn't make it any easier.

"Come out, I said. Who's there?"

"Coming! Hold your horses. My name's Tim."

"Tim, huh? The rest of you guys, wake up. We got a Tim stowaway."

Groans arose from different corners of the bus.

"Where's he from?" Sophia asked. "How'd he get aboard?"

Once over the seat back, I climbed into the aisle and thought I'd never get the kinks out. Stretching and backbends helped. The band crowded around me, staring as if a magician made me appear. No one said hello, how you doing, who are you, or anything. Talk about awkward. It looked like it was up to me to break the ice, maybe try to lighten things up. My days at the joke shop when called upon to entertain impromptu came in handy. Left with no choice, even though I hadn't practiced ventriloquism lately, I made my hand into a puppet while working the thumb up and down as a bottom lip, then cleared my throat in preparation to sing.

"That's how to raise a spoiled brat;

Yee-gads, not another spoiled brat."

To my surprise and delight, everyone roared. Instead of putting me off the bus, the band asked for more. I sang the refrain from Sophia's song over and over, not moving my lips except to join in the laughter. Afterward, while still using my hand for a puppet, I told a sad story about a mean-hearted cowboy who put a boy off in a thunderstorm; how the poor youth came close to dying from exposure (instead of freezing); how a sweet girl with a hydrant of hair rescued him and drove him to a concert, which, by the way, he thought the best he'd ever heard; and finally how he got on the band's bus to get out of the rain and ride in comfort to El Paso.

"El Paso!" the band members cried in unison and laughed hardest of all.

"Denver, you mean," Sophia said finally. "Our next engagement is in Denver."

The look on my face brought the house down, but all in all, things turned out better than expected. They ended up sharing their breakfast snacks—peanut-butter crackers, chips, apples, and sodas—and even passed the hat. After collecting the incredible sum of four bucks, we said emotional good-byes on the side of a Colorado highway.

Once again standing on a gravel shoulder of a blacktop with my thumb out, I felt there was little to complain about, seeing as how I had food in my stomach and money in my pocket. Added to the five bucks Hect gave me from the old man in the '48 Chevy, my savings amounted to a grand total of nine whole dollars. The only worry now was that my next ride might take it away from me, so after folding the bills into a tight square, I hid the wad inside my sock in the arch of my foot. A little uncomfortable, to be sure, but the feel of a lump in my shoe reminded me that, come what may, my nest egg was safe from misfortune.

It took all that day of short hopper rides to reach the Colorado border. From there, an Olds '88 took me to Albuquerque. The driver, an ex-supervisor of a road crew, had just quit his job that morning and left his wife and kids to "find his inner self". On the drive, he told me the tale of what he called the "New Mexico Department of Transportation Boondoggle."

"State bungle crats," as he described them, "spent millions on a new four-lane highway that went from Las Cruses all the way north to Albuquerque, or at least that'd been the plan. The problem arose in the last couple of miles because of an Indian reservation. The chiefs initially granted access, but then changed their minds and broke the deal at the last minute. As a result, the highway began at the bottom of the state and ended in a field of wildflowers. To get from Albuquerque to the ultra-modern highway, a car had to wind along a lumpy dirt road, part of which went through a trailer park; next, navigate open pasture land; and finally, climb a steep, man-made hill. After we traveled that same detour, the Olds turned around for Albuquerque, leaving me standing next to the brand-new highway with the lights of the city visible across that very field of wildflowers.

As I waited for cars on that lonely shoulder, night slowly enclosed me in a pair of black jaws, and I, standing at the edge of the throat, or that's how it felt anyhow, awaited the swallow. Far away, mountain silhouettes could be distinguished from the dark heavens only by the lack of stars. My knees knocked as I braced for whatever hungry man-killer might leap out of the quiet forest behind me.

When a car finally climbed the steep hill on the last part of that detour, it arrived like a ray-eyed dragon from the underworld—first, waving beams of light shot upward, along with a growling engine and tires clawing gravel. Next, a shiny grill appeared with what looked like chrome-capped fangs, all the while accompanied by the sounds of a gunning motor and rocks scooped into the wheel wells. By the time drivers negotiated all that, they raced by as if more in the mood to run down a hitchhiker than give him a lift.

Just as it seemed things couldn't get any worse, they did. All at once, as if by a starter's signal, the air filled with flying things out of the forest. Millions of vibrating wings hummed in the air all around me with the inevitable head-on crashes into my face and neck and down my shirt collar. I slapped all over, tore grasping claws out of my hair, jerked my shirttail out, and ran in circles among a blizzard of bugs.

Unnoticed because of my panic, a fancy car had parked on the shoulder. When I finally did see the Cadillac, I set an all-time personal record for the dash to catch up to it. Never in a million years would I have guessed such an expensive car would stop at this time of night, but who cared? At finding the back door locked, I sprang for the passenger handle, while swatting wildly at the swarming creatures, and dove inside.

Thankfully, a grandmotherly woman sat behind the wheel. Thoroughly winded, I couldn't speak at first. In the overhead dome light, the old woman's face had wrinkles covering every inch of skin, all of which seemed to smile along with her lips.

"My goodness, child, you're so out of breath," she said in a crackly voice. "Are you all right? Are you hurt?"

I heaved and blew.

"Gracious sakes alive, what is it? Is something after you? A wild animal?"

"Worse." I panted. "Much, much worse."

"A pack of vicious dogs? A black bear? What's frightened you so?"

"Just in time—you stopped." I managed in between breaths. "Saved me."

"A mountain lion! Oh, no, a panther. Yes, they're around here, I've heard, and can be dangerous too. A little girl was attacked once. Thank heavens you escaped."

"No, no, flying things—sharp claws. They bite, too." Actually, I couldn't remember being bitten, but it seemed reasonable. I finally got my wind. "Lucky, I kept moving—otherwise stung. They're all over out there."

"Oh, them," she said, sounding relieved. "You mean, moths."

"Moths?"

"You scared me half to death, child. I thought no-telling-what might be after you."

"Just *moths?*" I was glad we sat in the dark, as I felt heat rising in my cheeks. "Regular moths? Do they bite?"

"Oh, no-o."

"Sting?"

"Lands, no, they're harmless, child. They're just plain old moths. They swarm after a rain this time of year. They'll be gone in a day or two."

Lights from an oncoming car showed crushed smears on the windshield; plus a few of the fluttering insects had come inside with me. Blushing until my ears rang, I would have said about anything to save face. "But they fly real fast, like Tommy-gun bullets, and when they hit, they sting." It was only making things worse, though, so the best idea seemed changing the subject. "Thanks for stopping. I was sure glad to see your brake lights."

"I'll bet you're hungry, aren't you?" she said and switched on the interior light. "Have some chocolates."

"Gee, thanks." I took several from a box of Millionaires, glancing up to make sure she didn't mind. Once again, the many creases zigzagging all over her face smiled with her lips.

"*Grandma!*"

I jumped so the chocolates went flying. When getting into the car, I hadn't looked at the backseat, being too much in a rush. Now I did. Among piles of books and pamphlets sat an older man, in his twenties maybe, sitting like royalty with legs spread wide, sporting dark glasses and holding a white staff. Then it hit me. Besides being blind, he also couldn't hear well, judging by the wires from his ears leading to a device in his shirt pocket.

"Grandma!" he cried again in the same shrill, irritated voice. His accent sounded foreign and unfamiliar. "I smell damp air. Did you pick up some riffraff again?"

I moved to introduce myself when the elderly woman put a finger to her lips and shook her head.

"No," she called, switching off the interior light and guiding the big Cadillac back onto the highway. "I opened a window, that's all." She reached over and touched my shoulder, either saying hello with a pat or else assuring me she had done no wrong in telling a white lie.

"Answer me, Grandma. No more good-for-nothing waifs riding for free, I told you."

"I did answer you, Ichi. Just now. I didn't pick anyone up."

"Grandma, answer me! I swear, we can't go anywhere without you picking up a smelly, penniless, unwashed vagabond. This is the last straw. I won't ride in the same car with highway trash. You better listen, or I'll have you committed and make the judge appoint me guardian."

She reached over the back of the seat while guiding the car one handed. A hollow thud followed.

"Ow! Not so hard. OK, OK, but it's your fault I had my hearing aid off in the first place. You and that confounded old geezer music."

"Classical, not old geezer, and I've told you twice already that I didn't open the door and there's no one else in the car but us. I rolled down my window."

"All right, but next time warn me. You know how I detest independent acts and simply will not tolerate them."

"Yes, Ichi," she said. "Now then, practice your lecture for tomorrow, and I'm going to listen to Beethoven's 'Moonlight Sonata,' so turn off your hearing aid."

The elderly woman drove so fast the telephone poles flew by and moths hit the windshield like spitballs.

"Ichi?" she called. "Oh, Ichi?" A quiet followed. "Well, child," she said and by her tone meaning me, "we can talk now. Ichiroh has his hearing aid off. He's a war orphan. Supposedly, his father led the generals who tried to stop the emperor from making peace at the end of World War II. My son came across him in Tokyo and adopted him.

— 88 —

Since then, we've done everything in our power to meet his every need and anticipate his slightest want to make it up to him for all he's been through. As I'm sure you'll understand, Ichi is suspicious of strangers and somewhat touchy to communicate with at times. So then, I'm glad to have another person to talk to for a change. Now, tell me, why's a boy like you way out here at night all alone?"

I worried that the hearing aid in back might not be off completely.

"It's OK," she said. "My grandson can't hear us. Without his listening device, he lives in his own silent world, and quite frankly, he prefers it that way. Except for me, Ichi doesn't like people much, and at times, I worry about me."

"Thank you!" the grandson in back announced before I could respond. "Thank you, thank you. You're so kind!" He spoke loud enough to be addressing an audience. "No, really, please, that's enough. Sit down, do sit down, please. Oh, a standing ovation, how thoughtful. You're so kind, thank you." He cleared his throat and paused as if allowing time for his listeners to settle. "The purpose of our gathering today," he piped in an accent like nothing I'd heard growing up in West Texas, "is to enlighten modern parenting duos on recent advancements in child rearing. The title of my unbiased lecture is 'Corporeal Punishment by Parental Thugs on Innocent kids.' The, ugh…The, ugh… Ughmmm, that is…"

"Ut-oh, poor Ichi's lost his place," the elderly driver explained. "But don't worry; it'll come to him. So tell me, child, where's your home?"

"I've left home."

"I thought as much." She heaved a sigh. "When I set eyes on you beside the road, a little bird whispered in my ear that boy has been mistreated."

"Ayeee!" the voice in back yelled, followed by short, choppy exclamations that to me sounded like a percolator coffeepot, only angrier.

At first, I feared his fury directed at his grandmother or even me until remembering he didn't know I was in the car.

"Poor Ichi," she said. "He gets so frustrated when he forgets something that he scolds himself in Japanese, but don't pay it any mind."

"Oh, yeah, yeah!" he cried. "Now I have it!"

I relaxed a little.

"It's a proven fact, ladies and gentlemen," he went on, still at the tops of his lungs, "and verified by every reputable polling agency in America, that ninety-eight percent of all children are irreparably harmed by paddling. The other two percent end up serial killers." He chuckled to himself as if he thought that quite the cleverest aside. "Thankfully, though, my own organization is working to ban corporeal punishment. If enough people give generously to my cause, congress can be swayed to pass laws that prevent parents who discipline their children. We…We…We… That is…"

"Oh, my, that's twice now he's lost his place," the older lady observed, sounding worried, "but he'll get it, you'll see. He's very smart. Ichi wrote his first best seller about raising babies at the age of thirteen without ever having a child. Now he's in demand for speaking engagements at universities all over America."

Another burst of Japanese.

"Child?" she said, lifting her voice above her grandson's. "Don't you think your mother's worried about where you are?"

"Of course!" he yelled so loud my ears rang. "Worthy citizens, listen to me. Recently, I've received good news. There's been elected to the legislature a sympathetic leader to our cause. We simply must get behind Congressman Gustav with our support. He has come under attack by the forces of unreason for his bold statement that 'Any parent who paddles a child ought to be taken out and shot.' With such ardent passion, Congressman Gustav is working his hardest to promote juvenile emancipation. There are signs of…signs of…Oh, no…er…"

"We'll be in Ruidoso before long, child," the woman said over the mumblings. "That's where my grandson's giving a lecture at the college. I'll let you out there."

"Aaagggh!" The exasperated yelp sounded in pain. More Japanese.

The grandmother's remark just now hit me. "Ruidoso? I know Ruidoso. My parents and I vacationed there many times, but I thought you were traveling farther than that."

"…S-s-signs of *hope* on the horizon, that's it!" the grandson cried in triumph. "Outside the narrow-minded borders of this backward country, progressive nations have outlawed…have outlawed…let's see… oh, yeah, have outlawed corporeal punishment. One Scandinavian country is so progressive, children are encouraged to form groups and retaliate against their parents."

The luxury car swung around a bend in the road and entered a resort town. Even in the dark, I recognized the mountain village. I'd been to Ruidoso often on weekend trips to escape West Texas heat or else in the winter to hit the ski slopes. As we drove under a streetlamp, I looked at the kindly old lady, wanting to ask if I could stay on, wishing I didn't have to get out, but she didn't look my way.

"Best of luck to you, child," she said, steering the Cadillac to the side of the road. We stopped. "Here, take this before you leave."

With my door already open, I accepted the fistful of bills.

"Grandma!" the young man in back yelled. "I feel a draft again!"

After mouthing a silent "Thank you," I eased the car door closed.

13

The Pines Diner

AFTER THE LUXURY car drove off, leaving me on a dark, quiet street, I felt empty and lost, but not hopeless. I still had my ace in the hole, my nest egg, my one bit of security. Thanks to the six dollars from the lady in the swank car, four more from Sophia's band, and the five from the old man in the '48 Chevy, I would eat once the first restaurant opened. Fifteen whole dollars should be more than enough for three squares and a place to spend the night. Why worry beyond that? Instead of dreading tomorrow, I couldn't wait for it. Only a couple of hours more to go and I'd be home free. Oh, the horrors of being penniless.

After passing rows of dark shops, I came to a wide-open grassy area with a playground, a fenced-off swimming pool, and a lawn enclosed by dark pine trees. The park brought back many memories. No telling how often I'd played on that swing set or slid down that slide, but without the cries and laughter of kids, the place seemed as creepy as a cemetery. Even creepier, a life-size gorilla stood with its arms lifted like King Kong in back of the park's lone bench. Many times I'd had my picture taken hanging on the ape's arms and never once thought of it as a place to spend the night. Nevertheless, I curled up on the cast-iron bench, but, unable to stretch out, my knees wound up under my chin. With King Kong's arms hanging over me and the park so gloomy and lonesome—talk about a place to give a guy nightmares.

Once I got still, the mountain air really cooled off. It reminded me of the last time I felt this cold, right before the girl whose name I couldn't remember came by. It seemed like weeks ago she picked me up, not the day before yesterday. One thing, though, at least I'd learned that being a little chilly didn't mean freezing to death.

Despite being so tired, I couldn't sleep. My mind was troubled and wouldn't let me shut my eyes. What if a robber lurked in the shade of those pine trees just waiting for me to doze off? He could creep up and steal my nest egg while I slept. Maybe he wouldn't find the stash in my sock, but maybe he would. While putting my arm under my head for a pillow, I felt a crevice in between one of the bench's slats and the metal armrest. No thief would have time to take apart the bench. My savings would be safe there. After taking off my sock and folding the bills into a tight square, I wedged them into the gap. Relieved, I closed my eyes, worry-free for once.

That next morning, a barely risen sun put out so little heat that it'd be laughed out of the state of Texas. Forced to sit up by such cold, I rubbed my arms and shivered, but what I saw in front of me added to my misery. The street ran bumper to bumper with traffic, and not a single passing motorist bothered to look in the direction of the cold, hungry figure on a park bench. The gorilla could've come alive and bitten my head off, and no one would've cared. It taught me that busy people in a rush don't see outcasts like me.

Of all the comforts I could think of, none compared to sleeping late just one more time in my own bed, but cold and hunger didn't allow wishful dreaming. I had to get moving and start the blood flowing and generate some body heat. With every joint stiff and aching, I stood up and slapped my arms while stamping frozen feet.

None of the restaurants had opened yet, so I walked in front of them and looked in the windows. At one time or other, I'd eaten in them all. Back in those days, my parents and I chose eating places based on mood—Mexican for fun; Italian for special occasions; steaks to celebrate; Oriental for a difference—but not one had ever been chosen based on gut-wringing, grinding hunger like I felt now. My only comfort was in my recently discovered knowledge that skipping a few meals meant distress, not starvation.

Main Street ran the town's length with the usual tourist traps—pinball parlors, pool halls, go-carts tracks and miniature golf courses. Narrow side roads ran down to a creek with motels and rental cabins along the water. When we used to drive from one end of town to the other in the family car, the distance seemed like nothing, but now on foot, the road wound endlessly up the mountain.

An aroma floated on the air as sweet as that of a pretty girl trailing perfume, only bacon flavored. I stuck my nose up, my heartbeat quickened, and I followed that scent as if love struck. Off the main drag and a block over, sure enough, a building had more parked cars around it than the Buick dealership back home. The mouth-watering fragrance got stronger until I spotted a run-down building with what appeared to be a hand-painted sign over the door:

THE PINES DINER

Once past a screen door, a room full of square tables had booths lining two walls. Smells hit me first—sausage, bacon, and onions frying—while my eyes lingered on such feasts as plates of fried eggs, scrambled eggs, stacks of pancakes, hash browns, waffles, and biscuits, along with steaming cups everywhere. Even more astonishing, the customers, who should've been shoveling food in with both hands, preferred to waste time talking.

"Table, hon?"

I jumped sideways. So distracted had I been by all the sights, I failed to notice the cashier counter. Behind the cash register, a woman filed her nails, hardly paying me any mind. She had bleached white hair and wore a name tag on her blouse that read "Snowball." As she hadn't yet looked up, I couldn't be sure whom she meant. "Huh? Or, pardon?"

"A booth then, if that's your pref, hon." She shrugged and glanced up disinterestedly. "Your choice. This way."

At a booth with a street view, she handed me a menu, but I didn't have time to look it over and ordered on the spot. Waiting for breakfast to arrive, I drummed my fingers on the table and watched the first shoppers mill around out the window.

My food came steaming hot and smelling good enough to skip a knife and fork, but I used them anyway. The first mouthfuls burst into flavors of meats, potatoes, butter, and eggs. Chewing was a blissful grinding up of those tastes while adding sweets of syrup, jams, juices, and mixing in bread and pancakes. But then, hardly before I got a good start, my plate lay bare. Except for those initial bites, I hardly remembered enjoying any of it. Disappointed, I picked at the last crumbs and dragged a finger over smears, licking off the jam.

Snowball brought the tab. Heavy-hearted at having to reduce my savings for a meal that went by so quickly, I searched one pocket, another pocket, and then my back pockets. Beginning again, sure of some oversight, I went through my pockets one more time. Sweat broke out on my forehead. Every nerve in my body tensed. I dug through them again, this time being extra careful and finally stood up and pulled all my pockets inside out. Next, I slipped off my shoes and felt in my socks. Snowball watched the whole time with one eyebrow cocked.

"I had it. Honest. I swear." I looked at her, about ready to drop to my knees and beg. "You've got to believe me. Word of honor, I had it."

Her eyes narrowed. "*It?*"

"I'm not lying, either. Please believe me. I had fifteen dollars. A friend gave me five before we split up, and a grandmother and some musicians gave me ten more. I had enough to pay for breakfast last night on a park ben—" The memory hit so hard it knocked me into my booth. I lay my head on the table and wished I could pull my brain out and slap it.

"Look, hon, up to me, I wouldn't care...but it ain't up to me, so why bother? You pay, or I call the law, which is it?"

I jerked upright. "Law! Oh, no, not them. Please?" I imagined the warrants that'd be discovered back in Texas. It crossed my mind to make a run for it, but how far would I get? While putting my shoes back on, I wondered if Snowball had a soft spot.

"Listen to me, please." I looked up at the waitress, hoping to appear pitiful. "I hitchhiked here, and this jerk cowboy in a pickup let me off in a driving rainstorm. Because of that no-good, dime-store cowpuncher, I got soaked and almost died in a…" Noticing her bored expression, I decided to switch tactics to a more businesslike approach. "Could you ask the owner if he'd take an IOU with my personal signature?"

She rolled her eyes.

"I'll pay back every cent, honest. I'm good for it, too. I just need a little time to run back to the park and get my money, but if it's security you want, I've vacationed here many times with my parents." Uncertain how that secured a debt, at this point, I threw in everything. "Could you at least ask?"

The blonde wagged her head. "You don't want me to, honey, believe me. He's in the worst mood ever today. He lost his dishwasher this morning, and he's having to bus tables by hisself, so you're only setting yourself up for the riot act."

"Can you at least ask him? Please?"

"All right, but don't say I didn't warn you." She half turned while keeping one eye on me. "Eli!"

The customers inside the diner quieted and looked toward us.

"Eli, get out here! Now!"

A big man in a dirty apron burst through swinging double doors along the back wall. The diner customers turned toward him. He took off his cowboy hat, pulled the apron over his head, rolled down the sleeves of his flowered shirt, brushed off his padded vest, and put his hat back on. One look at the bird feathers, wood matches, and toothpicks in the hatband, and I about slid out of my booth.

"Hey, Snow," the man whooped. "What've you dug up now? That there's the one I told you about. You 'member me telling you—I give him a lift, and he wouldn't say where he was headed, 'cept only west. So I took him west, all right."

My eyes bored into Snowball, trying to read if she'd reveal my earlier hasty remarks regarding her boss, which I now deeply regretted. She winked as if to say not to worry. The cowboy strode through the crowded diner. "Bucko, did you get wet out there t'other day?"

"Soaked actually." I managed a smile.

"Aw, don't take it so hard. From the look on your face, someone might think you're fixing to bust out bawling. T'wasn't but only water. Not like it'll hurt you."

"Yeah, just water."

The cowboy arrived at the table. Compared to how I remembered him from the pickup, he looked ten times bigger. He wiped huge hands on his wadded-up apron and offered to shake. His meaty mitt swallowed mine. "You ort'ta said you was headed here, Bucko, 'stead'a being so secretive. I'd'a brung you to town. Now I feel bad."

"I should have, you're right. You're, um, you *are* right, all right."

"My ranch ain't but only a mile or two over the hill before the turnoff that takes you to Albu-querk."

I chuckled, doing my best to hide a rising terror, knowing Snowball would speak any second. I looked at her and saw it coming.

"He can't pay," she said and yawned while patting a wide open mouth.

"Can't pay!" The cowboy's face hardened but just as quickly relaxed. "Shucks, if I didn't feel so bad about letting you out in the rain, I'd horse collar you and acquaint you with a good ole country drubbin', but I feel guilty. So you need a job, do you?"

"A job?" Caught off guard, I felt there'd been a miscommunication. "Oh, I've got money. Fifteen dollars, in fact. If you'll just allow me time to go to the park and get it, I'll be right back."

"Only place you're going is back yonder to the kitchen, bucko." The cowboy held out the greasy apron. "Either that, or come outside, and I'll work off some of this steam I got built up."

"A job, huh?" I took the apron, realizing all negotiations had ended. The material felt wet. "Why, thanks. Thanks a bunch."

"It don't pay nothing, so don't go getting your hopes up, leastwise not till you pay for that high-dollar meal."

"Fair enough. Only, I've never really managed a restaurant before. You'll have to show me how to run it."

"Ru—!" He choked as if the word caught in his throat, then bellowed hilariously. "Hear that, Snowball? Bucko's got him a sense of humor, he does. Yep, you'll run some'n all right—*run* the glass-washing machine, *run* hot water out'a the tap, and be sure to turn them glasses upside down 'fore you *run* them through too. But ain't no employee of mine goes hungry, so when you *run* them scraps into the disposal, e't all you like."

I lifted my shoulders agreeably.

"Look at it this way," the cowboy said. "In jail, you'd be washing out cells. Here, you're washing dishes. It's a whole lots better."

I followed the man into the kitchen under the watchful eyes of the entire diner, expecting to see a few dishes needing washing. Instead, I found pans, pots, bowls, plates, and skillets piled from the counter against one wall in a food-crusted avalanche, along with heaps of silverware. As soon as the cowboy left, I made a beeline for the back door but found it locked. Trapped, I resigned myself and put on the wet apron while filling a bathtub-size sink with water.

Surprisingly, the job went faster than I thought. Every item had been separated, rinsed, and stacked—wet, of course, but they'd drip-dry soon enough. Eli returned and, except for the glasses that went through the automatic washer, made me start over, this time with him standing watch. How was I to know to scrub with soap and hot water, rinse, and towel dry, having never washed a dish in my life? Doing the chore the way Eli wanted took all morning, but it taught me a valuable lesson that doing a job twice is more than twice as hard.

No sooner had I finished the breakfast dishes than the noon crowd arrived. By the time I washed all those, the dinner rush showed up. I got my first taste of the real hardship of manual labor: unchanging repetition.

Besides hard work, I experienced other new things, such as eating leftover scraps off the customers' plates. A good appetite overcomes any hesitations about that. I did pass on all but the untouched pieces—an unbitten chicken breast, a whole corn dog, the second of a two-pork-chop dinner, a few pieces of fried catfish, and, of course, fries by the bushel. Despite the scraps being cold or lukewarm, I never enjoyed food so much.

Eli seemed not displeased with my work. He even told me I could bed down in a booth that night, although I had a suspicion that, rather than out of the goodness of his heart, he wanted a free night watchman—that, and maybe to make sure I showed up for work in the morning, but he really needn't have worried. I liked having a roof over my head and the hope of an income one day.

By the time the kitchen had been cleaned and all the dishes put away, my hands had the feel of mushy steak fingers with skin like mashed potatoes. Eli left early to hit the honky-tonks. Before we closed up, Snowball gave me a lift to get my fifteen dollars, which I thanked her for over and over. She then drove me back to the diner and locked me inside. I turned out the lights and settled in for a pleasure I'd never known my whole life—the sleep of a working man.

14

Amateur Scammers

AFTER T.J. BACKED the truck on top of the car and got carted off to jail, Hect hoped Becca would trade her starry-eyed visions of being a movie star for practical concerns. For one thing, they needed to find shelter by nightfall, not to mention something to eat, plus some way to earn money, and a place to stay until T.J. got out of jail. She would listen to none of that, though, and instead made a beeline for the Mexico border. Except for her stubbornness, he would've told her about the five dollars he had hidden in his pocket from the old man in the '48 Chevy, but he knew she'd just fritter it away trying to get to that movie set in Juarez.

On the way to the international bridge, they stopped off at a bus station café. Bypassing the buffet line, Hect went straight to a condiment table and made lemonade out of sugar, water, and lemon slices and then grabbed a handful of soup crackers. Once at a table, he assumed Becca would do likewise and gawked when she arrived with a full dinner of meatloaf, mashed potatoes, and gravy on a tray. She'd skipped the cashier, but before either one could get a bite down, the skinny lady who ran the place, or acted like she did, came up and laid into them both.

Becca dropped her fork, still with a hunk of meatloaf on it, and shoved the tray full of food away. "Don't look for me to recommend this dump to my friends."

"Good," the long-faced woman shot back. "They're likely mooch-ers too."

"I wouldn't eat here for free."

"Well, Miss Sassy, I figured you two was down'n'outers and, as such, hadn't intended to call the cops, but now I think I will."

Becca stormed out in a huff, but Hect lagged behind. "I'm sorry, ma'am," he said, being extra pleasant. Judging from the hard look on the woman's long face, her threat had not been an empty one. Hoping to change her mind, although it broke his heart to do it, he fished out the five bucks he'd been given by the old man in the '48 Chevy and handed it to her. "Maybe this'll make up for what she taken?"

"What's this?" she asked.

"A five-dollar bill, ma'am. Whatever you figure she taken, it's all I got."

Her face relaxed and drew down even longer. "Keep it, but that smarty gal friend of yours needs a lesson in how to speak to her betters. She's too snippy for her own good." She patted my shoulder. "But you seem like a nice enough sort, only if I was you, I'd get shed of that little twit. She'll do you wrong in the end."

"Yes'm," he said and put the money back in his pocket. "Thanks for the advice."

"If you want the meatloaf, go ahead. No charge."

"I better not." He didn't feel right to eat without the girl.

Outside, Becca acted impatient and irritated. "What's taking you so long, and why're you gabbing with old horseface?"

"Aw, she's not so bad," Hect said. "But how come you to grab a plate like that?"

"I'm hungry," she said as if that justified it. "And we're wasting time! Let's go."

Hect walked beside her although he had to break into a trot now and then to keep up. "In the morning, we'll see if we can get T.J. out?"

"Psshaw!" Becca spat, as out of sorts as ever. "The truck's impounded, we're broke, and we got nothing for bail. I barely got a sniff of that meatloaf. 'Sides, he got his own self into jail—let him get his own self out. It's his fault I don't have my movie magazine with the directions. How'm I to find the place now?"

He hardly knew what to say. She seemed to care more about her movie career than her own flesh and blood. "But we can't just leave him there."

"He's grown. He'll take care of hisself. Anyhow, we show up at the jailhouse, they're liable to arrest us too, who knows?"

Now that he thought about it, she had a point. Even if they didn't get arrested, a curious jail clerk might nose around in any visitor records. Hect sure didn't want that. As far as Becca being content to leave her father sitting in jail, he explained that away with the excuse she just had her head full of all this movie-star nonsense. Besides, how often did a guy meet a gal so outright gorgeous? Her beauty covered up any defects he could see, and those he couldn't see, he ignored.

As they neared the international crossing, they talked of how grand a sight it must be with flags waving and the bridge being built out of special stones like marble maybe and no telling what all kinds of ornaments and decorations. They also discussed what the Rio Grande River must be like, so blue with ships sailing back and forth.

Once they got there, though, they both stopped and stared like they'd seen a princess turn to a frog. Not marble or special stones at all, but chipped-up gray cement formed the bridge, and in place of waving flags, trash blew everywhere. The only ornaments consisted of hand-painted drawings so nasty that, to keep from facing one another, the two ran and looked over the edge.

More disappointment. Down below, the Rio Grande water flowed muddy brown with an oil film atop the surface that didn't look normal. Come to find out, Juarez pumped its raw sewage into the river. Brown-skinned kids stood up to their chests in the moving water, holding buckets on the ends of long poles. Tourists tossed coins down and the kids caught them in those buckets. A lady heaved a whole handful of change. They couldn't snag all the coins, but quick as water bugs, they dove beneath the greasy surface and came up grinning, holding high the silvery pieces to show that none found the bottom.

At the customs station, Hect asked an agent if anyone matching Tim's description had been seen, but the man just pointed to the masses milling back and forth for an answer. Becca asked how to get to the movie set and got bad news as well. The guard said the place wasn't in Juarez but miles out in the desert somewhere.

Across the international bridge, the crowds got even thicker. The couple could no longer walk side by side on the sidewalk, so Hect trailed after her in the gutter. Smoking taxis crawled bumper to bumper next to him on so narrow a street that he tightrope-walked the curb now and then. While watching his feet during one such time, Becca stopped short and the two collided.

"Watch it!" she snapped, although distracted by something inside a restaurant window. "Look'ee there, would you."

Hect moved next to her and leaned toward the glass pane. "Crowded, ain't it?"

"Not that. Right in front of you, dimwit."

Disregarding the name-calling, he cupped his hands to the glass. "Oh, yeah, all that food, man-oh-man."

"Are you blind? Right there—the fella that's all busted up."

A man sat at a table next to the window. Except for the glass, Hect could've touched the sling that held his arm. A plaster-of-Paris wrap began at his wrist and went up past the elbow to his shoulder. Underneath the table, a pant leg had a slit up to the hip exposing a second white cast. Crutches leaned against his table. On a platter in front of him sat a juicy T-bone steak, but instead of eating it, he had his head cradled in his free hand, looking low-spirited.

"Got him a settlement out of that broke arm and leg," Becca observed, "and the dope has throwed the money away at the dog track too. It's our luck he ain't gone broke yet. The sucker's ripe for plucking, or I ain't the judge of character my poppa raised."

"How you know all that?"

"By looking, naturally. Hadn't he bought him a steak he ain't got the appetite for? Would he order one and leave it sit if he was broke? Not likely."

"No, the part about the race track?"

"You sure don't notice much, do you? Look at the racing form on the table. See how it's twisted like a wrung-out dish towel. That's what he's done to his innards losing his settlement. Look at him. He sure ain't no winner."

"But the dog races?"

"Greyhounds. Durn. Sometimes I feel like I'm with a fourth grader. The greyhound track is over in the ritzy section of Juarez. They got palm-tree-lined avenues and ritzy hotels and fine homes. T.J. goes over there and throws his money away too."

"OK, OK, but what's all that got to do with a settlement?"

"No one gets rid of cash quicker than a lawsuit winner. T.J. says so. He even has a saying, 'Greenbacks easy got is cheaply thought and slickered for naught.' I've seen him do it lots." She took Hect by the arm, "Now I ain't had nothing to eat hardly, so I'm about to talk that sap out of his steak. You fall in behind me and do as I say, but being a greenhorn, you're liable to mess me up, so don't say nothing. Just to be sure, I'll do T.J.'s old trick and make you deef and dumb."

"Why not just ask for his steak? He's not eating it. Maybe he'll give it to you?"

She glared like she never heard anything so stupid and entered the restaurant. At a table where the man sat hunched over, Becca took a chair as bold as if she'd been invited. Uncertain what to do, Hect sat down as well.

"Here, Mister, let me help you commit suicide," Becca said, picking up the man's knife and fork. She cut his steak, and once the blade passed through the char, red juice filled the plate. She held the bite out for him.

The man looked up with bloodshot eyes. "How'd you…?" His sad face frowned. "Say, *what?*"

"Sure 'nuff. I'm glad to lend a hand to a fool set on killing hisself."

"But…?" He broke off. "Listen, young gal, you've mistook me for someone else."

"So you say." She held the bite-sized piece of steak between them, dripping red juice on the table. "You're the only one 'round here smooching up to the Grim Reaper, ain't you?"

His frown deepened. "What are you talking about, for Pete's sake?"

"Ever hear of a blood clot?"

"I have, if it's any of your concern."

"Eating steak in your condition, unable to move an arm and leg, you're asking for a blood clot that'll hit your brain like a lead slug. If your doctor didn't warn you, then you got cause for a mis-practice suit, unless you're going against his orders."

"Bull!"

A tiny puddle of red juice formed on the tabletop. Hect had an urge to lunge forward and snap that bite of meat off the fork.

"Bull?" she repeated. "Well, it's certain sure you know a lot about it. Are you medically trained? I'd say no, eating a slab of poison like that."

"Bull!"

"You sure say that a lot. You must be in the cattle business. Me, I'm a doctor's daughter. Ain't that right, Hecty?" Still holding the fork, she made hand signals with her other hand.

He nodded and made hand signals back.

"Doctor's daughter, my foot." The man smirked. "You ain't either, but, here, you fresh snip, don't you eat my steak."

Too late, she already had the bite in her mouth. At the same time, she rolled her eyes as if put upon. "It's for his own good, ain't it, Hecty?" She made hand signals.

He nodded and made hand signals back.

Becca slapped her hand atop the table, causing the two seated with her to jump. "That's it! I quit! I can't do it! Hecty, you think this fella's falling for this line of hogwash? Not hardly. He ain't no more believing one word of what I say than nothing."

Uncertain how to react since he wasn't supposed to be able to hear, Hect looked at her with an injured expression. She, in turn, cut another piece of steak and scraped the meat off the prongs with her teeth. "Don't mind him, mister," she said, chewing. "As you can plainly tell, he's a born liar. Puts on like he can't hear or talk, but he's faking it. Myself, I can't tell a fib. He's the one put me up to this. Anyone could tell by the look on your face, you're way too smart to be fooled. I seen you looking around for the manager. Another minute, and you'd have set the law on us. The honest truth is, me and my brother here is flat busted. I begged him to let me ask you straight up to help us, but he made me perform this 'doctor's daughter' routine." She cut a third piece of steak and, her mouth working, surveyed the two.

Hect looked at the man and couldn't believe what he saw. At first frowning, then smiling, and finally breaking into a horse laugh, the man banged the table with his cast. He grimaced and hugged the hurt arm to his chest while still gasping hilariously. "Little gal," he called, chuckling. "I bet you nursed on chili peppers when a babe. I've never seen a gal with so much spunk. How's that steak, missy?"

"Burnt."

"I been sitting here feeling sorry for myself, so glum the idea of hanging myself sounded fun, and you come along and hit me like a pitcher of ice water. Picked me right up, you did. I'm sure glad. I s'pose now I got to buy your charlatan friend here a steak?"

"He'd eat it, I bet."

The man ordered two more steaks. They all gorged themselves as Becca told one bald lie after another and so angelic faced that Hect, who once thought T.J. the master at deforming the truth, had to admit his daughter mangled it even better. After she finished, the man broke down in tears and ended up handing Becca a ten-dollar bill.

Barely staying long enough for good-byes, the couple left and hired a cabbie who could speak a little English at least. After a long ride into the desert, they came to a gigantic object in the middle of nowhere. The structure looked real from a distance, just like an old-timey prison, but up close became a movie set. The walls had ivy partway up them, no doubt fake, and guard towers on top. Two massive gates blocked the entrance. The cabdriver parked, saying in broken English, "Movie go broke. Me drive sad actors to airport."

Hect asked why he hadn't told them that *before* they left Juarez, but the cabby no longer understood English. It took the rest of their money to get back to the city. Once again penniless, the dejected couple walked back to El Paso with hardly a word passing between them.

15

An Unhelpful Rummy

Back across the border on the American side, Hect noticed the area of El Paso nearest the bridge looked the same as over on the Mexico side. Narrow streets threaded among a honeycomb of shops; card tables full of wares blocked the sidewalk so shoppers walked single-file in gutters with taxis only a hairsbreadth away; old men pushed handcarts selling tamales or popsicles; and a constant racket of people haggling over prices arose everywhere. It sounded the same whether they bargained in Spanish or English.

"Time to get us some jobs, lazybones," Becca said with her usual charm.

He looked puzzled. "Ain't no jobs in this place. And even if we got lucky and found one, wouldn't pay nothing."

"Oh, there're jobs, all right. You just gotta know where to look."

"I *am* looking," he said, perturbed for a change. "And I'm tired of you acting like I'm the dumb one all the time. These shops around here hire their own kind, not us. We don't even speak their lingo."

"There he is!" She bolted into the street, starting and stopping in between car bumpers, bobbing and weaving like a running back on a football field. "There's our jobs," she called over her shoulder.

Stunned, he watched her run all the way to the other side of the street and zero in on a lone derelict shuffling along.

"*Him!*" Hect gasped, thinking she'd lost her mind. He ran after her, cutting diagonally across the street.

The shambling hobo, meanwhile, rounded a corner and trudged down an almost deserted side street, hobbling stooped over, his head bobbing as loose as if his neck muscles had come undone. Just before Becca caught up to the shabby figure, Hect grabbed her arm, pulling her a safe distance back. "Just what'a you think you're fixing to do?"

Her pretty eyes narrowed. "About to ask that rummy for a job."

"You ain't serious?" Hect snickered. "Tell me you're joking—*that loser?* Why, if he ever had a job, we wasn't born yet. Plus, I can smell the wine clear back here."

"Just the same, he knows where to find work." She jerked her arm free. "And he's almost got away, thanks to you."

"Oh, no you don't." He grabbed her again. "I'll take care of it. This ain't no job for a gal. If anyone takes a chance around here, it'll be me, not you."

"You know these sorts, do you? Have you growed up with them? Have you had supper with them and had them for playmates and invited them to your birthday parties, 'cause I have. I know them like my own kin."

"I can ask a simple question good as you. I told you already; quit acting like I got the sense of a billy goat."

"Rummies ain't the same as normal folks, you know? They don't swap pleasantries like the average Joe on the street. They're none too good at small talk on account they've marinated their brains in hooch."

"I said I'll handle it. Stand back and watch."

She bowed in a mocking gesture and backed out of the way.

He ran ahead and caught the dismal figure. After he laid a hand on a skeletal shoulder, the bum turned slowly around. One look and Hect fell back a step.

The man's face had been brutalized. Possibly a prizefighter at one time, he had eyebrows of hairless gray scars above a flattened nose pushed off to one side, frog eyes that looked like gun sights on a battered pillbox, and mangled lips that'd been stitched together too many times.

"Huh?" the hobo croaked in a hoarse voice.

"Hey, there." Hect put on his friendliest manner. "What're you doing?"

"Wha'…?"

Because of the hobo's cauliflower ears, he guessed him to be hard of hearing and so leaned in closer. "I said, what're you doing?"

"*Wha'…?*"

Hect could feel Becca's eyes on him, and it made him feel awkward. He decided to slow his words. "I…said…what…are…you…doing?"

"*Wha'…?*"

"*What…are…you…doing?*" he shouted at the man's beat-up face.

The bum's mismatched nostrils flared as he drew a breath. "*Wha' 'm I doin'—Wha?*"

Baffled momentarily, Hect realized he'd been misunderstood. "No, no," he said, lowering his voice. "Not what are you doing, like trying to find out *what* you're actually doing. It's my way of saying 'howdy.' Most folks answer back with something like—'Not much' or 'Same ole.'" At the sound of Becca's giggling, he tensed up and tried a different tack. "So, *how're* you doing?"

"Wha'…?"

"I said…how…are…you…doing?"

"*Wha'…?*"

"*I…said…how…are…you…doing?*" by now yelling.

"*Wha'…?*"

In the background, Becca's stifled laughter caused Hect to blush until his ears warmed. He took a deep breath and screeched, "*How…are…you…do…ing?*"

"How'm I doing—*wha'…?*"

Becca stepped between the two, grabbed the short wino, and shook him. "Tell him how you're doing, rummy."

"Hey, hey," he cried, losing his combative tone. "Leave off me, you."

"He asked you a simple question, now answer him before I box you one upside that flea-ridden head of yours. Tell him, I said, or I'll straighten out that funny nose."

"Le' go, le' go! Wha's wrong w'ich you?"

Becca shook him. "Tell him how you're doing. Come on, say it."

"Fine, fine. I'm fine. I'm good. It's a beautiful day, ain't it?"

"Don't get smart." She released him. "Now that's more like it. You only need help with your manners, 's'all. Now tell us where we can find work. Hey, don't doze off, pay 'ttention. Where can we get hired out?"

The bum partially lifted his arms as if afraid of being hit. "Wha's it to ya?"

Becca grabbed him. "I'm warning you, rummy."

"Le' go, le'go. No need to get rough."

"Out with it. Where're they hiring day laborers? Speak up."

"A work café. Not far. You can hire out there. They got jobs."

"Where? I said. Ain't you got ears?"

"Down the street. There's a big sign out front says 'Fast-One's'. Can't miss it. Jobs, rooms to let, meals—all on credit. The gal who runs the place keeps a tab, and if you don't take care, she'll charge for breathing her air too. Now leave off me."

Becca walked by him without another word.

In passing, Hect could not resist one final remark. "How you been?"

"*Wha'...?*"

Becca pulled Hect out of earshot of the bum's railing.

16

Fast-One's Café

The building at one time had been an old movie house. A marquee above the entrance stuck out like the bow of a ship overhanging the sidewalk. On either side of the ticket booth, cobwebbed posters in glass cases had the picture of a sneering cowboy pointing two six-shooters. In its heyday, the building's second story may have served as offices, but now laundry hung out of opened windows. Big black letters on the marquee no longer advertised a movie but instead displayed the sign:

FAST-ONE'S CAFE

MEN ONLY

One look and Becca spun around, shielding her face. "Sorry, ole, drunken sot," she fumed. "That rummy knew they didn't allow no gals here. Keep walking, Hecty."

"What sort'a place is this?"

"A work café." She kept her back to the front windows until they'd made it past. "No cash needed here. Everything's done on IOU's. Most big cities that got a skid row have one, my mom says."

"Never heard of such. At towns in West Texas folks help each other for free."

"Momma ran one on the docks of Houston. The pickups come by every morning and hire however many workers they need that day. All the company paychecks went to Momma, and she taken her cut before the guys could hit the wine shops. No one got rich, but everyone worked and ate and had them a place to lay their head at night. She run hers that way anyhow, but trouble is, this place don't allow but only guys."

"What'll we do?"

"Bulls make steers, don't they? Why not the opposite?"

"'Bulls make ste…'?"

"Never mind, just watch. First, we got to find us a Salvation Army or a pawn shop or mission store, some'n. They're always around these parts if you look hard enough."

A block over at an army-navy store, Becca traded a gold bracelet and a zirconium ring for a woolen cap and an extra-large khaki shirt. She stuffed her hair into the pullover cap and left the shirttail out so it hung to her knees. "All that's left to give me away is my voice," she said, while studying her outfit in a full-length mirror. "So, now it'll be my turn to be deef and dumb. You'll do all the talking."

"Me?" Hect thought of his recent episode with the rummy. "Aw, I don't know these guys like you do. Just deepen your voice."

"All it'd taken is one slip up, and we'd be done for, maybe even arrested. I got a feeling you don't want that. Seeing your face every time we happen onto a lawman—the way your eyes bug out, and you look this way and that like searching for a hole to jump into, I don't know who or what you're running from, but it's some'n."

Hect clammed up after that.

The café had only two customers inside. One sat in a booth shaking a finger at an empty chair and another slept with his head on top of the counter. A large, round woman dried dishes behind the low bar while belting out Tennessee Ernie Ford's popular song "You Load Sixteen Tons." Her width looked equal to her height, reminding Hect of a medicine ball, and her jolly disposition contrasted with the place's drab interior of patched walls, stuffing hanging out of furnishings, and large gaps in the floor linoleum leaving bare cement. All in all, she looked a refreshing sight, considering the endless procession of glum faces out on the streets, a sort of oasis in a desert of sad sacks, but, as he would soon find out, an oasis can be a mirage.

The beefy woman looked up and quit singing. She grinned, exposing two canines in her otherwise toothless lower jaw. Smile lines enclosed her lips, and laugh lines crinkled the corners of her eyes. "Look'ee here what's come dragging into my lair, boys," she boomed in a voice as large as herself. "Have you a look-see, I say. Why, they ain't no more'n kiddos. I'm so used to ole, wore-out roosters, they're like newborn chicks." Her body shook with her rollicking.

Hect and Becca halted and traded looks that expressed wonder at so robust a greeting.

"You ain't got to be scare't of me. Come on in this place. I'm as good-natured and fun-loving as you two will ever meet." She threw out her arms as if awaiting a hug. "Call me Fast-One. What'll I call you?"

Neither moved. Becca elbowed Hect, who edged away from her. He couldn't think of anything but the rummy on the street and, as such, was unable to get a word out.

The woman's grin lifted her whole face, and in place of hugging them both, she wiped her hands on her dish towel and blotted the back of a fleshy neck. "Say now!" she said, breaking the silence. "If neither of you orphans got a tongue, we're in deep vinegar on account'a I don't know no sign lingo." She reared back and hallooed.

The joke gave Hect an out. With no time to weigh the pros and cons, he turned and made hand signals at Becca. The girl gawked. He wheeled back to face the round woman, who showed similar astonishment, and pointed to his mouth with a shrug.

"Why, strike me cross-eyed, a pair'a mutes!" the woman howled, exposing her bottom fangs. "Must be my lucky day—a sign some'n good's bound to happen to me." She whooped like it already had. "So, neither of you two can talk, huh? Leastwise, you can't be liars." This really set her off as she grabbed her sides. "Don't mind me, I'm always having fun. That's why they call me Fast-One on account'a I pull comical gags on the boys around here, and how they do love it too. Life's hard, but with a little effort, you can have a ball is my motto. But, here now, you two no-speakies, just let Fast-One know what it is you want. Besides having a good time, I'm one gal full of the milk of human kindness. Need a place to lay your head?—I'm your haven in times of trouble. What about some good honest work?—I'll get you jobs. Hungry?—I'm a chef deluxe. Sit right down, and I'll fix you a meal this instant."

Hect reached in his back pocket, intending to show the woman he had no money, but it had the reverse effect.

"Put that back, scalawag!" she threatened, shaking the fist holding the dish towel at him, her index finger pointed as menacing as a gun barrel. "Money," she spat. "Did I ask for money? You both sit down this instant before I get my feelings hurt, and I'll fry up some hot hamburgers, plus we got okra gumbo left over from lunch."

She put two meat patties smothered in onions on the grill that sizzled and dipped gumbo out of a bowl onto plates. The couple watched hungrily; the steaks they'd eaten earlier a distant memory.

Fast-One glanced over at the man asleep on the counter. "Shove over, booze-hound, and give place to these tongue-less strays."

Instead of moving, the slumbering fellow snored on. After winking at the couple, Fast-One slid the towel off her shoulder and twisted it into a tight braid. "Here!" she hollered. "No flies allowed in my diner." And she snapped the rat-tail on the sleeping customer's ear.

The man leaped up with a painful yelp and clapped a hand to the side of his head. Fast-One laughed and, at the same time, made a shooing motion. He slid down a stool, flashing such a glare beneath a sulk, it should've left a scar.

"The boys are worser'n kids," Fast-One crowed, after delivering two plates of hot food. "I've always got some little practical joke to get their minds off their dreary lives. They act like they don't like it, but deep down, they love my horseplay. You might say, I remind them of the old ladies they run off from back home." She reached over playfully and tousled his shaggy head. He glowered up at her. Finally, he laid his head back down and soon began snoring again.

"Dirty, sorry, and smelly as they are," Fast-One went on. "I wouldn't trade for none of them." She leaned with both hands on the counter and winked. "Ain't none would take for me neither."

Hect clutched his throat with one hand and sat bolt upright. Becca pounded his back as if to dislodge whatever might be stuck in his throat. He waved her away and spit a mouthful onto his plate, then drank an entire glass of water. His eyes watered, and his face turned as red as if he'd swallowed a hot rivet.

Whooping merrily, the round woman moved out of the way of a shelf behind her. A line of bottles had surprisingly professional looking labels on them.

FAST-ONE'S VOLCANO SAUCE

"Didn't I say they was *hot* hamburgers? It's my own creation," she boasted. "It's all the alkies around here can taste. Homemade hot sauce. Why, I concoct stuff down in my basement you'd never believe. Make my own moonshine too. Even got the newest label machine. A few drops of my hot sauce and you'll howl at the stars." She gasped with laughter. "Me oh my, there ain't nothing like good clean horseplay to pass an afternoon. If it wasn't for jokes and acts of charity, I couldn't hardly stand to put up with the ornery, long-faced boozers around here."

Hect nibbled at the fiery food, chasing it down with gulps of water. Becca did likewise.

"Looks like you ghetto gypsies lost your appetites," the merry café owner said, drying a plate. "But don't worry, I got a room for you tonight. I'm the onliest gal what'll house the likes of garbage-gardeners that populate this neighborhood. I feed and clothe beggars, put a roof over their heads, and even provide work gloves. And what thanks do I get?—None, naturally. All I get is gripes about the fees I got to charge to keep the place open. Like I'm going to do all this for free, like I'm a church, but I don't mind. It does the boys good to grumble, and it don't bother me none. The more they gripe and fault-find, the more I tease and play jokes on them; that's just the kind'a gal I am. I ain't about to stop enjoying myself and get grouchy. Just too durn good-natured."

Fast-One presented each with a slip of paper. She fetched a nub of pencil out of her hair, motioning they sign. The receipt listed her services and all the charges but one.

Cost for 3 Meals $ 2.50
Room Rent $ 4.50
Job-Finders Fee $ .50
Room Cleaning Fee $ .50
Lenders Charge $ .25
Extras Charges $_____
    Total Charges $_____
    Signature_____

Before signing, Hect read the receipt. All the expenses looked reasonable other than the blank space after "Extra Charges," but how much could that be? Adding them in his head, he came to a total cost of $8.25 per day. Any temporary help job Fast-One found them would pay minimum wage, $1.25 per hour, meaning for eight hours he'd make $10.00. Subtracting $8.25 from $10.00, he should clear $1.25 per day. Not bad. Not bad at all. He touched the end of the pencil to his tongue and signed his name, adding a fancy loop at the end of his signature. Fast-One drew a line through the "$2.50" for '3 meals a day' and handwrote in "$.85 for one meal" to the side, lifted a cashbox from underneath the counter, and put both IOU's inside.

Afterward, the couple began a long wait for the café to close. As ten o'clock drew near, more and more customers filled the tables until the place packed out. Everyone had the same meal—okra gumbo and red beans—although Hect and Becca passed on the Volcano Sauce. As they finished eating, the men stacked the dirty plates on the counter, and Fast-One submerged them in a sink full of grimy water and turned off the grills, but then, she did something peculiar. She spread two handfuls of coins on the still smoking grills where earlier she'd fried hamburgers. She even flipped the loose change with a spatula. The coins soon turned a dull red.

As the clock reached straight-up ten o'clock, Fast-One slid the blade of her spatula under the coins and carried them to the front door. Curious, Hect and Becca followed. Outside the café, lying along the sidewalk like dozing alligators on the banks of a black river, bodies stirred and yawned. The woman cocked her arm back, careful not to spill the coins, and then underhanded the spatula in a motion similar to a softball pitch, lofting the change into the street. The winos sprang to life and followed like crocks after ducklings, swearing as they fought over the change, swearing worse as they tried to pick up the near-molted metal pieces. They managed to get them into their pockets somehow and disappeared into the night.

"Off they go after bottles of port," Fast-One roared, standing in the doorway with hands on her board hips. "How that pack of rapscallions do love to play my games." She turned around and almost ran into the couple. "You two?" she said, winking at the looks of horror on each face. "It's onliest way to get my storefront clear for the company pickups tomorrow. Come on inside."

After locking up and turning off the lights, Fast-One led the men out the café back door. She climbed a wooden staircase up to the second floor with her ragged troop in tow. Somewhere along the way, the chuckling woman added a new touch to her outfit. A belt around her barrel waist showed the grip of a pearl-handled pistol in a holster.

Upstairs, a long hallway of rooms had four cots each inside, except for the first one that had a shower stall and toilet. Hect and Becca shared a room with two other men, both of whom reeked of wine. No one removed clothes or even shoes before climbing into the cots. The beds sagged badly, and the covers smelled of dust.

"Becca?" Hect whispered. All evening, he'd been worried over the way she refused to look him in the eye. "Psst, hey, gal?"

No answer.

"Becca? Psst, Becca?"

"Sssst!" she hissed back. "We ain't able to talk, 'member?"

"Aw, don't mind them two. They're so drunk, they don't know nothing. Everyone in here is plastered but us."

"That was the bone-headedest idea ever," she snapped. "What in the name of Sam Hill was the big idea of acting like *neither* of us can talk? Me, OK. Why you?"

"Not so loud. Fast-One might hear. Anyhow, it's just for around this place, not on the job. We'll talk at work." He felt her anger and wished he could think of some way to calm her down. "It seemed like a good idea at the time."

"Well, it warn't! Not by a long shot. Uncommon stupid, s'more like it."

"Shet ya trap, loudmouth!" one of their roommates slurred. "Anymore, and I'll shet that mouth 'a your'n. You'll be quiet as six feet under."

17

Skid Row

Hᴇᴄᴛ ᴄᴏᴜʟᴅɴ'ᴛ sʟᴇᴇᴘ. The surroundings were strange for one thing, but even worse, the man across the room kept hollering bloodcurdling threats. At first, Hect thought the warnings aimed at him and Becca, but when the two quit talking and the murderous outbursts kept on, he looked for some other cause. Then he saw it, or rather heard it. The other roommate—the one across from the enraged blowhard—snored so loud he shook the air.

Unable to shut his eyes, Hect kept watch on a single pulsing glow across the room in the direction of the man shouting death and destruction. The red cigarette ash whirled around crazily, sometimes two at once, as the chain-smoking windbag cursed and swore and waved his arms. He lit one cigarette from another and, judging from the height of the glowing ash, sat up in bed. His shouts grew loudest in between times when the fiery tip pulsed faster and brighter.

What happened next made Hect spring awake out of a drowse. The ash floated upward and hovered briefly at the height of a man; then floated in a bobbing motion, coming to a stop at the area of the dark room where the snoring man's bed was located. The red ash pulsed hotly, descended, and vanished.

Hect waited. Nothing happened. He saw only black. The ash didn't reappear, nor did the chain smoker light up another cigarette. But even more curious, for the first time that night, the threats stopped. Now *both* men snored.

Alarmed, Hect eased out of bed and crept to the bunk where he'd last seen the ash. He felt around atop the covers. At a suspicious wad of blanket, down deep in the crumpled covers, a sharp sting nipped his fingertips, and the smell of smoke choked him. Nestled like a cinder at the bottom of kindling, an ignited ring of fabric glowed.

After spitting on his burned fingertips, Hect pinched out the smoldering material, dropped the cigarette on the floor, and crushed it beneath the sole of his boot. On his way back to bed, he ground his teeth angrily. "Lame-brain wine-head," he murmured. "Did he think only the one bed would burn up?"

Once back in his bed and with the entire floor of men sounding as if snoring in unison, he couldn't sleep because of new torments. In his troubled mind, he saw the shack in the junkyard burning like a huge bonfire. He turned back and forth, trying to make sense of why he couldn't rest. Had he not just this minute saved a life? Hadn't he kept someone from burning alive, the very same crime he'd committed? By all accounts, shouldn't that even things? In fact, he may have saved a whole building full of men. Surely *that* should square things. Then why was he wide awake and restless while those two across the room peacefully conked out, except that he didn't get blind drunk beforehand like them? Here he'd saved dozens of lives, but it didn't matter somehow. All he could think of was the one life he'd ended as if, no matter how much good he did, he could never make up for the bad. But how was that fair? If there wasn't a way to even the score, then what's the use? One bad choice and the jig was up. The only hope was to never, ever do anything wrong. And who could do that? No one. So the system was rigged in favor of those who lived a perfect life. The rest of us had no chance.

The lights in the hallway turned on. Hect awoke with a start.

"Up an' at 'em, bed jockeys!" Fast-One's voice rang out. "The race's over, and all y'all lost. Get up! Baloney's frying, and mush's warming in the pot. Got you losers a special supper tonight, too—sow-ear sandwiches and collard greens. Don't it make your mouth water, though? Here now, come on. Up, up, up, I say!"

Despite his fitful night's sleep, Hect sprang out of bed and tightened the laces on T.J.'s boots. Becca rose with a groan. A sprig of hair had escaped from her pullover cap, but she drowsily tucked the lock back underneath. The wino who would've burned up except for Hect saving him struggled to sit up also, but the other one, the would-be arsonist, snored on.

Fast-One's considerable form entered the room. "What've we got here?" she said to the arsonist still asleep under the cover. She turned to Hect. "You reckon a caterpillar's 'neath them covers turning into a butterfly?"

He shrugged, but then to his horror, watched the woman draw her pistol from the holster and aim it at the still-slumbering form. Before he could react, a stream of liquid left the barrel, then another, and then one last squirt. The mound on the bed slept on undisturbed.

Clapping her hand over her mouth, Fast-One smothered a giggle and holstered her gun. If she had been expecting a squirt gun to awaken him, she seemed oddly amused by its failure. The woman left the room. Puzzled by what had just happened, Hect watched the bed.

The form beneath the covers twitched as faint wisps of smoke arose from different spots on his blanket. A moan emerged. The man flopped one way and then the other, did a complete roll, threw back the covers, and shot out of bed with a howl, swatting his body as if covered in biting bedbugs. He tore from the room and hollered all the way down the hallway towards the shower.

"Devilish ol' witch," the other wino muttered as he shuffled between the two still seated on their beds. "Somebody ort'a shoot her first thang in the morn with batt'ry acid."

Hect hurried into the hallway as overnight boarders lumbered out of rooms, yawning, and formed into a ragtag line. On Fast-One's signal, the men trudged after her in a shabby formation. Outside the barracks, morning broke gloriously as a not-yet-risen sun fired the bottoms of black clouds like charcoal briquettes. Hect noticed the shoddy troop acted no more energized from a night's sleep than when they went up the staircase the evening before. They moved like lost souls descending into the underworld.

Once out in front of Fast-One's café, company pickups lined the street down the block. Most had signs on the doors indicating work in the oilfields, but Hect also noticed trucks from welders, construction outfits, and other businesses. As the troop of overnight boarders waited to be hired, the café owner, already in high spirits, handed out coffee, a hard roll, and a sack lunch to the men along with tickets to sign. In a nearby tree, a mockingbird trilled a chirping melody until a wino threw a bottle at it and scared the singer off.

Hect and Becca got hired by the foreman of a local chemical plant. The two spent the day shoveling a thick tar-like gunk out of the bottom of a plastic-lined reservoir. That evening, they rode back to the café and after dinner, waited for the place to close. At ten o'clock, Fast-One played her usual coin trick, and everyone slogged back upstairs.

Each day, the couple worked at different jobs. Becca kept in touch with T.J. by way of the company phones at secretaries' desks during lunch hours. She and Hect hoped to save enough to post bail for the trucker, but as time went along, neither got paid a dime in actual cash. No one did. Fast-One held all the daily paychecks against the tabs, which always balanced out to zero because of that blank item at the bottom of the receipt marked "Extras." Of course, everyone felt cheated, and they said as much, but that was all anyone ever did, talk. No one had the gumption to take issue with the crooked proprietress. As far as the economy in this slum went, Fast-One held the monopoly. Nothing would've ever changed either, except that T.J. got out of jail.

18

A Fast One on Fast-One

During Becca's lunchtime phone conversations with T.J., she kept her father up to date on Fast-One's shenanigans. Unable to stand it longer, the outraged trucker burst out with, "'T'ain't no thing worser'n a thief!" which left Hect wondering how he justified the poison log routine. With nothing else to do in a six-by-ten concrete cell, T.J. put "every ounce of his genius," as he put it, in plotting how to get revenge on the crooked café owner. From then on, the phone conversations with his daughter consisted of her explaining the details of how Fast-One ran her operation, her habits, her personality, where she kept her savings, and even her hopes and desires in life.

In one of their last talks, as Becca told Hect, the trucker boasted, "I'm a natural-born't settler of scores, and I've come up with a world-beater of a scam, a real doozer, if I do say so myself."

Hect listened in on the secretary's phone along with Becca as T.J. outlined his plan, but neither could hear very well because of a guard in the background who kept shouting for the trucker to end his call, that time was up. "If my scheme works out," the trucker screamed while wrestling to keep hold of the phone, "it'll pay off our fines, get the truck out of hock, and get all them down-and-outers at the café even-stev—"

The line went dead.

The day arrived when T.J.'s sentence ended and Becca took an early lunch hour and raced to meet her father. Luckily, their jobs had been at a construction site near the jail. After she got back, she told Hect, as the two applied silver paint to a metal oil tank, that she'd left her father at a men's store where he'd been jabbering a blue streak, talking a young salesclerk into taking a personal check.

"That'll be the day," Hect chuckled.

"Oh, he'll persuade her, all right, and make her proud she done it, to boot."

"What's he buying—hunting stuff?"

"Not a man's store, dummy, a *men's* store—a fancy-pants place for dandies who dress up in fluffy silk vests, tailored suits, form-fitted shirts, and such duds. Why, if you'd seen T.J. trying on outfits, you wouldn't no more recognize him than nothing."

"What's he up to?"

"Didn't have time to find out, but it's got to do with Fast-One. He's aiming to knock her pegs out from under her."

"When?"

"Today. Soon as he can walk over to the café. I'd like to see him do it too."

"Let's quit."

"Our jobs?" she gasped, but her eyes lit up. "Soon as they find us gone, they'll call Fast-One, and she'll pitch a hissy-fit deluxe."

"She don't pay no-how. Look, they ain't back from lunch." He pointed at the construction trailer without any company pickups in front. "Being Friday, they're probably all boozed up, and we'll have to walk back to the café anyhow. Go to the trailer and write us up a couple of excuses on company papers."

Becca smiled and nodded. "I hate being a painter anyhow."

❧

THE CAFÉ HAD the usual late-afternoon loiterers inside. Fast-One perched on her stool like a mushroom. She held a newspaper spread out before her and looked up just as Hect and Becca entered. A frown marred her normally merry face. "Why ain't you no-talkies on the job?"

The two marched up and handed the woman the letters that Becca had written earlier on the secretary's typewriter. Fast-One took one look at the forgeries and wadded them up. "Jobs ended early, huh? Well, t'ain't the way it works around here. They hire for eight hours; they pay eight hours." She opened her newspaper. "Bad luck for you two. No supper tonight." She snorted as if to say justice done. "And you'll work Sunday for getting the afternoon off."

Hect patted Becca's shoulder as if to console her, but a twinkle in her eyes told another story. A booth near the front door gave the best view. They sat on the same side so both could see the entrance, although Hect mainly stole looks at Becca's face, wishing he could make a pendant of her profile to wear around his neck forever. When her eyes got big and excited, he knew who had just arrived.

T.J. wore a copper-colored suit, matching vest, white tie, and snake-skin boots with the pant legs stuffed in the tops. He carried himself with such dignity, no one would ever guess he just got out of jail. At the sight of his daughter, the well-dressed man winked. His suit and tie almost hid his potbelly, and his leather heels clicked on the linoleum floor. Fast-One, on the other hand, being engrossed in her newspaper, missed the trucker's entrance. Not until he got beside her did she look up, take a double take, and crumple the paper.

"Revival time, boys! Preacher's arrived." She laughed. "Say, you sure you're in the right place, Reverend?"

"Afternoon, ma'am." T.J. dipped his head in a polite bow. "Beg pardon, but I'm not in the ministry. Kindly inform the owner of this establishment I'd like a word, if you would."

She folded the newspaper and placed it on the counter. Her good-natured smile shriveled into a skeptical pucker. "That'd be me. Who's asking?"

"Forgive me, ma'am. Name's T.J.," he said, and his poise caused the couple across the room to trade approving glances. "May I know your name, if you please?"

"Fast-One's good enough for now," she said, no longer sounding friendly. "I don't give out my real name to strangers as a rule."

"Good enough. Anyway, back to my reason for being here. After asking around town, I hear you're in the business of hiring out temporary help."

"Look," Fast-One said, snatching up the newspaper and twisting it into a roll like a club, "if you're from the gov'ment, I ain't got nothing to do with employing this bunch around here, so don't go harping about tax money I owe Uncle Sam. They stand outside my place, 's'all. That sidewalk out there is public property, and can I stop them? If folks come by and pick them up, whether it's to work or not, is that any of my business? They're all deadbeats anyhow, so as a favor, I collect their money like a Good Samaritan, if you get my drift. Ain't none of them works for me, and I sure as tarnation don't have nothing to do with no unpaid payroll taxes."

"You've mistaken my business once again," T.J. said calmly. "I'm not from the IRS. I'm from Hollywood, California, and I'm in the moviemaking business. Producers hire me to staff their movies. But, I've walked a long way getting here. May I sit down?"

"Here!" She swatted a dozing figure with her rolled-up newspaper. "Move over a stool, you, and give place to this gent. Durn hobos, I ain't got the heart to run them off. I'm too dang kindhearted."

Grumbling, the sleepy man shifted down a seat.

"Might I get you a cup of Joe?" Her manner reverted back to her old jolly self, although there lingered an edge of suspicion. She lumbered around the counter and grabbed a coffeepot and cup. After pouring, she poked the coffeepot at the man so suddenly the liquid licked around the opening in a black tongue. "I get your drift, mister! It just now hit me. You're with that bunch what's making the movie over yonder in Juarez. Everyone 'round here talks about it, but they say the deal went bank-ruptured?"

"It's being produced by a new movie company," T.J. said. "Like I was saying, my job is to gather up a cast for the picture show. On this particular film, I'll need to hire lots of extras. We won't require any prior acting experience, only that they march around in prison uniforms and do like they're told. Since it's an independent film, no one will have to join the actors union, but our company pays scale just the same. Fact of the matter, if you'll take care of transportation to the site, lunches, and whatever other extra expenses might arise, we'll pony up twice the normal rate. Scale for extras is one dollar and fifty cents per hour, so we'll pay three dollars an hour, and we'll need at least seventy-five men."

Fast-One gulped as if she'd swallowed a gold ingot. "W-w-why, j-j-just so, j-j-just so. Er, L-l-let m-m-me see now, according to my ciphering, that—that figures to, well—three bucks at eight hours times seventy-five, that's, well, that's a daily rate of—*one thousand-eight hundred George Washingtons!*"

"Plus added expenses not covered like overtime and catering. Just bill us."

"Bull's-eye!" she squealed. "I'm the one to talk to; you hit the target square! Oh, I knowed my day would come. This is what I get for looking out after all these grapette guzzlers. The gal with a heart for charity finally gets her due; that's me. Yes, siree, you've come to the right spot. Temporary labor, that's me. I own this place. I'll get you your seventy-five workers, you bet. Just leave it to old Fast-One. I'll take care of you."

"There's one sticking point," T.J. interjected. "It's a matter of legality, you know."

Fast-One's merriment plummeted. "I knew it. I knew I'd mess this deal up. Too good to be true, I should'a known. I've ruined it all, ain't I? Too excited, huh? I shouldn't'a busted out in that stupid cheerleader holler. I'm sorry, honest. I didn't m...er, what's your name—P.J.?"

"Tee-Jay. But there's no need to get in a tizzy. I just require your full legal name. It's for the contracts."

The café owner surveyed the room, pausing on the two young people in the booth, but then she nodded as if remembering they couldn't tell anyone. She gently nudged the man at the bar with her rolled-up newspaper. "Good, he's asleep," she said to T.J. "This's just b'twixt you and me on account of I sure wouldn't want none of these wisecracking buffoons around here to get holt of the tag I got labeled with at birth. If any of these smart alecks ever found out, why, I'd never hear the end of it, got me?"

"Completely," T.J. said.

She looked around the room once more as if still uncertain. "It's, er, Gertrude," she said in a low voice. "But like I said, that's just b'twixt me and you."

"Gertrude? Gertrude, what?—For the contracts, you understand."

"Oh, well then, Gertrude Tootie, but do keep that top secret. Not a word to no one. This bunch of mule-faced mummies around here would love to find out that little tidbit, and there'd be no end of haunting me with it, neither."

"Now then," T.J. said, sounding official. "There'll be a lawyer along in a couple of days with contracts. He's a lawyer, like I said, but there's no need to worry. His job's to see to it that everything's been done proper. He's only going to make sure you've treated your laborers fair according to government regulations, that's all, and that you don't owe no one back wages."

The coffeepot exploded at Fast-One's feet like a landmine. Hect yelped at the sudden noise, and Becca whimpered. The two then traded looks, warning each other that they weren't supposed to be able to talk. Thankfully, the café owner still had her eyes fixed on T.J. Even the sleeping man at the bar rose up and gazed around before settling back.

"Sure busted, ain't it?" T.J. said, leaning over the counter. "Anyhow, like I was saying, there's always one or two soreheads in every outfit, I know, so you might pay them off with whatever sum gets them happy. That way, they won't say nothing ugly about you. Should that lawyer come up with any complaints, the bosses are liable to cancel this deal."

Fast-One made a grinding noise in her throat as if unable to get the words out.

"Was you about to say something?" T.J. asked.

Still making that grating noise, she threw her head side to side.

"There now." The dapper man stood to his feet and took a final drink of coffee. "Keep in mind what I told you. There'll be a lawyer by in a few days, so if you got one or two soreheads who might complain, you'll do well to pay them off."

After T.J. left, Fast-One hurried to the window and lifted the blind. She waited a short interval and then turned around to face the café.

"*One or two soreheads!*" she bellowed. "Every lousy one of these wine-guzzlers is a sorehead!"

For the first time since Hect had known the café owner, all trace of humor left her, and he even thought her close to tears. She came over to the booth the couple sat in and dropped down, squishing Becca into the corner. "Oh me, oh my, what's a poor business gal to do?" She dropped her head into her hands. "I'm undone. For a second, I thought I'd been saved from these overdone sourdough heads. You're the only two I can confide in. 'Sides, who're you going to tell?" She chuckled sadly. "My ship had come in, I thought, but it sailed away, leaving me at the dock. I always hoped a nice gent with a pocketful might come by one day and rescue me, but I never expected it'd be a glamour boy like that. Now here comes that meddling lawyer asking around and sticking his nose where it don't belong. Every last one of these thankless scoundrels around here will gripe, making out like I've rooked and rawhided them."

Hect recognized a crucial moment. The success of T.J.'s scheme might well hinge on his next move. Inspired, he grabbed the pencil from Fast-One's hair, scribbled on a napkin, and then slid the note over in front of the dejected café owner.

She read the note quietly. "Buy them off!" she croaked out loud and gave a little jerk that made her jiggle all over. She looked Hect in the eye. "You say—*buy them off?*"

He nodded.

A smile spread across her face until her two bottom fangs showed. She banged the table with a fist and just that fast her old self returned. "Who says it don't help to share thoughts with my two best pals? Why, I should'a thought of that. Not only do I make my own Volcano Sauce, but I also make a mean homebrew. Got bottles and bottles in the basement. I thought one day I'd retire and sell to the alkies around here, but I got a even better use for it now, all on account of you two. Don't think I ain't grateful, neither. Fact of the matter, I'm giving you both high-paying jobs. I'll print up a batch of labels on my label machine—tiny ads inviting all the wine-heads in these parts to my place for a meeting tonight. Mini-fliers that say some'n like:

"Fast-One's Lightning Strike
1 Bottle Free, Tonight, 8:00"

To every man who shows up sober, there'll be a bottle of my special-made, hundred-and-ninety-proof Lightning Strike. One drink and your dreams come true. No more pain, makes you strong enough to whip ten one-handed, the fountain of youth. Fast-One's wonder drink."

19

The Wonder Drink

HECT AND BECCA had their first real falling out over those flier-labels Fast-One gave them to pass out. Hect had the idea to break their silence and explain to the guys on the street in simple language about the meeting that night. He feared no one would bother reading them, especially since the print was so tiny, but Becca balked. She said she'd never be able to hide her squeaky voice and her secret would be out. Hect argued, but she wouldn't budge, as usual. The argument got so heated they finally split up and went separate ways.

After giving it some thought, though, Hect decided to do it her way. He didn't want to risk being responsible in case Fast-One found out about Becca's secret and put her out on the street.

Close to sundown, they met up again. As Hect predicted, every one of the flier-labels had been crumpled up and thrown in the gutters or else slung back in his face, unread. He knew what the outcome would be beforehand, but made up his mind not to tell Becca, "I told you so." He tried to encourage her instead. "Aw, don't look so glum, gal," he said, patting her shoulder. "Don't blame yourself for us getting treated so low and mean."

"Count yourself lucky," Becca snapped. "One of them pasted me a slap upside the head for my trouble, but I give it back to him, double. I laid one on his jaw that should'a loosed the last tooth left him."

As they discussed what Fast-One's reaction might be to the disappointing outcome of the afternoon's work, they came around a corner onto some men pitching pennies against a building front. The sight of familiar faces from the café gave Hect an idea. Here was a chance to do what he'd wanted to do in the first place.

"Watch this," Hect whispered aside to Becca and pulled a crumpled flier from his back pocket. "I got one left. Wait here."

"Oh, no. Ain't you learnt nothing yet?"

Despite her warning, he strode up to the group. One of the men, who'd had his back to him, turned around. Hect could hardly believe his luck. At the sight of the ex-prizefighter, he let out a whoop. "Well, I'll be!" he cried, clapping the other's bony shoulder. "Don't you worry one bit, neither. I ain't about to ask 'how you're doing' this time." He laughed and waited for some kind of reaction, but got only a lifeless stare.

The response came out of the crowd of gamblers. "Why, dip me in turpentine, you're a fraud!" an angry voice called. "A scheming no-'count liar, is what you are. What happened to you're not being able to talk, faker?"

Hect didn't recognize the man at first as he stepped forward. He had black, stringy hair to his shoulders, bushy eyebrows, and a large blister on his forehead like a burn mark. Both his fists were balled threateningly. "What'a'ya think, boys? Hotshot here's been laughing at us the whole time, acting like he can't talk. Why, he's nothing but a hypocrite, making fools of us. Somebody ort'a take him in hand and learn't him some respect."

In a flash, Hect recognized the voice of the arsonist from that first night, the one Fast-One shot with battery acid. Because of the whitish pus sac on his forehead, the man's face appeared twice as furious. He came toward Hect, who now wished he'd listened to Becca.

"Leave off him, Jake." The rummy with the beat-up face stepped in between the two.

Surprised, Hect glanced over at the smaller man's beaten, expressionless face. Though he felt thankful for the offer of help, the shriveled little prize fighter appeared to have long ago lost any ability to defend anyone.

"Mind ya business, runt," the fire-starter snarled and shoved the smaller man to the side. "Li'l squirt, some pro boxer you are." He laughed. "Good for nuthin' but sucking down rum. Git away from me."

Hect's mind raced as he watched the bigger man circle in a gliding, sideways step, his fists rolling over each other as if to conceal which would lash out first. Of all things, the little, battered-face rummy stepped back and blocked his approach. "Leave off him, Jake, I said."

"Move, half pint!" He shoved the little fellow hard, knocking him to the pavement. "I'll bust up the both ya. I'll stomp ya like a couple'a spoil't melons."

The rummy tried to get up, but the bully kicked him, sending him rolling.

"Man makes fun'a me, he'll pay for it," the arsonist growled, turning back toward Hect. "Whoever heard of a man start talking all at once't. Why, it'd taken a miracle for that."

Hect had a flash of insight. It was a long shot, to be sure, but what else was there? "That's it!" he cried, leaping forward. "I'm cured!" He shoved the small flier into the would-be arsonist's chest, crumpling it. "Read it! I'm cured! I drank Lightning Strike and started talking. A miracle! Here, read all about it. It's the answer, I tell you. Now I can talk."

Jake shoved the paper away. "Get shed'a that. Now what're you blabbing about?"

"It's what I've been trying to tell you. Here, read it. Lightning Strike! It'll cure whatever ails you."

"You're making fun again. Dadgum your hide, you're a real flim-flammer, ain't you? I'll teach you a less—"

"Wait!" Hect cried, fending him off. "It's the cure! Why you think I'm going to all this trouble—to help you, that's why. It's free. One bottle for each man of one-hundred-and-ninety-proof Lightning Strike. The wonder drink."

At this last claim, the men behind the would-be arsonist got up and moved in close. The interest they showed spurred Hect on. "Tonight!" he shouted. "Each man who shows up at the café gets a free bottle of Lightning Strike. The wonder drink. One gulp is all it takes. It'll cure your pains, make your dreams come true, you'll feel young again and be alive once more."

"Bah!" Jake spat on the ground. "Take that for your cure."

"I didn't believe it either until I drank," Hect said, hurrying along. "Now I talk. Him too." He pointed at Becca. "Tell him you can talk, um, *Beck*. That's his name—Beck."

"R-Right," she said, lowering her voice. "Me too. I can talk."

"Yeah, well," Hect said, noticing the men glance at each other, "maybe *he* ain't all the way cured yet. His voice's still a bit chirpy, but one more drink ought'a do the trick. And, oh yeah, don't forget—a hundred-and-ninety-proof. Lightning Strike. Tonight, for free."

"Fast-One ain't never give nothing away," the arsonist growled, but his voice had lost much of its power, "but only trouble, so why start now?"

"She drank, and she changed. Not mean anymore. She loves everyone and wants only to share. One drink, that's all it takes." Hect found out selling wasn't so hard as long as his sales pitch stuck to what he'd want such a potion to do for him. "Clear away your troubles; make you whoever you want to be. No more guilt. No more shame. It's everything you ever looked for. Read the flier, it tells you."

The other men pushed past Jake, crowding him out, and began asking one question after another.

"What about feeling ornery? Will it cure that?"

"How about all the meanness I done—will I forget?"

"No more being mad at the world, you swear?"

"Will it make me glad to be alive and not so lowdown?"

"Me? Happy? Come on, you mean it?"

Becca circled around behind the group to the would-be arsonist. She looked up at him, her chin almost touching his chest. "Heals batt'ry acid burns too."

Of all the unexpected results, even his face lost its scowl. Hect noticed Becca had a way with grouches, probably because of all the years dealing with T.J. The group of men left in such a hurry, going different directions, no one bothered to pick up their pennies. Hect thought he better remind them one more time before they got out of earshot. "Tonight, seven o'clock!" he shouted. "Tell everyone. One bottle! Lightning Strike! The wonder drink! *Free!*"

The couple watched the last man shuffle out of sight. They agreed that word would now spread like wildfire. Becca grabbed Hect's arm. "Lucky for you they was winos. Normal folks would never fall for a line that says all that comes in a bottle."

✂∞✂

THAT NIGHT AT Fast-One's, Hect and Becca would never have gotten in the crowded place except for the penny-pitching group of men who guarded the front door. With Jake at the lead, they bulldozed a pathway to the counter. All the stools had been left vacant, probably because no one dared get within arm's reach of Fast-One. The couple had front-row seats.

A ceiling fan pressed down a strong wine smell that made Hect woozy. A combination of alcohol and cigarette breaths, plus body odor, left the room with almost no fresh air. Fast-One, meanwhile, busily played the politician, reaching over the counter into the crowd to muss men's hair, tugging playfully at their ears and pinching cheeks until they yelped. When she came to the seated couple at the bar, though, her cheer left her. She informed them she couldn't pay them like she'd said even though they'd done a "half-passable job." If they recalled her exact words, she'd said she'd pay for every "sober" man who showed up and "there warn't a teetotaler in the whole besotted batch." She then returned to the crowd, her old jolly self again.

Hect shrugged, no longer surprised by any of the cinchy slumlord's capers, but Becca half stood and scanned the crowd, looking worried. She leaned down close to Hect. "Where's he at?" she whispered, safely out of earshot of Fast-One. "Why ain't T.J. here?"

"Maybe he don't know?" Hect whispered, anxious as well.

"He knows. He told me he'd hang close-by to see how things went. He knows, all right."

"You don't s'pose we done all this for nothing, do you?"

"Durn his useless hide," Becca murmured under her breath. "Drinking again, I bet."

Fast-One cleared an opening on the low counter crowded with dark bottles of homebrew. Adding high drama to the meeting, the heavyset woman stepped in an empty stool and climbed up on the bar. After much exertion, she stood on the polished plank that bowed under her weight as the wood creaked and popped. Despite her presence above the heads of the men, all eyes in the room remained fixed at her feet on the bottles with the handsome label, "Lightning Strike".

Fast-One stuck two pinky fingers in each side of her mouth and whistled so shrilly Hect and Becca covered their ears. Here and there a pair of bloodshot eyes may have lifted because of the piercing noise, but most of the men stayed fixated on the bottles.

"Upon my honest heart," boomed the rotund woman's voice over the gathering, "I got a gold heart of more carats than a farmer's vegetable garden. I'm the only shepherdess who'll tend her shaggy flock of wore-out, old goats."

So far, the café owner had stirred little interest. She told of her sacrifices, her selfless generosities, how she cared for each and every one alike, how her only thought was for them. "It's the pure and honest truth," she cried. "I've never cheated no man on purpose."

At this bald-faced whopper, every head in the room lifted. Eyes bugged, replacing sleepy gazes, chins dropped, and mouths gaped. Even Hect and Becca rotated toward the woman above them and stared, marveling at such uncommon gall.

"I ain't one to complain," Fast-One continued unfazed, seeming pleased to have captured her audience's attention at last. "Everyone knows I turn my sorrows into fun. No man can say I ain't put a little pep in his step at one time or t'other, but I got to talk serious this one time. What I'm about to say is not for me, but for the sake of my family out there. That's how I feel about each and every one—*family*. You're my brothers, fathers, grandfathers, and great-grandfathers, and a few resemble relations who've passed on. This meeting is to announce one more act of kindness on my part. I've done you boys a good deed, a charity, and you'll thank me for it too. I've gone and got you all jobs, high-paying jobs, top-hand jobs, and it's all the doings of your Mama Fast-One. Each and every one of you is going to get paid in the grand amount of a dollar fif...a dollar fif...er, a dollar *thirty-five* cents an hour."

Hect and Becca rolled their eyes. One person applauded, but when no one joined in, the clapping died out.

"T'ain't interested!" a lone voice called from the back of the room. "Keep it."

Hect perked up. One look at Becca confirmed his suspicion as she nodded with barely hidden excitement and mouthed the letters "T...J."

"Hold on! Hold on, boys!" Fast-One cried. "Money ain't a real high priority on you boys' list, I know that. Think about retirement, though. Ponder the future, won't you? It's coming one day, you know—sickness, old age, gagging for breath, a pine box, but I'll sweeten the pay a bit, how's that? You're hard bargainers, all right. OK, you win. I'll go higher—a dollar-forty. That's five cents more. Think of it! You'll never see wages like that again. Now come on, where else can you earn such big bucks? But there's a catch, boys. We've got to win this contract. There's a sorry skunk lawyer due here who'll try to cheat you out of your money."

"Let him!" that same voice called, hidden in back of the crowd. "Who cares?"

The roomful of men followed that lead with disgruntled moans and catcalls.

"Steady work, bah! Who needs it?"

"Eight hours a day, not for me."

"Panhandling's better!"

"Here! Here!" Fast-One cried above the racket. "This won't do, boys. What kind of glum talk is this? All right, I don't blame you. You want more, OK. You know I can't resist you. I'm too much of a softy, but I'll sacrifice my share. I'll see to it each one of you gets a buck forty-*five* an hour, how's that? Has that got you excited yet? Are you raring to go?" The woman cupped a hand to her ear. "What's that? Is that the drumbeat of old wore-out tickers beating faster? Have I got you revved up and motor's racing?"

"Drop dead!" T.J.'s voice lifted from somewhere in back. "We'll never see no cash from the likes'a you. You want us excited? Cancel our tabs!"

The phrase resonated with the men who picked up the line in a chant.

"Cancel tabs! Cancel tabs! Cancel tabs!"

Fast-One waved her arms and tried to outshout them. Finally, she picked a bottle up in each hand and held them over her head. The room quieted. "Not one," she cried, "but two bottles of Lightning Strike to each man who'll work for me. Two, I say!"

A hurrah went up as the men broke into smiles and patted one another's back, but the initial exhilaration died out quickly as a lone call could be heard in the back of the room.

"No deal! No deal! No deal!" T.J cried. "Cancel tabs! Cancel tabs!"

Again the phrase caught on as the bedraggled group stomped their feet.

"Cancel tabs! Cancel tabs! Cancel tabs!"

Fast-One shook her fist, taking aim in the general direction of her heckler. "Step out, you! Show yourself, whoever you are! You ingrate, I'll crack you a good one, and you won't smart off so quick next time."

"You will, will you?" T.J. returned, still concealed in the crowd. "*Gertrude.*"

The woman's face melted like wax before a hot flame.

"Who?" an unidentified voice cried across the room. "Gertrude?"

"Gertrude Tootie," the trucker answered. "It's her real name, boys—Gertrude Tootie."

The gathering broke into an uproar. Laughter echoed through the room as the men clapped one another on the back; others dropped their heads onto the nearest shoulder and quaked uncontrollably. Fast-One, meanwhile, looked stricken.

"Cancel tabs!" T.J. called out. "Cancel tabs, Gerty Tootie!"

The crowd picked up the new chant.

"Cancel tabs, Gerty Tootie! Cancel tabs, Gerty Tootie! Cancel tabs, Gerty Tootie!"

Fast-One shouted her loudest, trying to overcome the noise, screaming for the cowardly weasel to show himself, to come into the open, but no one beyond Hect and Becca heard her. Finally, she waved a white napkin over her head. After clumsily climbing down, she took her cashbox from beneath the counter and began handing out bundles of papers. "There, boys! See how I've changed? We're even now. No one owes me nothing. Now you'll say good things about me when that shyster lawyer comes around, right? When he shows up and asks, you'll tell him Mama Fast-One never cheated no man, OK? Do that for me, won't you, boys? Stick up for your old pal."

"Back wages too!" T.J. hollered. "Pay what you owe us!"

As the crowd started repeating the chant, Fast-One waved them off.

"I give! I give!" the proprietress called. "You win, boys. I'm licked. I know when to cry uncle." She lifted the top drawer out, revealing a lower chamber. "I'll pay. I'll square up things! Here's the cash. Only take it easy now and don't get greedy. This is all I got in the world. Step up one at a time...Whoa! Stop! Back up!"

The men charged forward.

"Hey, boys, don't crowd! Don't grab! Stop! Easy! Slow down!"

The overwhelmed woman couldn't fight them all off. The men wrenched the box away, and despite Fast-One's shrieks, it disappeared into the crowd. The frantic woman followed the men out the door, yelling for the return of her life savings. Hect and Becca wound up sitting by themselves in the vacant café, the cashbox discarded on the floor, empty. The many bottles of homebrew had disappeared off the counter as well.

20

The Room Clerks

Just before sunset, Hect and Becca found T.J. near the clothing store where his daughter last saw him. The trucker had returned his "Hollywood dandy" duds by jimmying the back door lock. After returning the copper-colored suit and matching alligator boots, he left the salesclerk a sizable tip, courtesy of Fast-One. When Hect asked about the check he'd written, he brushed it off, saying, "Give to me by my trustee cellmate who works in the jail headquarters." A wry glint lit up his eyes. "He once't was a honest-Abe, do-gooder banker till he went freelance. Got 'em out'a the top drawer of the warden's desk."

The threesome walked the narrow streets of El Paso. With night falling, they needed a place to stay, but T.J. passed up the affordable hotels for a pricey resort on a bluff overlooking the Rio Grande. "Fleabags get their money paid cash up front," he told the couple instructively. "Ritzy ones are classier and wait till the next morn, making it easier to skip out."

Considering where they'd spent last night, Becca and Hect agreed the resort looked like a palace out of a picture book. In the lobby, two uniformed clerks, both burly types, eyed the three from behind a counter with looks not exactly welcoming.

"You drifters lost?" one of them snorted. A pipe smoker, he took a wood match from a box, struck it and sucked the flame into the bowl, pulling his lips back in a sort of snarl.

Despite the snide reception, T.J. spoke like they were all old pals. When the pipe smoker turned away, the trucker swiped the man's box of stick matches off the counter, leaving Hect to wonder why. After giving the three the once over like they had some sort of catching disease, the pipe smoker handed T.J. a room key.

After unlocking the hotel room door, T.J. jammed a wood match into the outside keyhole and broke it off. "There," he said with a satisfied nod, "now them two numbskulls can't catch us off guard with no master key. Plus, it'll give us a head start come morning, if need be."

The room had two large bedrooms separated by a full kitchen, but rather than enjoy the grand quarters, the father and daughter started a fuss. TJ said he couldn't wait to use "his stash from Fast-One's" to buy the truck out of hock and take off for a load of firewood." That ruffled Becca's feathers, and she shot back, "You mean *our* money, ole miser?" And here they went at it. She told him she'd had enough of the poison log routine to last a lifetime, and she intended to use her share for a bus ride to Hollywood.

T.J.'s cheeks reddened up, his neck veins bulged, and his jaw hinges knotted. "Daughter, your noggin's stuffed with fancied foolishness worse'n a schoolgirl." From there, they swapped hurtful names like "fat old boozer" and "dimwitted dreamer."

Hect stayed out of it. No one mentioned that he had a share from Fast-One's, so he saw no advantage in taking sides. Whoever won the argument, the loser might decide to take revenge and leave him behind, so he turned his back on the squabble and went to the window.

Their third-floor suite overlooked the hotel grounds, and directly below, a second-floor roof extended out to a pool surrounded by a cement walkway. An underwater light in the water, along with the surface being so calm without swimmers, gave the concrete bowl an empty look. In spite of trying not to eavesdrop, Hect couldn't help overhearing.

"Ain't you got ears, Daughter?" T.J. shouted. "I told you, I'm set for trial, but I can't stay on account of this being my sixth DWI. They're liable to lock me up this time 'cause of that newspaper car I backed over was the first in a long line going to the mayor's funeral. I caused such a traffic tie-up all them polecat politicians missed getting their pictures took at the service, and now they want my head. The upshot of it all, I got to get out of the state and that not much past sunset tomorrow."

"It's always about *you*, ain't it? What about me? The whole reason I come along was to get to that movie set over in Mexico. Go ahead and spend your life hauling logs, if you like, but I'm on my way to be a star on the big screen."

"'S'hat so? Well then, you've forced me to tell the straight of it then. You ain't going to like it, but here goes anyhow." He paused as if trying to find the right words. "Truth be known, Daughter, you ain't no actress and never has been. You ain't got the makings."

"Bite your lip, old fogy. Being an actress is my ambition. That's what parts my generation from yours. In your day, no one had a notion for nothing but pinching pennies and scratching by best they could, but today, kids my age got dreams. Big dreams. Great dreams. We don't give a hoot about working our fingers to the bone. We got grander ideas. And, before you say so, I've been warned by schoolteachers about naysayers like you."

"Common sense, Daughter. You ain't a actress on account of you're too much like your momma—not a trollop."

"Listen at you," she sneered. "Why, actresses are artists."

"Artists, bah! Ever hear of a painter's kid being a painter? Or a writer's kid being one too? No. Then how come movie actors have copycat kids all the time? I'll tell you why, 'cause being an actress is a trade like driving a truck, only the clothes is skimpier."

Becca made a disrespectful blubbering noise. "You're talking about the most elegant gals in our society."

"High-paid tramps, you mean. Anyhow, it's neither here nor there. I'm still your father, and you'll do like I say until you're married. When you got a husband, then and only then, I'll have no more say-so. Maybe old-fashioned, but that's how it is."

Hect turned from the window, thinking the argument ended, only to find the two locked in un-budging glares. It seemed neither would ever stop staring, when all at once, Becca's face softened as though she'd had a sudden change of heart. As he watched, her fury dissolved away, allowing her natural beauty to return. "Aw, why're we fighting like this, Papa?" she purred. "Oh, I s'pose it's to be expected, seeing as how we're together so much. 'T'wouldn't be normal for us not to get crosswise now and then. After all, we're human. And since you told me the straight of it, as you say, then I got to do the same even if it's something you mightn't want to hear. I *am* married too."

The potbellied trucker jerked. He opened his mouth, but no words came out. His features squinted up. He showed his front teeth beaver like, looking as if unable to make sense of things, as if what he'd just heard was too many for him.

"Hecty here's my husband," she explained, taking hold of his arm and drawing him to her side. Hect stiffened and stared at her with an expression similar to her father's

"We married while you was in jail." She smiled up at her 'mate.' "How'm I to know when you'd get set free? I couldn't sleep in the street, could I? A girl needs looking after; you said so yourself. I never thought as much, but maybe you ain't too far wrong. Anyhow, he's my hubby, and I'm his sweetie, and before you say it, don't ask to see no papers on account of young people these days don't need such. Love's enough."

Hect eyed the trucker to see what he'd do next. Until he knew for sure, he wanted all the distance he could get from the stocky man. As he watched, he saw a change come over T.J.'s face as striking and unexpected as Becca's had been. The old man's wrinkled forehead relaxed, his eyes widened, and the corners of his lips lifted into, of all things, a smile. Exactly the same as what happened to his daughter, some inner thought seemed to make all the difference.

The girl, meanwhile, laid her head on her new "hubby's" chest as Hect gaped down at her slender limbs tightening around his middle like a boa.

"Yep," Becca said, nuzzling. "There ain't no way to change it. Me and my love-boat here have made up our minds."

T.J. clapped his pudgy hands together, startling the couple. "Well, that'd be that. Ain't any use hunting eggs after the chicken's cooked, as they say. Your momma and me showed no better sense, married right about the same age. Here, let me kiss you good-bye, Daughter."

"Good-bye?" she sputtered, shoving Hect away.

"I ain't about to stay on the one honeymoon you two is likely to get. No, no!" He held up a hand. "Don't try and talk me out of it. This place's my gift to you two as your love cottage, so enjoy the few hours you got left. Remember, though, in these parts, they frown on couples your age staying overnight who ain't legal married, and those two clerks downstairs looked on the intolerant side. Oh, and one more thing before I go. If tonight don't turn out exactly like you planned, remember to forgive and forget."

Hect glanced at Becca, and both frowned at this last advice. They all said awkward good-byes, and before the trucker left, Becca gave him a long hug. Once T.J. had gone and only the two remained, neither seemed able to think of what to say for a while. Becca gazed around the room, looking lost.

"You OK?" Hect asked at last.

"I can't figure it," Becca said. "I never seen the fight go out of him like that. He should'a fussed around and had him a fit, and after he cooled down, I'd tell him I made the whole story up, and he'd be so glad that we'd do things my way."

"Can you blame him? You sprang it on him sort'a sudden like. Me too. About took the wind out of me."

A fist pounded the door. "Open up in there," a husky voice barked, followed by even heavier knocking.

The couple traded looks, each with their mouths in silent screams.

"Key don't fit," a second man growled, sounding even gruffer. "Something's stuck in the keyhole."

"Wood match," a third person offered, "'s my guess."

This last voice caused the couple inside the room to clutch at each other.

"*T.J!*" Becca hissed in a strained whisper. "Rotten old coot, I knew he wouldn't give up that easy. 'Forgive and forget'—that back-stabbing, slippery, no-'count, conniving…"

"Open the door!" The wooden plank bulged inward. "If I have to break it down, you'll pay for it."

Becca balled her fists and shook it at the door. "That cold-hearted geezer has gone and set those apes on us. Told 'em we're underage, for sure. Once we're arrested, he'll get custody of me and leave you to chalk days on a jailhouse wall. Dadblame his sorry hide, I'll never be a movie star now. Oh, what'll we do, Hecty? What'll we do?"

Something heavy hit the middle of the door that cracked the wood as the molding popped and peeled back.

"Hurry, Becca. Follow me."

The two climbed out the window and dropped a short distance onto the second-story roof. Earlier, the swimming pool appeared barely past the edge of the shingles, but now the sidewalk encircling the water looked wide as a parking lot. "Come on. Run for it!" He grabbed her by the hand. "Jump to the water."

She drew back.

"Don't be scared, Becca-gal. You can do it. Ain't nothing to it. Think of it as running off a high-dive at a swimming hole."

"Off a high-dive, there's water. That's concrete."

"We'll clear it, I promise. Jump with all you got. Don't hesitate. We'll hit water."

The door splintered behind them and slammed into the adjacent wall as the couple sprinted down the shingled roof hand in hand and leaped.

21

Together Again

THE PINES DINER turned into an education in more ways that just work, especially after a couple of weeks when the customers quit calling me "Tex." The locals started talking to me like one of their own, and I heard things that'd be news to most vacationers. When I came here with my parents, I thought all the villagers loved and welcomed us, but not so. Behind those smiling, "what-can-I-sell-you" faces, they really wished we'd never come, except for our money, and that went double for Texans. I heard my state labeled everything from a "dried-up tree-less dustbin," to a "sun-fried hive of dust-devils," to an "oily gasbag stinking of rotten eggs," always with an edge that Ruidoso measured one better than paradise. And here I thought snobs were just about riches. Not so. Scenery stuck-ups can be even snootier.

At the end of every workday, after standing over a sink, wiping down tables, sweeping floors, mopping until disinfectant became my number one aftershave, and worst of all, cleaning toilets, my mother's words rang in my ears. She'd said one day she wouldn't be around and I'd end up doing such chores. Her curse came true. Until I actually did the work, no one could've convinced me people actually did such jobs for a living. If anyone asked me how restaurants got cleaned in those days, I'd have to say this magic tide rolls in at night, washes everything down, and floats the trash away for all I know. Even so, the idea of quitting never seriously crossed my mind for the simple reason of not wanting to be broke and hungry again. I might never have left the job except for an event that happened one afternoon when we had few customers, which, according to Snowball, was the result of our being in between the busy seasons of summer and winter.

I sat in a booth in the empty diner with no one to talk to, so bored I resorted to reading leftover newspapers. Ruidoso, being a mountain village, had a bimonthly newsletter that stayed around until the pages tore or else someone spilt coffee on it. The front page of one such paper had a picture that caught my eye of a traffic accident in El Paso some weeks back. In the photo, a tractor trailer had all but flattened a small car. According to the caption, a funeral for the mayor had been disrupted when the flatbed trailer backed on top of the lead car belonging to the paper's news crew. Something about the picture struck me, and as I studied it, a couple stood out among the onlookers. The article said it was thought the pair had been involved in the accident and fled the scene. Looking so close my nose nearly touched the picture, I could hardly believe my eyes. One of the grainy figures had a round head like the cartoon character Charlie Brown.

I dashed to the kitchen, cut a hunk of ham off the bone, and grabbed a package of cheese out of the fridge along with a bottle of milk, all of which didn't amount to the day and a half's wages I had coming.

Once at the bus station, the price of a ticket to El Paso seemed like nothing compared to the bankroll I'd saved by not spending my wages. With two hours before my bus arrived, the station restroom seemed the wisest place to wait in case Eli came hunting me. Once I was safely on the bus, the ride lasted all night thanks to stops at every one-gas-station town along the way.

As we neared El Paso, morning light edged down the mountains like sweeps of a spray painter—primer orange before the final coat of dingy brown, but across on the Mexican side, a honeycomb of shanties climbed halfway up a mountain. The sight of those tiny huts reminded me of a shack back in West Texas. I saw again the man in the window covered in flames. What suffering I'd caused. The painful memory, instead of lessening with time, seemed to pop into my thoughts more often these days, and just when I almost felt happy.

In the El Paso bus station, while waiting on change for the snack-vending machines, I showed a long-faced woman behind the counter the picture I'd torn out of the Ruidoso paper in hopes she'd heard about the accident and could tell me something. She'd not only heard about it, but she'd met the couple in the picture. As I ate powdered doughnuts and drank Orange Crush, she told me about the encounter. The blond boy, she said, had been nice enough, but that sassy girl needed her mouth washed with a bar of Lava. I didn't know what to think about the mention of "that sassy girl," whether she'd been the driver of the Thunderbird or where she'd come from. The woman said the pair looked to be headed toward the border crossing into Mexico, especially as a policeman had come by shortly afterward wanting to know if she'd seen them. I thanked the lady and headed that way as well.

Juarez, Mexico had a reputation around school as being a place where age didn't matter. Supposedly, all it took was money to buy anything a guy wanted. I'd never been, but a few of the guys had older brothers who had, and they bragged about sitting in bars and drinking tequila like grown men. During the daytime, though, the place didn't look so fun. Worn-out, old women who looked like burlap bags full of rocks squatted on the sidewalks selling packets of gum; beggars with arms or legs missing were left propped up against building fronts; packs of near-naked kids surrounded tourists; and girls younger than me wore makeup and stood in doorways, leaving me to wonder if they'd end up selling gum one day.

One girl in particular caught my attention because she called to me in English. She wore a tiny skirt revealing meaty thighs tapering down to skinny calves like turkey drumsticks. Her flat face sank toward the middle to a button nose, so that her cheeks, forehead, and chin sloped inward. The poor, homely girl, a guy would have to be blind drunk to want her. When I tried to pass by, she motioned urgently to come closer.

"Why Americun boy early?"

"It's not what you think." Even if I'd been tempted, which I wasn't at all, the only way to get to my nest egg would be to take off my shoe.

In this neighborhood, that'd be plain crazy. "I'm looking for a friend of mine."

"Likee me?"

I thought I'd better change the subject. "You live in Juarez?"

"Si."

"You know the town?"

"Si."

"Where would I look for my friend? This city is so big I'm lost."

"Americuns all go one place. Boystown. Two streets that way. You find." She flashed a smile of gaps and broken, brown stumps. "You come back here." She pointed across the street. "No forget plaza."

By "plaza," she'd meant the park across the street, which looked out of place in this bustling city because of actual trees, fountains, and benches of old men sitting and talking. "I won't forget." At the same time, I thought there'd be no chance of me ever seeing that place again. Little did I know that one day I'd search for it as my last hope.

"Adios," she called after me.

Two streets over, the street peddlers surrounded me. Evidently, the first tourist of the day, the hustlers crowded in close with trays strapped around their necks, pushing in, elbowing each other for position. Impossible to see the wares of one for another thrusting his tray on top, I felt besieged. The cheapest and most useless trinkets ever, who in their right mind would buy such junk? Not me, but knowing better than to insult their offers, I pulled my pockets inside-out. The smiling faces turned to scowls like I'd done something rude. One pug-faced peddler sprang forward. "You gottee no dollars, Gringo? Geet ta 'ell out'a Mex-hee-co."

I broke through the ring of hustlers, spilling their trays, and ran down the street. Angry shouts trailed after me as I veered from street to sidewalk, darted in and out among shoppers, finally ducking into an open-front shop. Women's leather purses hung from the ceiling. While pretending to examine the handbags, I cautiously eased back out onto a busy sidewalk.

"There!" a voice yelled. "That's him!"

I stiffened.

"That's the rascal, there! It's him!"

I wheeled around and let loose a rowdy whoop. "*Hect!*"

"Tim!"

We broadsided one another and leaped around, laughing and throwing punches.

"I just this second talked about you," Hect cried. "And here you are. From your wide eyeballs, I scared the by-gollys out'a you too."

"Did not."

"Did so. Admit it. You thought the Mexico law had you."

"Not a bit of it."

Hect stopped wrestling and looked serious. "I wasn't for sure we'd see each other again. Back on Highway 80 when I was hitchhiking, I seen you turn off north in a pickup headed to New Mexico. How come?"

"It's a long story. I'll tell you later."

We laughed again.

"Why was you standing in among all them purses, huh? You buying one?"

"Hiding from you, is why. It's awful luck you found me."

"Yeah!" Hect whooped. "Now me and Becca will never get shed of you."

At this, we turned toward the girl, who stood with one hand on her hip. She had the corner of her lip stuck into one cheek, appearing neglected. Her hair hung down as if a bucket of water had been poured over her head. Her shirt had a tear up one side, and the dyes of her pants smeared together in different colors. Despite all that, she looked a stunner. Momentarily awestruck, I said the first thing that came to mind, which turned out a big mistake. "You two look like you've been run through the ringer on a washtub."

Hect and I laughed, but the girl didn't. She scowled, apparently taking it the wrong way, so I turned back to Hect. "Where're your shoes? You're barefoot."

"Swimming hole. They was too big anyhow. But here, say howdy to Becca."

We exchanged hellos, but her smile left quicker than a twitch. Anyone could see we'd gotten off to a bad start, but I had just the ticket to make everyone happy. Not wanting to look like a braggart, I didn't tell them outright about all the money I'd saved. Instead, I went about it roundabout. "Say, Hect, buddy. You'll not get far without shoes. I bet you wouldn't mind if a certain moneybags bought you a new pair of boots, huh?" I gave him a big wink.

"See there!" Hect cried, grabbing Becca's arm. "Didn't I say he was born rich? He's always got money. I told you so."

I couldn't keep from beaming. "And what about you, ma'am? Maybe you're in the market for a brand-new outfit if it was purchased for you?"

"'Ma'am?'" She giggled, covering her mouth behind her hand. "Don't he sound the butler, though?"

The wind went out of me.

"Aw, that's just how he is," Hect said. "He can't help it. He was raised mannered like that, but he don't mean nothing by it. Hey, Tim boy, where'd you come by all the dough?"

"Earned it." I left out the part about the kind of work I did. "Saved every dollar, too. Come on, I feel generous. Let me spend some on my two best pals."

We explored the shops. I spent money like mother was still around handing out fives, tens and twenties. Becca fell under the spell of some black slacks with sequins, a black blouse with a starry night design, and a pair of speckled shoes. She stepped out of a dressing room looking like the high priestess at the astrology ball, but something told me to withhold any suggestions. Hect, on the other hand, finally settled on a pair of ostrich-skin boots.

After our shopping spree, I had trouble staying in a good mood even though repeatedly telling myself to not be petty, to let it go, to forget the oversights, but nothing worked. My best pals, so-called, hadn't bothered to say thank you. Here I'd spent my money—money I'd slaved over a sink full of scalding water for—and would it hurt either one to show a little appreciation? Then again, maybe they forgot? Maybe their memories only needed jogging? Maybe prompting might work? "Those sure are handsome boots, Hect." I stood back, admiring them. "After you walked barefoot, I bet you're really glad to get them. Are they comfortable?"

"Pinch," he said curtly, sneering down at them. "Wished I'd got the pair I wanted. Why I let you talk me into these, I don't know—probably on account of we was spending your money, so I figured by rights it should be done your way."

I felt cut to the quick. Surely he hadn't meant it. "But, Hect, no one wears *blue* boots. They made your feet look like blood blisters. Those I picked out are much more handsome."

He grunted and shrugged.

Waving him off as a lost cause, I hoped to have better luck with the girl. "How about you, Becca? You really look snappy in that outfit." A white lie for the benefit of our relationship didn't seem too bad. "How do you like your new clothes?"

"Aw, they'd be all right, I guess, if they'd quit sticking me, especially the blouse. Might as well be wearing nettles. No wonder they was so cheap."

Cheap! Did she say cheap? If only she knew how many hours of sweat and backbreaking labor that blouse cost, not to say what my hands went through soaking in hot water all day. That did it. From now on, no more showing off. The price was too high for the return.

22

The Dog Track

ONCE THE SUN hid behind the mountains, Juarez changed personalities. Out the opened doors of bars, trumpets brayed a tune as shrill as factory whistles calling workers; strip-show barkers pestered any walking by like the street peddlers had earlier; and men dragged women about, girls mostly, in some cases offering them as their own family members. At sundown, Juarez's wicked side took over.

Amid the crowds, the noise, the hustle, I spotted what seemed a restful place and waved for Hect and Becca to follow me. Behind a low rock wall, a stone bench large enough for three offered a good view. From there, we watched the revelers reel and stagger, swear at the tops of their lungs, roar threats at those passing by, fight each other, and fall into the gutters, where they either lay still or else started retching. Only, not everyone took part. Here and there, a few men dressed in pale-blue uniforms stood among the commotion and yet at the same time stood apart from it. The policemen had bronzed faces, twirled bat-length nightsticks, and looked like sturdy pilings in a swirling current.

Oddly enough, none of the revelers showed the slightest interest our way as if we didn't exist. No one hollered threats or tried to get us to fight. Instead, the little rock wall seemed a kind of magic barrier. Curious, I swiveled around. Behind our bench stood a one-room building with chipped stucco walls and a battered exterior, appearing war scarred. Tiny, stained-glass windows offered no light from within, and on a heavy, wooden door, there remained the imprint of a cross. The place looked deserted. Compared to the neon-flashing craziness outside the rock wall, the empty church seemed to exist in another dimension—a tiny fortress that, for whatever reasons, either lost or quit the battle.

"Where to now?" Hect asked, breaking the silence.

A man shouting in the middle of the street waved his fists at who knows what, and I only hoped he hadn't noticed us. "We can't stay here tonight, that's for sure."

"El Palacio," Becca said matter-of-factly. "And you two can thank your lucky stars I'm along. T.J. goes over there lots when he has him a pocketful and wants to throw it away living the highlife. I never been, but he says it's as ritzy and upscale a place as you'll ever see over on the US side. You remember, Hecty, that fella with his arm and leg in a cast?"

"Tell him about it!" Hect boasted. "Tim, you never see a gal operate so."

She drew herself up and beamed. I'd seen that look before on others—every time the curtains opened and the house lights went up. Now talking with her hands as much as anything, she described her encounter with the man in the Juarez restaurant; how instead of resisting her interruption, he'd had the time of his life to the point he'd bought them T-bone steaks; how after listening to her woeful tale, he'd felt so sorry for them that he'd donated ten bucks; and how it worked to everyone's good because, rather than be depressed, his attitude shot right up, feeling, as he did, that he'd helped someone. Through the telling, Hect and I oohed and aaahed, and after she finished, everyone split their sides.

"Anyhow," she continued, looking as pleased as if hearing applause, "that dope had been to El Palacio. It's next door to the greyhound racetrack in a part of Juarez that's nothing like over here in this nest of weevils. Only problem, we'd have to go there by taxi. It's too far to walk, and 'sides, they'd never let you near the swanky place if you come on foot."

Becca knew good and well that I was the only one who had any money to pay for a taxi ride, and yet she refused to ask me outright. Still, leaving this place seemed more important than bothering with feeling snubbed, so I decided to volunteer. "I've enough left for a cab ride, if it's not too far."

"It ain't." She stood to her feet. "Come on; let's go."

Our ride began in the poorest of slums and finished among the richest estates. Out our taxi windows passed palm tree lined avenues, along with columned mansions with long circular drives. Armed guards stood in front of vaulted gates.

Once we reached El Palacio, we drove under a dazzlingly lit archway and parked on Mexican tile polished to an orange sheen. Before the taxi even stopped completely, my door swung open and a uniformed fellow bowed. Another man, whose costume included shoulder boards, ran up. "Señor is checking in, no?"

"Well, I..." Before I could finish, Shoulder Boards motioned to the cabdriver to meet the man who'd opened my door at the back of the vehicle. Recognizing what they were up to, I had to think fast and hurriedly get out. "No, no. No luggage."

"No?" Shoulder Boards frowned.

I realized my mistake. Authentic American tourists arriving in Mexico would have a suitcase at least.

"Señor has no baggage—*at all?*"

"Yes," I said, contradicting myself. "I mean, yes, there is luggage, only it's, well, it's just that it's...it's not in the trunk."

"Ah-ha." Shoulder Boards smiled. "Señor is already staying with us, forgive me. I must have been occupied when you checked in with your parents. A busy day today. Welcome back."

I sighed, thankful he provided the excuse I couldn't think of. "Yes, yes, that's it. You're right. In our room—the luggage, I mean—with our parents."

He nodded and extended a white-gloved hand.

I tensed at the sight, having spent my last money on the cab ride. "Oh, of course, the tip. Umm, let's see…" Once again I couldn't think of a dodge. "Can I, um…Can I catch you later, do you think?"

"Your key, Señor. Give me your key so I can show you to your room."

"Oh, the key! Of course." I laughed, even though I really wanted to run for the hills. "Not a tip, you want my room key?" Flustered, I turned to Becca. "Do you have the, um, key?"

"Nope," she said with a satisfied grin. "Ain't you the one s'posed to know it all?"

Ignoring her, I turned toward Hect. "What about you? Do you have our key?"

He shook his head and backed away.

Even if I could produce a key, once we got to the room, a tip would be expected for sure. With everyone staring at me, I did the only thing I could think of. "Oh, no! The key! It's in the room, too." I looked at Shoulder Boards, trying to guess what he'd be thinking. "I'm afraid, um, we forgot it."

"My apologies, Señor." He sounded as if the mistake had been his. "Would you like me to go to the desk and request another?"

"No, no, thank you. I'll handle it." So many close calls coming at once had destroyed whatever pretended calm I had.

The three of us bolted for the revolving door and jammed together in the same partition. Shuffling in half-steps, we made it to the lobby where we had a chance to catch our breaths. Mexican tile floors stretched before us so glossy we could see our reflected forms atop the reddish squares. Along the walls, floor-to-ceiling mirrors enlarged the room and chandeliers hung from the ceiling like crystal Christmas trees.

"Wow, Cinderella might'a lived here," Becca breathed, staring wide-eyed. "It's all my dreams rolled into one."

While my two partners gazed around, I noticed we'd attracted the attention of the guests in the lobby. If Hect and Becca stood admiring too long, we'd seem not to belong in the eyes of those to whom all this hardly amounted to a second look. I pulled them both close. "Lesson one, I've stayed in places like these, so I know what I'm talking about. You don't have to really have money; you only have to act like you do. Don't either of you dare walk up to that desk clerk like humble pie or we'll be out on our ear. Walk slouchy, look bored, throw in a sneer now and then, and pretend you've been in places like this until they're old hat. Never go eye to eye with any employee, and if one happens to speak, cold shoulder them. That way, they'll think we belong."

"Our clothes?" Becca gasped a little too loud. "Everyone's duded up to the hilt in tennis outfits, high-dollar sweats, swim trunks, and fashionable duds. Compared to them, we're right out'a Hicksville."

I had an urge to ask her why she had me buy her that ridiculous outfit then, but thought better of it. "Keep it in mind who you're supposed to be—rich American teenagers who don't give a hang what other people think. In fact, we want disapproval. In order for this to work, you must get your mind-set right. Let's see, how can I best explain it? I know, think of it this way—don't be pleasant. That's a dead giveaway. Be offensive. Now we're going over to that desk clerk and demand our room key, like it was a bother, like we're put out with the trouble of it."

"How 'bout money?" Hect whined in a low voice. "We're broke, 'member?"

"A room key *is* our money. It automatically makes us members— gets us wherever we want to go—swimming pool, the work-out room, the sauna, the gift shop. We only have to walk up to the clerk behind the counter and insist on a replacement key. Once we got it, we're in, and that includes the restaurant."

"Good," Becca breathed. "I'm starved."

I hated saying what I had to next because of what was bound to follow. "Not to eat." Sure enough, her face scrunched to almost unbecoming. "Look, try and understand, our purpose is to give you a chance to do your damsel-in-distress routine, but in the meantime, we can't risk being arrested for stealing food. Before anything, though, we have to get a room key." I looked from one to the other. No opposition. "That'll be up to Becca. No desk clerk would think of doubting a young lady, but Hect or I are a cinch to get grilled. You said you came here to be an actress, well, here's your chance. Think you can play the role of a snotty American debutante?"

Becca's eyes brightened. "Just you watch. I been wanting to be one ever since I was old enough to know there was such queenly gals."

"OK, but remember, we're spoiled brats, so act it. Here goes."

I shoved Hect and punched his arm, pulled Becca's hair until she screamed, and took off running. They both gave chase. We played tag throughout the lobby, shouting, circling a couch, and brushing a waiter, almost spilling his tray of drinks. A man hollered at us, but we pretended not to hear, dodging one another by using chairs where people were sitting, all of whom glared daggers at us. Finally, out of breath, we ended up in front of the reservations counter.

A clerk talked with a young mother, who busily dealt with a child in a temper tantrum. The tot fell to the floor, shrieking. His mother pinned him there with a foot on the small of his back as he kicked and pounded the floor. The mustachioed clerk glanced in our direction and lifted his shoulders. The mother lost her hold as the child rolled out from under her foot. Still talking to the clerk, or trying to, the woman held the toddler at arm's length, avoiding roundabout hay-makers and kicks at her shins. I elbowed Becca.

"Senior! Senior!" she called, rapping the counter impatiently. "We ain't got all day down here, you know?"

The mustachioed clerk smiled as if he loved being ordered about by teenagers. With one final glance at the occupied mother, he moved down the counter. "Good day, Señorita," he said in surprisingly good English. "With your permission, the correct way to address a man in Spanish is señor, pronounced—sin-YOR."

"Not from where I'm from. It's *senior*, pronounced—SEEN-yer. Anyhow, we got business, Pablo."

The man blinked. "Beg pardon, Señorita, my name is Juan."

"Pablo, Juan, it's all the same. I can't keep them straight no-how." She shut her eyes tight as if thinking. "Now see what you've made me do? I've got mixed up and forgot what I come up here for."

I nudged Becca as a warning not to overplay her part, but she shoved right back. "Oh, yeah," she said as if remembering. "Senior

Pablo-Juan, whatever, fetch me my room key this minute. I've lost mine. Either that, or left it in the room, I disremember."

"Si, Señorita," he said, smiling as if the conversation so far had been a delight. "And what room number, may I ask?"

Becca hooked a finger in one corner of her mouth, obviously at a loss. All the while, I'd been searching the key slots behind the clerk for a room. Half the honeycomb boxes had no keys, which limited my choice, but still there remained so many. Unable to decide, I leaned over the counter to speak privately to the man. "Pardon me, but my cousin's so absent-minded. She can't remember a thing. Her parents checked in not too long ago and then went to the races, along with mine and my brother's here, and they took the keys with them." The whole time I studied the face of the clerk for any glimmer of recognition. "You couldn't possibly...?"

"I don't recall two couples taking the shuttle to the racetrack today," the clerk said, looking thoughtful.

I had to think fast. "One couple. Hers. Mine hit the shops."

"Only the couple from three-o-three took the racetrack shuttle, but..."

"That's it!" I never felt so relieved.

"...they're too old to have..."

"Grandkids!" I shouted, causing the clerk to pull back slightly. "We're all here together. Parents, grandparents, grandkids—one big happy family reunion."

The toddler next to us broke free from his mother's grip and fled. The woman snatched her shopping packages off the counter and gave chase and both disappeared around the corner into the lobby.

"Guests forget their keys quite often, Señorita," the desk clerk said while bending down under the counter. Once back upright, he carefully matched the key to the book register opened before him. "The name, Señorita, with your permission?"

Had the clerk looked up, he would've seen the color drain from Becca's face. It was luck he didn't. Meanwhile, I couldn't move, not only because of being unprepared for the question, which should've been obvious had I the time to think about it, but one look at the stricken faces of my friends showed they were about to bolt and run for it.

"For security only," the mustachioed clerk explained, still looking down at his register. "It is my duty, you understand, to make sure the room number matches the name."

The silence hung heavy. Had I been in Becca's shoes, I'd have flown into a rage or acted insulted or stamped my foot and tried to throw the clerk off his game, but instead, her eyes got wide, and she looked ready to keel over in a dead faint.

The clerk looked up and flinched. Beneath his narrow mustache, a smile faded as he searched each of our faces. I could think of nothing and smiled despite a desire to run like the toddler had earlier. Just as it seemed all was lost, the clerk reached over and patted Becca's hand in a consoling way.

"Gibes, Señorita," he said softly. "The name is Gibes."

Becca squealed happily, and Hect and I joined in. Even the mustached clerk tittered.

"Cousin, I've seen it all now." I took the key from the clerk. "To forget the name of your own grandparents." Then to the clerk, "She's never known them as anything but Gramps and Granny. Scatterbrained?—why, she takes the cake for being airheaded."

"Yeah," Becca put in drily, "and you take the cake for being Bossy Big Britches."

I laughed at the clerk as if it'd all been a funny joke. Once we reached the elevator and stood waiting, I couldn't keep from boasting. "Didn't I tell you? Act like you belong here, and they can't believe you don't."

23

Arrest

On the elevator ride to the third floor, I realized something that, had it not been obvious, wouldn't normally deserve a second thought. I'd ended up the leader of our group. The idea first occurred to me the minute I said we had to go upstairs and locate room 303 in case we got asked about it. No one argued. Then again, when Becca wanted to use 'our' key to sneak into the room, shower up, fix her hair, and "borrow" some makeup, and I'd said no. She'd puffed up, glared and got sulky, but that's all. Worried over her feelings, I'd explained about Hect and me being on the run from the law back in Texas, although not naming the reason, but for good measure, I threw in that, if we got arrested, jail in Juarez was rumored to be the filthiest nest of vicious murderers on earth. She'd shrugged and pouted but nothing else.

In the time it took to become familiar with the outside of room 303—how far it was from the elevator, what the hallway looked like, or anything else we might be asked about—and get back on the elevator, our group had changed. Hect and Becca began to act like a couple, talking privately, whispering, and giggling, leaving me the odd man out. Was this what it meant to be a leader? No one appointed me, of course, and odds are Becca would be first to veto the idea, but it didn't change anything. I also found out why practically no one wants to be one.

Becca would no longer walk close to me, and when I talked to her, she had her bottom lip stuck out. I could tell this troubled Hect. On the elevator ride down, she told him—with her back to me, naturally—that she couldn't wait to order a square meal for a change. My heart sank, but I had to butt in and nix that plan. I tried reasoning with her. What if the waiter knew the people in room 303? Or what if the 303 couple showed up unexpectedly? No telling what all could foul up. Despite my best efforts, Becca started acting like a real movie star.

"Phooey!" she spat. "On second thought, I ain't in the mood to be no actress for the likes of you. I'm half-starved and about to expire for a soak in a hot tub, and a lot you care. Find your snooty debutante somewhere else."

I could see our whole plan unraveling. "Aw, come on, Beck, don't be like that."

"Who said you could call me 'Beck'? Not me. And why should I take a chance on getting arrested? You just got through saying you wouldn't. Find someone else to do your dirty work."

"Look, you won't get arrested. I know these rich types, believe me, I grew up with them. They'll do anything to avoid a scene. A few tears, some tasteless boohooing on your part, and they'll pony up big to get rid of you."

"You do it then, if there ain't nothing to it. I'm taking all the risks while you sit there a rocking-chair supervisor."

"No one cares if Hect or I are in distress. Only a beautiful girl can pull this off." I threw in the flattery for good measure. "Come on, like you did when the guy bought you steaks and gave you money. It worked before."

"That was my idea; this is yours. Besides, I felt comfortable in that Tex-Mex joint, not this highfalutin' place."

Such back and forth could go on forever. That was obvious. Nothing I said from here on would ever win her over; not anyone that stubborn. A new approach was called for. If I couldn't persuade her, she'd have to convince herself, but how? The question answered itself. "You're right, Becca, of course. What's the matter with me? You're the expert. You tell us what to do."

Her pretty eyes lit up. "If you had half a brain, you'd know. You can't treat rich folks like that hung-over dumbbell at the eatery. These 'round here is smarter. You got to stick to the facts so they can't trip you up. Say, some'n like, this gal comes here because of a movie magazine to get hired on the set over yonder in Juarez, but the film went bust. The poor gal, not having had a bath or nothing to eat on account of this hardnosed bully of a boss she's with, needs a loan to get away."

Personal references aside, I couldn't have been more relieved to have her cooperation. "Good. That should work. We'll go with that."

"I didn't say *I'd* do it."

"Come on, Becca. Who else? Will you, please?

"Since you put it that way." She shrugged and walked off.

Inside the hotel restaurant, the tables were covered in white cloths that hung down to a wood floor as shiny as a basketball court. Black-jacketed waiters with white napkins draped over one arm stood along the walls or mingled among those dining. Everyone dressed to the hilt.

A short maître d' blocked our entrance. Thickset and broad, he eyed us up and down with his nose tilted up, exposing his nostrils. "I beg your pardon," he said, although coming from him, the phrase sounded anything but apologetic. "Gentlemen wear ties here. Snacks can be purchased in the basement coffee shop."

Hect and Becca wheeled about to leave, but I stayed put, having run into this same situation before. "Then provide two, my good fellow."

A flicker of disappointment crossed the man's eyes as he reached in back of his podium and gave Hect and me clip-ons. "Follow me," he said, snapping up menus. "This way."

I noted looks of admiration in the eyes of my companions. On the other hand, while we navigated through the tables, scornful glares came from every direction, or so I imagined. At a table behind a banana tree, the maître d' pulled a chair back for Becca, but instead of taking it, she pulled one out for herself. "Is he joining us?"

I chuckled at the maître d'. "She's joking."

Without cracking a smile, the man shoved the empty chair back and handed us menus. "Your waiter will have the pleasure from now on," he said with a ring of insincerity.

Becca opened her menu and stuck her face into it. "Hubba-hubba! Have a look-see at them prices, boys."

"They're in pesos." I spoke low while glancing around at nearby tables.

"Says here, it'll cost twenty-four of them pedros to get one lousy tamale dinner."

"Not pedros—*pe-sos*, and it takes a dozen to make one dollar, so a tamale dinner costs around two American dollars."

Hect groaned.

I smiled at those watching us and turned back to my companions. "Listen up, you two. We've been over this already, but it bears repeating. These people think we are who we act like we are. No one knows we're broke. They may hate us, but they'll tolerate us just as long as they think we belong here."

Becca slapped her menu down. "Rally, dearies, my gizzard's plumb bare," she crowed in a nasal version of a rich lady, although I had a feeling the performance was to spite me. "Hecty, dearie, is that your belly I hear growling or a dogfight?"

He giggled.

I envisioned us being thrown out on our ear. If we were to have any hope of staying, I'd better split these two up, and fast. "Cousin, you go ahead now." I made a shooing motion. "Take care of the matter we agreed on. Go! Go on!"

She leaped out of her chair, her eyes flashing. "I'm going," she hissed. "But only 'cause I'm sick of being ordered about by a head-honcho sourpuss like you."

Stung to the quick, I watched her storm away while wondering what I'd done wrong.

"Aw, don't mind her," Hect said. "She's high-strung, that's all."

A waiter arrived to take our orders. We asked him to come back. He did, and we put him off by saying we still weren't ready. The third time he approached our table, I hurriedly left for the restroom. We kept this up until Hect noticed him talking to the maître d'. Unable to stand it longer, I told Hect to go find Becca.

After twiddling my thumbs forever, Hect appeared walking at a fast pace. The look on his face alarmed me. "Run!" he whispered in a strained tone, causing people at tables separating us to stop eating and turn. "Now, run!"

"Why?" I no longer worried about who heard us.

"Gone!"

"Who?"

"Becca!"

A commotion across the room made us look over. A group of adults, each with a grim expression, marched our way—the maître d' and a white-haired couple, plus two uniformed policemen. Becca trailed behind. Tension electrified the air between us. The white-haired woman from the couple stepped forward, pointing an accusing finger. "Are these the villains, darling?"

Without looking up, Becca nodded.

"Officers, arrest them! Throw them in jail, and keep them there until they rot."

24

The Juarez Jail

Arrest at any time has to be upsetting, but in a foreign country by foreign police speaking a foreign language and the shock cannot be described. It put me in mind of a time when as a kid, in the skies above my hometown, a Piper Cub got creamed by a B29 Bomber. The impact off the collision boomed all over town as metal pieces and body parts rained down. Now I knew how the pilot of that Piper Cub felt.

A policeman jerked me out of the chair, twisted my arms behind my back, and pinched the flesh of my wrists in steel rings. Across the table, a silver-haired lady stared with eyes like carving knives at me the trussed-up turkey. She spoke in Spanish to the policemen, who bowed and took a step back.

"I told the officers to desist," she announced in English. "I want to have a word first before they take you two away."

A spark of hope ignited. Here might be a chance to tell my side of the story, but when I opened my mouth, she turned away. So quick had been her about-face that her hairpiece hadn't kept up and cocked off to one side. She straightened the wig but, without a mirror, left it at an angle, leaving it off-center. "Darling," she said to Becca, "I've already spoken on your behalf to the authorities, and they've agreed to release you into my custody. I have influence around here because of all the business I'm bringing to the region…oh, and him too," indicating the shorter, silver-haired man.

He brightened. Much thinner than the woman, he wore a toupee that matched hers in cut and style. They also dressed alike, same colors and same satiny material.

"Now then, um…" She hesitated. "Oh, tell me your name again."

"Becca," she murmured.

"Yes, yes, I don't know why I want to call you Becky. Anyway, I've told these policemen that you're the victim here. Anyone can tell, such a sweet and striking face would never invent a cock-and-bull story like you told me. Some ne'er-do-well behind the scenes had to think up such a line. Thankfully, after I told you who I am, you trusted me enough to confess what I already knew to be true. You poor dear, you must have suffered so in the grip of these heartless rogues."

Becca's eyes roved every direction except at Hect and me.

"But don't worry," the silver-haired woman said, her tone hardening, "these two won't manipulate you ever again, I promise you that. They'll not deny another young lady such basic necessities as a bath and hot meals. Why, when I gave you my dinner, I'd never seen a girl with such a ravenous appetite. I want you to know, you've done a service in taking these two off the street. That's why, while you ate, I slipped off and had the maître d' call the police. I'm sorry to have to trick you like that, but I worried, if you knew, you might signal these rascals to runaway out of fear of reprisal."

I waited for Becca to speak up, to take a stand for us. Instead, she kept her head down. My hopes sank.

The woman patted the girl's shoulder. "What you said at the table about being an actress is a worthwhile goal that can lead to a better life. As I promised, I'll help you all I can once our company's finances are finalized, and we resume shooting the movie. You'll get your part in the film—that is, if you go through with what you said and press charges against these two."

Even with her head down, Becca's cheeks moved, betraying a smile.

In a burst of clarity, everything made sense. I connected the dots of a childhood dream, an influential contact, and a career in the movies.

Seeing it from Becca's point of view—her once-in-a-lifetime chance for stardom had arrived. I had an impulse to go on the defensive, to point at Becca and say it'd been her idea, not ours; that she'd been to blame, not us, but I resisted. The silver-haired woman had her mind made up, anyone could see that. If there was a chance for us, it'd take a strategy different from anything natural. "I beg your pardon, ma'am, but could I say a word, please?"

The older couple looked at me, and the woman's face turned stern. "If you're ready to confess, you may."

"Yes, ma'am." What other choice did I have? "You're right, my friend and I did wrong, but please try and understand. We haven't eaten a square meal in days, like Becca here, although I'm glad to hear you shared your dinner with her. I only wish someone had been so kind to Hect and me. Then none of this would've happened. But please try and put yourself in our place. My friend and I have goals too, just like Becca wanting to be an actress. That's why we put her up to doing what she did—so we could accomplish in life something, as you say, worthwhile."

"*Worthwhile*?—what a crock." The crooked-haired woman sneered. "And exactly what worthwhile does a shakedown artist like you want to accomplish?"

I again resisted an impulse to disagree. "You've a perfect right to doubt what I say, but won't you at least give my friend and me a hearing? Shouldn't two young men with their whole lives before them be allowed to tell their sides of the story?"

"Enough, enough," she said, lifting hairless eyebrows that appeared drawn with a black crayon. "All right, you've got your chance, but it better be good. Tell me one of your *worthwhile* ambitions."

"Thank you. I appreciate the opportunity. It's kind of you to give me a chance to say, er, what I have to say." I rambled because, having been so intent on persuading her, for the life of me, not a single meaningful ambition or goal came to mind. It was as though I'd been wandering through life without a thought for the future until this very moment. "It's, er, my ambition to...to one day, well, to go to college and get an education."

"And end up an even smarter shyster than before, eh? Not particularly 'worthwhile,' in my opinion. What about your partner in crime here?"

Fearing I'd undershot her expectations, I thought I'd aim higher. "A doctor."

"Really, you don't say? My, my. I'll be."

I couldn't tell from her tone whether to take her as impressed or sarcastic, but there was no stopping now. "The world needs doctors, I'm sure you'll agree, so, please, ma'am, if you'll kindly speak to the police on our behalf, as you did for Becca."

"Enough malarkey, young impostor. Let's now hear from your accomplice. So then," she said to Hect, "it's you're ambition to become a physician, is it?"

I sensed trouble. "Yes, my friend just wants to help his fellow m—"

"Quiet! One more word out of you and it's off to jail, young Machiavelli."

"Like he said," Hect mumbled, his voice quaking. "Mostly, I just want to help my fellow man."

"Admirable indeed, but I'm curious, exactly in what area of medicine do you plan to specialize?"

Wincing, I wished I'd chosen a profession a little less scholarly. "Most all of it, I reckon."

"It's a personal vanity, I know, but I pride myself on being able to intuit other people's professions." She lifted and adjusted her hairpiece, revealing a mostly bald scalp.

One look at Hect's gullible gaze, and I stared a warning at him, but he wouldn't turn my way.

"I'm not sure why," she continued, "but you strike me as a person who'd want to specialize in a field requiring a unique ability like, oh, say, excrementology."

Hect glanced at me finally, but his frown indicated confusion.

"Now that you mentions it," he answered. "I might be inclined in a direction of that sort."

"I thought so. But now, I'm fascinated why people develop the interests they do. I suppose as a young man you spent a good deal of time in this field of study, correct?"

"Un-huh." A note of caution crept into his answer.

"Probably as a child you were always carrying some in to show your mother?"

His face turned deadpan, but too late. He cast his eyes down, evidently having caught on at last.

"I've heard quite enough," the silver-haired woman snapped. "It's obvious to me the truth is as unfamiliar to you two morons as morals."

After speaking to the policemen in Spanish, the woman turned to Hect and me. "Being in trouble is certainly not unfamiliar to either of you." She jabbed a finger at each one of us in turn. "So, I've instructed these officers to notify the Texas authorities. I have a feeling they would be interested to know your whereabouts. In the meantime, prepare yourselves to find out how the Mexico criminal justice system works. You'll find it is as corrupt as it is harsh."

25

Ju

THE VIEW OF gated estates and palm-tree-lined avenues looked different from the backseat of a Mexican police car than it had from a taxi. I'd been comfortable among all the grand scenery in a cab, but now everything seemed out of reach like my membership had been cancelled. As we drove, the passing mansions shrank in size. Circular drives, gates and guards all vanished. Next, stucco homes without lawns or shrubbery went by, and then finally, we arrived among slums so poor I actually began to feel better. Not that my spirits lifted, because they didn't, but the sight of so much misery lessened the feeling of being an outsider.

We stopped at a building with barbwire in front and a parking lot full of junky police cars. Hect and I got out, still in handcuffs. Our driver, a short, squat policeman in a wrinkled, faded uniform motioned us inside. Another policeman sat behind a desk, also in an un-ironed, blue uniform. He removed our handcuffs and indicated we empty our pockets, which I did first, having only a few coins in change left from my savings and some mints I'd snagged at the hotel restaurant. The policeman pointed at my wristwatch, a ring, and an ID bracelet that'd been given to me for Christmas, which I removed.

Hect's turn came next. He took out a rusty pocketknife, a beer bottle opener, a beat-up matchbook that brought back memories of the junkyard, and a paper folded into a tiny square. The policeman opened it, and I gasped. *A five-dollar bill!* I recognized instantly where it'd come from—the old man in the '48 Chevy.

Meanwhile, the seated officer mumbled something unclear and scooped all the items into a desk drawer.

I leaned close to Hect. "What's that?"

"Our fines," he whispered back. "He's taking our stuff."

"No, not that. I know that." I noticed the seated guard glance up at our whispering and lowered my voice even more. "The five bucks, you rat-holer! I spent my whole wad, and you offered nothing."

"Silencio!" The guard jumped up from behind his desk and shook a fist while the other one shoved me. But it was worth being pushed around for the chance to tell off my best pal, so-called. I didn't feel as bad losing my stuff for the satisfaction of seeing the miser lose his stash.

We all three walked down a long, silent corridor. On either side of the hallway, rusty iron doors lined urine-stained gutters. Peep sights on the doors had little pocket-watch covers. I feared the powerful stink might bring on an asthma attack, while at the same time dreading the prospect of ending up in one of those concrete tombs.

At the end of the corridor, the policeman unlocked the last door. To my great relief, it opened to the outside. For a brief second, I had hopes of freedom, when the guard grabbed my shoulder and hurled me through the opening. Far from free, I stumbled into an outdoor pen. Groups of prisoners huddled together throughout the yard. While we'd been inside the building, a stinging sandstorm had blown in, which allowed only quick glances to get oriented as I had to keep ducking away and shielding my eyes.

Hect collided into my back, propelling me forward. Behind us, the door slammed. With no explanation where we were, what to expect, or how we should react, we stood among clumps of prisoners, perhaps hundreds, spread throughout the yard.

About the size of a rodeo arena, the open-air holding pen had canvas covering one corner. The tent snapped and flapped in the wind-driven cloud of dirt. By cupping my hands around my eyes, I saw that on two sides of the yard, barbwire ran along the tops of high wooden fences. At the farthest end, though, only strands of wire swayed in between iron poles that curved inward on top. As flimsy as chicken-wire, it struck me as odd that none of the prisoners had bothered to climb over and escape? If things got too bad in here, that's exactly what I planned to do.

Most convicts had grouped together beneath blankets, except for those fortunate few who chatted and reclined underneath the tarp. Judging by all the empty space under that tent, I figured those who enjoyed its protection must have a special status. As a result, I knew better than to go there and pulled Hect within earshot. "The good spots are all taken."

He nodded, shielding his eyes. "They give us these blankets."

I took one he offered. It felt coarse and had to be nasty. By holding it up as a shield, I could survey the yard. "Over there. Next to the wire."

"Say louder!"

I cupped my mouth with one hand. "Over there!" I pointed. "Let's go!"

We bowed our heads and held up the blankets. As we got nearer, I noticed signs with lightning bolts hanging on the wire. So that's why none of the inmates scaled the fence and escaped—one touch amounted to an instant electric chair.

At a spot away from the rest of the prisoners, we spread out a blanket and sat Indian-style with the second one draped over our heads against the stinging dust. Hopefully, the fabric wasn't lice ridden. I didn't know which was worse—the rasping sand on my skin or the smothering heat beneath the cover.

As I sat there, breathing the same hot air over and over, trying to process all that'd gone on so far, a feeling came over me. A tiredness, almost like the time in the desert when I'd run until unable to take one more step, sapped my last bit of energy. Was it a sickness? Had my brain had a stroke? Whatever, going any farther seemed impossible. "Hey, Hect?" The wind howled outside the blanket in a deafening whistle. "I'm through."

"What's 'at?"

A weight lifted off me just saying so. "I give up. I'm going home."

"You ain't serious." He snorted. "I'd like to know how. You think they let you out on account of being homesick?"

"I'm not homesick, or maybe I am, who knows? Anyway, we never should've run away to start with. We'd been better off staying put."

"'Staying put—in the slammer, you mean."

"We're in jail now." My exhaustion returned, only this time in regard to persuading my negative friend. "What've we gained by running away?"

"We ain't in the big house. There's a difference, you know? This here's jail. In jail, they let you out by and by, but not the big house. You'll stay there the whole long term—till you're old—if you live that long."

That gave me pause. "All I know is, ever since we ran away, I've felt miserable inside, and things have gone from bad to worse. I don't know how exactly, but if I get the chance, I'm going back home." I pointed at the building we'd come out of. "If I have to walk in there and confess everything."

"And what about me? What's that do for your best bud? Don't think they won't haul me right along with you. If they ship you to Texas, and you end up in Huntsville strapped in Old Sparky, I'll fry in the very same electric chair."

It was time to tell him. I'd tried a dozen times before, but how to start? Should I say, "We won't have to go to prison, maybe. It's possible that all we've been through has been my fault and that seeing a man on fire in that shack might have been a hallucination, same as the night I saw the phantom." And then what should I say next? Something like, "Gee, sorry about all the trouble you went through, but I've been afraid to say anything." He'd be mad, all right, might even start swinging, but it had to be done. I took a deep breath. "Hect, I've got to tel—"

His arm shot out straight, a finger pointed at the building. "Look-it!" He jumped to his feet. "What's going on?"

I'd been too intent to notice men from all across the yard walking with blankets draped over their heads like monks. Everyone seemed headed for one spot behind the building. I got to my feet as well. "Where're they going?"

"Chow time, what else?" Hect picked up the second blanket and shook out the sand. "Better hurry, or we'll be last in line."

I threw my blanket over my head—glad for an excuse to put off confessing, even if only temporarily—and trotted after him. Two policemen came out the back door with a big cauldron between them. They set the iron kettle atop an unsteady, three-legged stool as prisoners shuffled into line. Those quick enough to be up front got a tortilla along with a dipperful of refried beans ladled out by a policeman in a chef's hat.

Had those lucky first prisoners kept moving, trouble might've been avoided, but instead, they huddled and ate their meals while hot. These prisoners, I noticed, were the same who'd had the privileged places under the tent, and they seemed content to leave the rest of us to get by as best we could. Crowding and shoving resulted. Meanwhile, I stood on tiptoes and watched those ahead make a burrito in one hand and use the other to hold their blankets up to keep prison-yard dirt from seasoning their food.

A logjam slowed the line to a near stop. Angry shouts in Spanish broke out until I feared missing my turn. What if I didn't get my share? How often did they feed around here anyway? Did those in charge even care? Judging by what I'd experienced so far, it was doubtful. Would the result be the strong ones stole food from those of us too weak to resist? Were there any laws? Any justice? Or was it all dog eat dog?

Here and there, shoving fights broke out. Burritos got knocked to the ground, a few of which I almost made a dive for until they got trampled. Mud stuck to my shoes as refried beans mixed with the dirt made it slippery to stand. While I struggled to hold my place, a lone voice stood out among all the rapid-fire Spanish. Whoever the voice belonged to, his words came out different—measured and clipped with an accent that didn't sound like the others at all. Had I not known better, I would've guessed the person came from a country other than Mexico—one I knew, but couldn't quite name.

The pushing matches worsened as packs of inmates taunted one another. From the looks, the squabble over dinners spread to old rivalries. I got anxious someone might mistake me for one of the enemy. Not alone in that concern evidently, everyone in line turned away from the food table, taking up defensive postures. This opened a clear path to those serving, so I grabbed Hect and pulled him along, squirming ahead. After being handed a tortilla, it took all my strength just to stay steady enough for a dipper of refried beans, which turned out to be boiling hot. The scalding steam shot through the thin bread, searing my palm and, while adjusting my grip, I got a closer look at what I'd been served. Horrified, I threw the tortilla straight up along with what I took to be a boiled rat. The burrito rose above the convicts, hung there for the briefest instant, and then dropped, sticking like molten plaster on the nape of the man nearest me. He screamed, spun around trailing a roundhouse right hook, but I ducked. The fist traveled over my head and landed square in the middle of the cook's face. Tiny red jets of blood squirted out either side of the ball of knuckles.

A full-scale brawl erupted over me, making it impossible to stand back up. Aware there stood a good chance of my being blamed for beginning the riot in the first place, I dropped to my knees, desperate to find the cooked rat in among shuffling feet. Digging in the mud while trying to keep my fingers from being mashed, to my dismay, I found, not a cooked rat at all, but a hunk of tree bark. Worse yet, on closer inspection, the bark didn't even look close to a rat. Who would believe me now?

Directly overhead, the cook cupped a bloody nose with one hand, while swinging a bean ladle with the other, catching the prisoner who'd hit him upside the head. The blow staggered the convict, who spun, reeled sideways, stepped back, and tripped over me. He collided headfirst on the hard-packed sand and didn't move. A pair of hands slipped into my armpits from behind and lifted me to my feet.

"Good show, old chap."

I recognized the voice at once as the one that'd sounded so different from all the other Spanish-speaking brawlers. Because of the press of struggling bodies, I couldn't turn around to locate him.

"Cold-cocked the hooligan, you did! Well done, well done."

It took everything I had just to stay on my feet, but I turned my head enough to catch a glimpse of a black man. A head shorter than anybody else, he cupped his mouth with one hand, yelling at me, while with the other hand, swung his fist at an opponent. "Thanks for the assist, although none needed, but glad for the effort nonetheless."

I started to explain about the boiled-rat mistake, but a fist brushed my chin so close I felt the wind off it. In recoiling back, I dropped my bark piece as the wad of knuckles landed in the middle of Hect's back, propelling him forward into the three-legged table and toppling the vat. Gallons of refried beans splashed into the mud, sloshing all directions. The uniformed cook fell with the table, and on top of him stacked a dog pile of men punching one another.

Guards poured from the building, swinging bats, and clubbing heads, backs, legs, arms and whatever else. Someone ran into me, and I slid down. Of all the luck, my piece of bark lay half-submerged in the gunk. Managing to struggle up on my feet, I started to show someone the bark evidence when a line of uniforms sliced into the melee, cutting me off. The prison guards, still raining blows, herded a portion of brawlers into the building.

Shots rang out. The whole yard dropped to the ground and pulled blankets over their heads, looking like pill bugs. One of the last to get down, I crawled over next to Hect. From underneath our covers, we pecked out in time to see the cook gouge handfuls of mud from his eye sockets; then glare with such rage, the bean paste on his face seemed ready to boil. Afraid that he might be searching for me, I motioned to Hect, and, still under our blankets, we crawled away along with the other prisoners.

On the way back to where we'd first made our beds near the wire, a pair of legs blocked our path. The black man stood with arms folded across his chest, feet planted solidly apart, and taking no precautions against the stinging sand. "I say, old boy." He grasped my hand and pulled me to my feet. "Terribly decent of you to interfere in that scrap. Had you not meddled, a human life might have come to a violent end, as I planned on snuffing that cheeky blighter." He laughed and helped Hect up as well.

I shielded my eyes against the dust, surprised at how small his height. He looked older, maybe as much as thirty. Then it hit me. "You helped me get back on my feet back there."

"Right-o, chum. During the knockabout."

"Knoc…oh, yeah, the brawl."

"Frightfully plucky of you to dump your bean pie on that blighter's crown, and I might add, more than a little amusing, eh?" He chuckled. "Then, of all the ways to cap a scrap off, to pull that old childhood stunt of getting on all fours behind their hit man and spill him onto his noggin. Quite the act of a champion, I must say."

I started to correct him and say the whole thing had been an accident, except that he'd called me a "champion." I liked that for a change.

"Hit man?" Hect gulped. "Did you say hit man? What *hit man*?"

"Paid assassin, old boy. I assumed you chaps knew who you were dealing with. He and his ilk murder for the pleasure of it inside this clink, but on the outside, they're paid a stipend to kill. And quite the lucky turn for the pair of you—getting that whole pack of bloody cutthroats carted off to the punishment chambers."

I suddenly felt sick. "What kind of chambers?"

"Solitary. Surely you noticed those cells on your way out to the yard, eh? Not a flicker of light in them. The occupants get a bowl of watery broth once a day, a concrete floor to nap on, and bedbugs and fleas for bunkmates."

I shuddered, imagining what that'd be like.

"Aye, laddies," he continued, "this'll teach those malingerers what to expect if they tangle with the likes of you, eh? Good riddance."

"You mean…" I swallowed hard. "You mean, they'll blame *me*?" Already the term 'champion' lost its glamour. "But, why?"

"No need for modesty, old boy. I was right there when you dumped your pottage on their leader's head. Why, that sly jackal thinks he's a mean one, he does. He'll gut a bloke quicker than you can scoop the bowels from a cod, but you got the better of him this time. Only, you'd do well to fashion a weapon before he gets out. He's sure to have his knickers in a twist. In your place, I'd attack the entire bunch before they know what hit them. That way, you'll lessen the odds by one or two."

My legs went rubbery when, out of nowhere, a hand clapped my back and my knees all but caved. A prisoner, smiling a mouthful of rusty teeth, walked around in front. It took a second to realize his backslap had been friendly. Another arrival shook my hand, and then more gathered around, some slapping me good-buddy-like and a few hugged my neck. They spoke in Spanish, of course, but I could tell they were expressing thanks, whatever for, I didn't know, but they put a little strength back in my legs at least.

"You're a hero, lad," the black man said. "That bloody ruffian and his gang of hooligans have tyrannized these downtrodden jailbirds—pilfering their food, pummeling them for the slightest infraction, and generally making their lives frightful. That's what caused my scuffle—that shifty galoot tried to snitch my bean pie. In a manner of speaking, you saved us all."

A hand from out of the blanket-covered prisoners thrust a burrito at me, though his face remained hidden in the hood's shadow. I begged off at first, but the hand kept jabbing. Finally, believing it'd be rude to do otherwise, I took it and bit off a chunk. Cheers erupted. The shouts arose again with every mouthful thereafter.

The prisoners wouldn't allow Hect or me to return to our earlier spot in front of the wire, but instead escorted us under the tarpaulin, now vacant because the thugs were in the punishment cells. We spread our blankets, made sand pillows under one end, and got comfortable, or as much as possible under the circumstances. The tent offered excellent protection since, as the wind let up, a heavy drizzle of sand fell to earth.

"Call me Ju," the black man said. "It's short for Juweel in the language of the Afrikaans and means jewel, or really a 'gem.'" He smiled a set of white teeth. "There's no need to bother about surnames. What are you chaps to be called?"

"I'm Tim, and this is Hect."

I shook his hand, but Hect turned away. Unsure what to make of my friend's behavior all of a sudden, I tried to cover up for it. "From your accent, Ju, I'd guess you're from South Africa, correct?"

"I no longer lay claim to any one country, old boy—nationalism and all that rot," he said, losing his grin. "My patriotism is to a government without any boundaries. We're not limited by rivers or mountains or oceans. For the present, my home is in whatever country doesn't know I'm there." His good humor returned. "Come now, that's enough of me. If you lads don't mind me giving you some advice, I'd employ a bit of discretion the next time before I got the vilest bunch of assassins in this place after me." He chuckled as if he thought the remark humorous.

I managed a half smile; Hect didn't even try.

"Tell me now, lads," Ju continued. "What are two such game steeds doing in this foul, wretched place? And, for heaven's sake, don't give me that old saw about selling subscriptions to cricket magazines, eh?" This witticism really set him off.

Before I knew what happened, Hect grabbed up a handful of sand and flung it, causing prisoners nearby to duck. "What's the use?" he yelled loud enough that everyone under the tarp looked our way. "We're finished! Done for! Why jabber like nothing matters no more? Don't you see it? After that riot, they're sure to look for who started the fight and it won't take long to find out neither. They'll check our records back in Texas, and once they know we're wanted, they'll ship us home in leg irons." He slumped into his former sulk. "Who knows? Maybe we'd be better off on death row than in this chicken-coop dump."

I couldn't believe my ears. He'd exposed everything we'd been trying to keep secret all this time, and I had not a clue how to cover up such a reckless outburst.

"Death row?" Ju gasped. "You can't mean it? *You two?* Well, bowl me over; my original estimate of you chaps needs revising, it seems. I had you sized for a couple of nanny-worriers, but you say you popped off some bloke?"

"Don't listen to him, Ju." My mind raced for an excuse. "We didn't do anything wrong…at least, I didn't."

"There!" Hect yelled, pointing at me, his finger shaking. "I knew it! Sooner or later, I knew you'd crawfish and push the blame off on me. I seen your true colors all along. Well, it won't work. Remember, the one who lights the fuse goes up river same as him who throws the Molotov cocktail."

"Blimey! You don't mean to say you two barely-shavers are actual bombers?" Ju reared backward. "Why, bless my blind eyes, don't tell me you blew up some poor bugger, and you're now on the dash for it? And here I had you pegged for a couple of mum's tots."

Hect pulled his blanket over his head.

"You know, Tim lad, his point may well be valid. Now that you're incarcerated, these Mexican bobbies are sure to check with Texas authorities. If you two really are fugitives, you could be on your way north of the border by morning. But, what if I told you, there might be another way? After all, you helped Ju, and he never forgets a favor. Should things work out the way I think, we may be departing soon, if you get my line."

A gust of dust made me avert my eyes. I rubbed them until they watered enough to wash the sand out. "Gee, thanks, Ju, but I don't think so. It sounds risky."

"I'd ponder my offer, laddie. Keep in mind, once those bloody ruffians get out of their punishment chambers, they'll want to settle old scores, and Ju may not be here to assist you."

I hadn't thought of that.

"Good point, Ju. In that case, I change my mind. Whatever happens, it's bound to be better than staying in here."

"That's the spirit, lad. And what about you, Hect? If you got the chance, I dare say you wouldn't mind seeing the last of this, as you call it, 'chicken coop dump.'"

One look at Hect, and I knew I'd better jump in. "Of course, he would."

"Good enough. Time to shove off now, chaps. The guards will take an interest if we talk too long. But now, watch yourselves, and as soon as it gets dark, keep on the alert. That's all I can say for now. Cheerio, lads, and watch that the whiptails don't crawl in your beds." Ju picked up his blanket and left.

I got up immediately and shook my blanket out before spreading it again. Why'd he have to mention scorpions, or whatever he'd called them—"whiptails." Had it really been necessary to put that thought in my head? Now how was I to sleep?

By evening, the wind let up entirely, leaving the air so powdery dry, my throat tickled and each breath finished with a little cough. All around us, prisoners snored, most having gone to bed without anything to eat.

"I don't trust him," Hect's head poked out of his blanket. "Do you trust him?"

I didn't answer.

"What about you, Tim? Do you trust him?"

I busily brushed off gritty cheeks and ruffled sand out of my hair.

"You're mad, ain't you? All right, I needn't'a pitched a temper like that, maybe. It just kind'a come over me, you know? I couldn't keep from it. You know, Tim?"

He wouldn't quit asking, of course. The silent treatment never worked on him. No matter how many times he got ignored, it just never occurred to him to apologize.

"You know what?" Hect asked, sounding as if changing the subject. "I think he's got it in mind to bust out of this place tonight. Don't you? Is that what you think? Well, is it?"

I patted my shirt, raising puffs of dust with each slap.

"Hey, Tim?" he said like I hadn't heard. "Don't you think so? Well, don't you?"

He'd win in the end like always. We both knew it. I could never outlast him.

26

Jailbreak

I'D SEEN ALL kinds of sand—beach sand, the desert sand in West Texas, sandboxes, sand dunes, even the pure white sand in the golf course traps at the country club, but never anything like the sand in this prison yard. Instead of coarse or grainy, it felt like fine flour. The granules embedded in my skin like talcum powder, only dirty feeling. It seemed no amount of soap and water would ever wash the grimy feel away.

I couldn't sleep. For one thing, everyone around me snored like they were choking to death. Even worse, the path to the latrine went directly by my bed so that whoever walked by kicked up sand onto me. Even though it meant leaving the tarpaulin, Hect and I picked up our blankets and went back to our old place in front of the electric fence. We made our beds and scooped a sand-hump under one end for a pillow.

"Ho-there!" Ju's voice rang out from the direction of the tent. "Not there, chums! Choose another spot to build your nest."

Just about to stretch out, Hect and I traded puzzled looks.

"Get cracking now, lads. Spread your knapsacks somewhere else, I say. Move down a tad away from the wire. Come on, hut-hut. It's far too drafty there."

"Drafty?" Hect whispered, bunching his round face like a deflating ball. "Has he lost it? We're in an open yard. The whole place's drafty."

I shrugged. "A joke, maybe?" I'd given up on the silent treatment. It took too much effort to waste on someone who could care less.

"Lads!" Ju called from somewhere. "Quit your gasbagging now. Be quick about it. Move down, and you'll do fine."

Without understanding why, we picked up our blankets and moved.

"No, no, still won't do, lads. Farther down yet. Away from the wire completely."

We did as he said and fixed our beds away from the electric fence altogether. Ju must have approved, because he stopped shouting. Finally, we could get some sleep.

During the night, I got restless and rolled off my blanket, inhaling a nose-full of powdery dust. Choking and gasping, my nostrils burned as though I'd sniffed hot ashes. After a spasm of snorting and sneezing, I could finally lay back down.

The scratchy wool blanket made sleep difficult, but even more distracting, a view above took my breath away. A black-velvet sky seemed stretched in front of a powerful light that shown through tiny pinholes. Despite being weary, I couldn't shut my eyes. A science teacher once said all this came about by accident, a freakish mishap without design or purpose, but how could that be? Accidents involve wreckage, spillage, breakage—not what I saw—so quiet, composed, and orderly.

Three shooting stars crossed the heavens. No ordinary meteors, the glowing lights flew in formation, streaking across as bright as three smoldering, flameless matches. Incredibly, they lit up the whole prison yard. I'd never seen anything that compared to it. Even more remarkable, the brilliance blotted out the starry sky itself.

Sensing danger, I flipped onto my stomach in time to see lights— two below, one above—coming fast, along with a terrific roar. For an instant, I thought the shooting stars curved around and now traveled parallel to the ground, aiming dead at me. A metallic "*crunch*" rang out as the lights crashed into the wire fence, followed by an ear-wincing scraping. Amid sparks and blue arches of voltage, the wall of wires and iron poles collapsed partway. Had Hect and I not moved, we would've been pinned beneath the fireworks display.

A cloud of dust swept over us until nothing could be seen, making the roar all the more terrifying. Once the air cleared, a truck stood on its back wheels with its front tires off the ground and headlights shining almost straight up. With a fresh growl, the truck backed off, stopped, and charged forward again, this time climbing nearly over the wire. The truck's tires, three times the size of regular ones, more like balloons really, kept the arching electricity away. For a second time, the huge truck backed up and made another run, this time crushing the leaning fence flat. An even thicker dust cloud swept over us. When I could see again, a truck half the size of a locomotive had parked just inside the fence with a spotlight atop the cab, along with headlights above a front bumper that had tires strapped to it.

Gunfire cracked as prisoners scattered in all directions. The spotlight on top of the truck swept along the back of the building, pausing on guards aiming their rifles, making them duck away. The shots sounded at first like harmless pops until one whizzed overhead, followed by several more sizzling whines. Tiny sparks multiplied along the building. A familiar figure ran hunched over into the truck's headlight beams.

I recognized the form. "Ju! Wait! Ju!"

"Hurry, mates!" He circled the truck's cab and climbed up one of the bulging back tires onto the bed frame. "Trolley's departing! All aboard!"

With no time to think, only react, Hect and I sprinted for the truck and climbed a huge rear tire by grasping whatever handholds came within reach. The back brake lights enabled us to see enough to tightrope the steel rails of the bed frame amid zinging noises all around. Once at the back of the cab, I made the mistake of grasping hold of an exhaust pipe, scalding my palm, and leaving me with only one hand to hold on with.

The truck lurched backward, throwing us forward. We drove in reverse over the mangled fence as wire strands clawed against the metal sides and snatched at our pant legs. Once over the fence, the truck braked and then accelerated in a U-turn. We sped along the dark roads of Juarez as occasional streetlights flew past in bright balls within clouds of trailing exhaust smoke.

Once outside the city, we traveled through what appeared from my angle, a tunnel of light encased in a black tube of night. The ride went fairly smooth for awhile after that. We rounded a curve, and our headlights swept across a hulking structure in the desert.

"There!" Hect hollered.

I looked in time to see a massive shape against a starry sky back-drop with the lights of Juarez distantly behind it. Something about the place gave me the willies.

"That's the place!" Hect screamed above the wind.

I aimed my ear closer to his mouth.

"The prison movie set! Where me and Becca took a taxi to!"

I nodded and turned for a second look, but the truck veered, leaving the highway; then straightened and sped up. A strong pull tugged me to the right, trying to drag me off, and with only one good hand, I held on for dear life. The pulling sensation didn't stop as we made a full circle, or almost, then sped down another straightaway. The same drag tugged again, only this time on the opposite side, throwing me to the left against Hect, and unexpectedly swung back to the right as I almost lost my grip. Despite the pain in my hand, it was either hang on or fly off the side. I spread my feet, crouching in a baseball player's stance, prepared for any quick change in direction. However, this time, the truck slowed.

After a familiar rumble that I'd heard many times going over cat-tle guards in West Texas, we bucked so hard all three of us left our feet. Afterward, the ride really got rough. Dust boiled up. I coughed and wheezed until it seemed I'd never get a breath that wasn't half dirt. With my burned hand, I pulled my shirt collar over my nose and mouth.

Since the pace had slowed considerably, it felt safe enough to lean over and try to make myself heard by Ju. "Where to?"

His response blew away.

I leaned in closer. "Where to, Ju?"

"Camp!"

"*Can't...*what?"

"Not can't! *Camp!* C-A-M-P! Camp!"

I nodded, too ashamed to ask more, even though who knows what he meant. What kind of "Camp" could possibly be out here? Not a kids' camp, for sure. Any attempt at an explanation would be useless on the back of this truck in the wailing wind. Besides, the way he teased about everything, it might be another one of his unfunny jokes. Who knew?

Overhead, a slice of moon hung at a crooked angle in what looked like a half smirk. Even the moon seemed disapproving, no less. I could imagine the clever remark behind that mocking smile, something along the lines of, "My, my, look what you're into now."

The truck braked, catching me off guard, and I sailed forward. A white flash burst inside my head along with a crackling sound down my neck like stepping on gravel. Umbrella showers of bright colors appeared and then the sensation of falling and tumbling.

⛬

MY HEAD ACHED. Afraid to move, I lay still and stared straight up at a dome of stars. That sliver of moon still had a know-it-all grin, but the last time the wiseacre had been straight above, not over on the horizon. Had I been out that long? And where'd the truck gone? Why hadn't they stopped? What happened to Hect? I sat bolt upright. Hit by a throbbing, I dropped back on one elbow and massaged pounding temples.

I'd partially awakened one other time. Back then, everything had been blurry. I strained to wake up all the way, trying to escape semi-consciousness, but unable to, sank down into a murky depth. Before slipping under completely, though, a fear gripped me of some unidentified danger nearby.

Now, fully awake, I sat up ever so slowly this time and gently felt a lump atop my head. The hair around it had matted and felt sticky. I also discovered a blister on my palm that felt the size of a Vienna sausage, proving the escape from a Juarez jail hadn't been a dream after all.

All around, a black formless desert stretched far away to starless mountains. On either side of me, deep tread impressions in the sand helped make sense of things. I must've fallen through the truck frame, and the balloon tires kept the rear axle high enough to pass over, but why hadn't they stopped? How long would it have taken? Had they assumed I'd been killed? Or else, had they been too afraid of whoever might be in pursuit? Or, could it be the driver hadn't known, and when he found out I'd fallen, they'd come back? Only, considering there were no headlights anywhere on the horizons, that wouldn't happen anytime soon. And yet, Hect would never abandon me—if he had a choice, that is.

One thing was all too clear; to sit here and wait would end badly. Anyone who'd lived in the desert knew, headache or no headache, once the sun arrived, this place would turn on all the burners at once. Even if the truck did come back, they'd surely follow the same route, so I would keep to the tire tracks no matter what.

Finding water was a must, but a far more immediate problem had to be dealt with before anything. Which way to go? Would it be best to follow the tire prints to wherever or retrace them back the way we came? After imagining what it'd be like to wander lost in the desert, only one choice remained: a clear destination. Once the sun came up, maybe the view of the mountain above Juarez would be enough to keep going.

No telling how much time was left before sunrise. With one eye on the horizon, I kept in the left tire track. Any change in the sky to a lighter shade would start the countdown. After that, both water and shade had better be close by. Finding one without the other would only prolong the agony. On this flat griddle, the chances of finding them together were slim at best. Hurrying didn't help either, as breathing faster only dried my throat, making cottonmouth unbearable.

First light didn't arrive as I figured. Instead of the dark turning lighter, a jagged edge of mountain peaks revealed the eastern sky. It took a while for that truth to register, but when it did, I clenched my fists against the urge to run and forced myself to walk at a steady, unhurried pace, refusing to look east any longer. Instead, I hummed tunes and searched a pastel sky in the west for a cloud. Any cloud. Oh, for an overcast day. Better yet, a rainy day. Surely, it rained in the desert sometimes. Why not today? If only I'd get lucky for once. What I wouldn't give to be in a downpour like the one in the mountains of New Mexico. How wonderful to get soaking wet, to walk with my mouth open, letting the cool rain trickle down my throat.

No luck. A purplish sky contained not a single cloud. Not one. Instead, bronze rays shot overhead into blue skies like outstretched fingers reaching for me. I set my teeth against rising sobs, knowing I couldn't afford the water loss. A nagging sense of not getting anywhere dogged me. I quickened my pace while in my mind, the same phrase kept repeating, "The sun! Oh, the sun! Oh, no, the sun!"

If anyone had told me something could make me stop in my tracks, I'd have called them crazy, but something did. Afraid to move or so much as blink, my eyes stayed glued on one spot.

There! There again! And there again! To the west, up above the horizon, on what must be a foothill—a light! No, two lights. One blue—no, red—the other white. From this far away, they appeared tiny as fireflies and just as fleeting. One second the lights appeared; the next they were gone. First one, then two, then none, other times more. But what could they be? A farm house? Cars on a mountain road? Some kind of warning flares? Who could tell?

I started in that direction, but froze again. Going toward the lights meant leaving the tire tracks, something I'd sworn not to do. Afraid to shift my eyes away from the lights for fear they'd disappear, I had to decide. But who would not go toward them? Who in their right mind could walk away from their one chance of rescue? Especially as the western sky had by now lightened to a pale blue? Left with no choice, I took the risk.

Walking got harder after leaving the packed-down tire print as the sand gave way under my feet. Sometimes I missed a step and stumbled but didn't dare shift my stare away from the multicolored specks. As if things hadn't been discouraging enough, a memory came to mind of the Marfa lights. Every kid in West Texas had been on a school trip to see the wonder at Marfa, Texas. A teacher once told our group that no one, not even scientists, could figure what caused the lights on the horizon. She'd said Air Force jets had flown out trying to solve the unexplained mystery, and nothing. What disturbed me most was they'd looked very similar to these, more like colored sparks. Were these an optical illusion too?

A warm sensation on the back of my neck told me what happened without having to look. I did anyway. The sight of an orange eyeball peeking over a rugged mountain staggered me. The fiery Kilroy seemed scouring the desert floor for lost victims, but when I turned back around, something far more disastrous occurred. The lights had vanished. I dropped to my knees, dug my hands into the sand, still cold from the night before, and squeezed it through my fingers, while at the same time writhing inside, agonizing over such stupidity. I should've known. Why hadn't I thought of it before? Of course, the sunlight would erase them. Now what? No water, lost, a sun on the way ready to suck the last drop of moisture from every living thing, and no idea where the tire tracks might be. What had I done to deserve this? Everything in life backfired and left me in worse shape than before. I'd gone through the same dull plot of temptation, double-cross, and defeat, but why? For what reason? What could possibly be the point?

I lay down on the ground for a last feel of cool before the sand got hot, except a memory wouldn't leave me alone. Once before I'd given up. Only that time, it'd been next to a highway in New Mexico. If that girl with the hydrant of hair hadn't passed by, I might still be there. And yet, the situation hadn't been anywhere near as bad as I thought. In fact, just the opposite. Instead of being freezing, the temperature had been in the seventies with Ruidoso a mile or so over the hill. What if this turned out the same? What if, a little farther over the next rise, an undreamed-of rescue awaited? Wasn't it worth a try?

Enough to get me back on my feet; I walked in what seemed the general direction of the oversized tire prints. Shade from the mountains shrank away like a herd of black animals running for cover. A blazing heat swept the desert floor in a virtual hot wind as I tracked whatever sand ridges even closely resembled tire prints, but they all melted away to nothing. Cactus, yuccas, and squat gray sage looked the same in every direction. At last, I crossed fresh footprints and my initial thrill collapsed into even greater despair at the sight of my own shoe prints.

The sun's heat intensified, although not yet full strength. All my life I had been warned of the symptoms of heat stroke. By the time chills, dizziness, and nausea set in, it was too late. And yet, as far as the eye could see, not one spot of shade offered a hiding place to wait out the day or an overhang to crawl under or even a boulder to lie next to. Everywhere, flat, shrub-less sand stretched on forever. I pulled my shirttail over my head for a tent.

Of all things, a breeze kicked up, but the air felt fresh off a brush fire and only meant the shifting sands would erase the tire tracks faster. What difference did it make, though? Even if the prints appeared, how long would I be able to follow them? To the limit of my vision? And then what? Another vista? And yet another? Who knew, I might even be walking in circles, judging by my earlier footprints.

I climbed a small rise and looked each direction, seeing only far-away mountains. Above, a ball-of-fire sun bore down with a savage intensity that would only worsen as the day went on. I knelt in the sand. "Oh, God!" My voice frightened me, wheezing like some sick old man. "Help! Don't let me die, not like this, not out here alone."

The prayer blew on as meaningless as the sand. How many such frantic pleas must arise from all over the world every day– from Asia, Africa, Europe, and South America? Why should mine get noticed? What'd I done to earn special attention? If only there was some way to make mine more meaningful. Urgency? No, all such prayers were urgent. Then how? How to get to the front of the line, so to speak? A promise? Or an oath? Better yet, a vow? Maybe. A vow might take my prayer out of the ordinary. I even knew what to promise as Hect and I had talked about it right before we escaped.

"I'll go back!" I'd spoken out loud, even though the effort amounted to no more than a raspy croak, but actually saying the words, rather than just thoughts, seemed more sincere. "I'll go home and take my punishment. I'll confess! Whatever they dish out, I don't care. Only help me, God."

Again, my words seemed drowned by the whistling wind. Nothing happened. How then should a prayer go? Were there magic words? I thought of that girl, the one who'd picked me up on the side of the road. She'd believed in God and even tried to convince me. "*Zelda,* that's it!" Her name came to be out of the blue. All that time I'd tried to remember it, and nothing. "She'd called a name like she knew God. *Jesus!*" The cry came off chapped lips barely above a whisper. "If you're real, Jesus, help me."

Dust hit me in the face, and I ducked away, rubbing my eyes. No tears came up to wash the sand out despite how hard I rolled the balls of my fists in my sockets. I caught glimpses of a whirlwind meandering off in between gritty blinks, wiggling its many hips, spinning up to the clouds and throwing off bits and pieces.

As I watched, something about the mini-tornado attracted me. Most of the debris settled back to earth, but a few specks hung in the air, circling. By continually wiping and rubbing my eyes, my sight improved. At first, I thought the sand left specks on my vision, but no, the flecks actually hung in the air. Only, what could defy gravity like that? Not buzzards. They were too small. Then what? Doves, maybe? Only, what would doves be doing way out here in this barren desert with hardly a shrub? Hect and I used to hunt doves with his uncle's 12-gauge, but always in a field of sunflowers or else at a…

I dared not finish or even allow the word into my mind. A person could go insane from such disappointment. Still, the mere possibility got me moving.

Before long, there appeared on the desert floor something that, from this far away, looked the size of a mole. After a hurried walk, the bump formed into a tuft of bare sticks. I broke into a stumbling trot. The bushes had died obviously, but at least it indicated a sign of life I hadn't seen anywhere on the sands so far.

No longer able to block the word, "Cowpond!" popped into my mind. Where else? That'd been the only place Hect and I ever hunted doves besides in a sunflower field. When the birds flew in for a drink, we'd pick them off in flight. And yet, that didn't make sense. No livestock existed out here. How could they survive? Without so much as a blade of green grass anywhere, only scrawny, straw-like broomweed, what livestock could live with practically nothing to eat?

I broke into a stumbling run, but it didn't last long. Wild imaginings filled my thoughts as I dove into a cool, clear pool, splashing around, drinking my fill, and swimming laps. Adding to the fantasies, on every horizon, heat waves appeared as water sparkled in shimmering silvery blue lakes.

The sun's position had reached directly overhead, meaning regardless of what that clump turned into, there'd be no going any farther. Whatever lay ahead would either become my rescue, or else that's where they'd find me. As if things weren't hard enough, a hot wind blew as sand hurled in my face, forcing me to duck away and wait for the blinding gusts to pass. One hopeful sign, a short tower rose out of the dead brush— almost certainly a windmill. Cautiously joyful, the sight kept me putting one foot in front of the other.

As I got closer, this windmill, unlike the metal ones back home, had legs and crossbeams of wood. A tube ran down the center, only the pump rod hadn't moved the whole time I'd been watching. Worse yet, the propeller hadn't turned, and it was obvious why. Instead of facing into the wind, the fan faced away. Any West Texan knows the spinning propeller lifts the center pipe up and down, pumping water to the surface. Except why then the circling doves? One last hope remained—that the tank held enough water for a drink. That was all. Nothing more; one drink. If slimy, stale, or stagnant, who cared? I'd chew moisture out of pond scum, if need be.

At the windmill, I collapsed against a weathered cross brace and carefully slid down one splintery windmill leg. Too afraid to look at first, I sat there and tried to work up my nerve. The tank was as big around as a child's wading pool with metal sides about waist-high. Water didn't flow from the fill pipe or else there'd be splashing. I shut my eyes tight and crawled to the tub, which felt hot at the bottom. A bad sign. Had there been water, it would feel cool. Oh, but if only a drink was left. Just one.

Before daring to look, I prayed like never in my life, and then rose up on my knees, put my hands and chin on the rim and ever so slowly opened one eye; then both opened wide. Dry.

27

Uninvited Guests

Was this the result of prayer—to end up a laughingstock by an empty water trough? Had the whirlwind been part of a gag with the punch line being a broken windmill? Would whoever finds my bones get the last laugh? And yet, why the doves? How to explain them? Doves want water, but they wouldn't stay where there was none. Had there been a pond recently and the birds stopped by for a drink out of habit? Or, did they know something I didn't? Whatever, the ordeal seemed so meaningless until, that is, the answer hit. Of course. The whirlwind, the doves, the windmill—all combined to outsmart me. My past wrongs really had been kept track of, after all, and now came time for payback. I'd been lured out here. Just as the poor hobo in the shack had burned alive, so my life would end in the same awful agony.

The desert sun didn't allow lingering, though. Heat bore down hotter than any I'd ever felt lying next to the country club swimming pool. Those tanning beams had been gentle, but these harsh rays stabbed right through my clothes, stinging the skin. Because of the unrelenting burning, I crawled into the dead bushes for the slices of shade beneath the leafless branches. Not only that, but when the end did come, it'd make it harder for buzzards to spot me.

A wind rattled the dead twigs above me. On the other side of the brush, a dry pond had deep cracks in the surface. I imagined what it must have looked like when full. Sparkling blue water so clear that fish could be seen swimming along the rocky bottom. Truthfully, no such pond existed in the desert, certainly not in West Texas, but then who wanted to dream of green slime mixed in a brown, watery slop? Not me. I saw glacier waters tumbling over boulders, ending in a chilly pool.

My fantasy ended abruptly. Within one of those dried-up mud cracks, something stirred. At least some living thing found a way to survive this wasteland.

Two claws the size of crab pinchers poked out of the crevice, followed by a creature so ferocious that I drew back and shuddered. Black as a piece of char, a giant scorpion crawled out, stretched wide its pincers, and straightened a poison-bubbled tail as though just waking from a nap. Never had I seen one of such size. In West Texas, a large one would be a couple of inches, which was bad enough, but this one measured three times that and with a curved stinger big as a fishhook. I shrank into the bush as far as possible without getting into direct sunshine, praying the creature would not come my way. Thankfully, it scampered back into the dark crack.

Not about to daydream now, I kept a wary eye out. Sure enough, another scorpion crept out, this one not quite as large, its color more a brownish yellow. It scooted across the dry bed and scampered underground. In no time, a third appeared, but on her back rode six babies. As I watched, a total of five ugly critters made an appearance, until I realized underneath the algae crust, there must be a whole colony. It didn't take long to figure out why. The dry mud covered enough dampness to enable them to thrive, which would explain why the doves came around—they smelled water. But how to find out for sure? The obvious answer would be to crawl out there and look, except for one problem: the scorpions.

As a kid, I had nightmares about the terrible pests, and if I so much as thought about one before bedtime, I had to first inspect my sheets. I'd heard no telling how many tales, true or not, of the painful deaths the stings caused. And yet, none of that affected the choice now facing me—them or me?

I looked for a weapon. A pointed stick should do the job, or maybe a rock large enough for crushing, but it occurred to me that even if I got brave enough to go out on the dry bed and battle one, they'd all come out. What then? In my mind, a picture flashed of being surrounded by the venomous fiends, their pincers open and stingers cocked. The image convinced me that, no matter what the weapon, crawling on a thin crust that covered poisonous insects to the most likely spot to find water, the middle of the pond, would be impossible.

While I sat there and cursed my cowardice, that first huge scorpion came out again. By now familiar enough to think of a nickname, I called it Blacky. Something struck me as curious about Blacky. What about the creature so thoroughly defeated me that I'd be willing to sit here and die of thirst? Its size? Monstrously large, true, but still no bigger than my hand. Well then, it's pincers? As sharp looking as scissors, but how hard could they pinch, really? How about its hideous looks then? Half spider, half centipede, but it's not like the thing had jaws full of sharp fangs. No, it was the stinger. That poison-loaded gaff ready to crack like a whip, bury its hook, and sink liquid fire into soft flesh. If not for that, I'd swept the varmint aside by now with no more care than a grasshopper.

I threw a small rock to see what would happen. Blacky squatted and spread its claws wide while opening and closing its pincers, the terrible tail cocked with stinger at the ready. I threw another, feeling some slight satisfaction at being able to harass it from a distance. Blacky spun about, its wide-open pinchers stretched as though daring an attacker to come within reach; the dreadful tail curled down, touching its shell back. I found a twig and tossed it. Quick as could be, the insect whirled to meet the enemy from that direction.

Could it be that Blacky had a weakness? Hect had a name for such a maneuver when we played war. Let's see... "Flank attack," that's it. Might it be that an approach from the rear stood a chance? To test my theory, I broke off a twig long enough to reach the pond bed. No sooner had I touched the dirt than the alert insect whirled and lashed its tail almost faster than eye could see. A touch on the other side got the same results. However, a theory was one thing; acting it out for real was altogether different. Still, what choice did I have?

After several breaths, while sealing my mind against discouraging thoughts, I set my jaw tight and crept to the edge of the pond. Blacky, either feeling vibrations or sensing movement, whipped around to face me. A shiver went through me, followed by an unexpected calm, from who knows what source. With a steady hand, I scratched the dirt. As expected, Blacky lifted its rear so its shell back curved into a cocked tail. As I lightly twiddled the dirt with my left hand, I slowly reached around with my right to the side and behind Blacky. Before losing my nerve, knowing better than to hesitate, I struck, clamping down with thumb and forefinger and trapping its tail and stinger. Waves of revulsion almost forced me to let go as its flexing tail twitched within my grasp. Blacky's eight legs scrambled at the dirt trying to pull away. I hoisted up the writhing bug, surprised by its weight. Thrashing and twisting in the air, its pincers couldn't reach far enough behind to get me. Of all its weapons, none compared to its menacing looks. From deep inside, a feeling rose up. I might've kissed Blacky except for its repulsive features, and so smiled instead.

Not about to give the insect a second chance, I dug my thumbnail into its upper tail and sliced off the stinger. A couple of drops of jellied liquid spilled but didn't sting, and I flung the remainder away. The desert would make short work of such a paper tiger.

Four more had to be defanged on the way to the middle of the pond bed, and I began to think myself fairly handy at it. After lifting off a crust of dry mud the size of a manhole cover and a short dig—Water! Slowly, the hole filled with a runny sludge, which I lowered my head into and sucked up, straining grit through my teeth, while spitting out solids, or most anyway. Unsure how my stomach would react to all the mud, though, I sat back and considered the pond and the nonworking windmill. Two more scorpions had to be disarmed and a relative of Blacky's, judging by its size and color, crawled out but quickly turned and hurried out of sight.

Considering the amount of moisture that remained under the pond bed, the windmill had to have worked not too long ago. Besides the doves flying around, the pond's outer sandbanks had animal tracks, plus droppings here and there. Some sort of desert life had been stopping by to see if the water returned. And yet, the windmill itself, with its rickety fan blades curled up the same as a wilted sunflower, hardly appeared workable. A ladder going up one side lacked half its rungs and ended at a platform that tilted badly to one side.

Having grown up among windmills, it only took one look to figure out why the fan faced the wrong way. The tail fin, which acted the same as a ship's rudder, had broken loose one of its anchoring chains, leaving it folded to one side, uselessly. Anyone could see how to fix it. The tail must be straightened and its anchoring chain reattached, so the sail fin could catch the wind and swivel the housing around. In order to do the repairs, though, some fool had to be crazy enough to climb that house-of-cards contraption—crazy enough or thirsty enough.

The rusty rungs on the ladder looked too untrustworthy, so I climbed by placing my feet on the angled cross braces while hanging on to one handrail. No sooner had I gotten halfway up than the blister on my palm popped. By wrapping my belt around the wound, it enabled me to climb using both hands.

Once at the top, I balanced on a platform so wobbly any hope of muscling the housing around was out of the question, but at least the entire unit wiggled back and forth enough to show the bearings hadn't frozen. To attach the chain link, after the one that'd broken off, I only needed an inch or so to reach the hook on the arm, but considering the manpower it'd take to stretch those unyielding metal links, it might as well have been a mile.

Discouraged and needing a breather anyway, I sat on the sturdier part of the platform with my legs dangling off the edge. A hawk drifted on the wind. What I wouldn't give to have a pair of wings like that. I'd fly back to Texas nonstop and take whatever punishment without grumbling. The hawk folded its wings and dove toward the desert floor like an arrow, but just before crash-landing, opened its wings and shot straight up toward the clouds. A few times of that and the hawk's motions gave me an idea.

I got up and checked the metal arm. Sure enough, a latch. Why hadn't I thought of that before? Although not a windmill mechanic, I'd taken sailboat lessons and knew, in a high wind, there must be a way to collapse the canvas to make repairs. The tail fan of the windmill had to work on the same principle. Otherwise, how could it ever be repaired on windy days?

I undid the latch, and the arm folded, bringing the tail fan within reach. Another catch on the broad plate doubled it over as well. With hardly any effort, then, I reattached the chain, and once the fin reopened, both latches locked automatically. The two chains snapped tight, and the bearings squeaked as the wind turned the housing. All that was left for me to do was to step over the arm as it swung by. The propeller, now facing the wind, turned with that familiar click-bang, click-bang, click-bang.

As soon as my feet touched the ground again, I put my hand in front of the fill pipe and felt faint puffs of air as soft as breathing, interrupted by occasional moist coughs. A mist coated my palm. During the fragile process, I didn't so much as move as a glistening bead trembled at the edge of the fill pipe. As pretty as any diamond, the drop fell and sizzled to nothing on the hot metal tub bottom. Others followed until a steady drip turned into a string of silver beads. I didn't dare put my head under for a sip, fearing that might somehow interrupt the flow. Now and then, gusts of wind shred the delicate stream.

Unable to stand it any longer, I eased my head underneath and tasted the first cool trickle splash inside my mouth, nip my dry tongue pleasantly, and trickle down an oh-so-parched throat. In a kind of delicious torture, the dribble wound all the way to my stomach, leaving a chilly path. I drank until a cramp in my neck forced me to stop, and then let the soothing liquid dribble on my sunburned skin. One scary moment occurred when the water turned bright red as the dried blood in my hair dissolved.

By late afternoon, the depth of water in the tank had risen above my fingernails. I lay down in it, turned over and over, and imagined swimming in the Z-shaped pool at the country club back home, although that clear, sparkling water never felt half as refreshing. A little before sunset, I knew better than to stay wet. The desert at night got as cold as the day had been hot. Back under the bush's meager shade, the splashing sound in the tub echoed like a waterfall hitting a tin basin. I had a hard time going to sleep for fear every thirsty animal within hearing distance would arrive by morning and suck up all *my* water.

❧❧

I AWOKE IN pitch dark, terrified. The branches above me had moved but not by any breeze. Something brushed against the bush, something big. I lay motionless; trying to think what animal out here could be that size. What else? Coyote! Now what to do? Should I try to outrun it? If I couldn't outrun Mauler, I'd never outrun a coyote. Worse yet, the scavengers often hunt in packs. Normally afraid of people, there's no telling what might happen if they thought me injured or dying.

At a wet blubbering sound, like something blowing its nose sloppily, I would've wept, except for knowing better than to make a peep. After a dull thud and a ring that sounded like a hoof knocking the metal side of the water tank, I eased onto my stomach. Another snotty snort was followed by an answering "Heee-ha-aw." Obviously, more mules than just one had arrived. All at once indignant, knowing exactly what they wanted, I had an urge to shout, "Hey! That's my water! Get away!" But then, just as quickly, I relaxed.

No telling how long I'd have stayed still like that, afraid to make the slightest movement, except that the animals kept stomping around. Any second, one might accidentally step on me. In the pale moonlight, three four-legged shapes kept plunging their heads into the tank next to the windmill. Because of their short legs and even shorter necks, the water level had not risen high enough for a drink. As if to prove my point, tempers flared as one mule shouldered another and then swung its heads like a mallet, while the third pawed the tank as though to turn it over. One of the quarrelers reared and backed away, coming near stepping on my head. That did it. I stood in a half-crouch and then eased up until full height.

Clearly startled, two mules sidestepped away while the one that had almost trampled me sprang to the side and galloped a short distance. Their long, jackrabbit ears perked, neither of us moved, but after a while, either they realized I meant no harm, or else their thirst got the better of them, and they returned to the tank while turning their heads now and then to look my way.

As I watched, one mule with only half an ear wheeled around and kicked the tank with both hind legs in several loud bangs. Seeing a way to help, I edged out of the bush and crept to the opposite side of the trough from the mules. They, in turn, backed away. Slowly crouching, I grasped the bottom of the tank and lifted the side, tilting it enough for them to reach the water. None of them moved. Maybe they didn't understand? Bracing the tub on my knees, I splashed the water. Half Ear trotted forward first, bobbed its head several times as if to make sure of no tricks, and then began lapping. The other two joined in. I suspected once they drank their fill, they'd leave, so I gently stroked each ones furry foreheads and removed burrs from their hair and untangled small knots.

All during this time, I'd been plotting how to improve our relationship. While petting Half Ear, I noticed stiff spines at the tip of its nose that, when touched, caused a whimper and a head toss. I could guess what happened.

Half Ear, possibly driven to recklessness by thirst, tried to nip off the juicy red fruit of a cactus and wound up with a pin-cushion snout full of needles. Anyone who'd ever picked those treacherous pears, as I'd done for my mother to make her prickly pear jelly, knew how badly the needles stung, but would Half Ear allow me to take them out? This wouldn't be easy. I'd learned the hard way that the arrowhead spines hurt when pulled out, but knowing the mule's agony, I had to try.

I set the tank down, which, judging by its weight had about been licked empty anyway, and began parceling out dipper-size handfuls from beneath the fill pipe. When Half Ear's turn came, while its rough tongue lapped water, I moved with the same quickness I'd used on Blacky and clamped thumb and forefinger on one of the spines. The mule jerked its head back, removing the needle. Half Ear reared up and let loose a painful "Hee-haaw!" and then dropped back down and shuddered. Surprisingly, the mule stood there. As tenderly as possible, I located each spine by feel and yanked out one after another, while at the same time patting the animal's furry neck, stirring up puffs of choking dust.

After removing all the needles, I scooped out the little water left in the tank and wet Half Ear's hot back and smoothed its musty pelt. The whole time, the same question kept going over in my mind: Would Half Ear allow me to climb on? I washed down all four knotty legs and used my fingers to comb through its fur while, ever so gently, reaching farther across to the opposite side of the animal's back, each time applying more of my weight. Whatever the mule's motive, whether the water, the cactus spines, the bath, or just plain good natured, Half Ear stayed still as, with a quick hop, I ended up seated in the middle of its back. The spinal column felt about as comfy as a row of sharp rocks, but even worse, we didn't move. Now what? Not about to risk a kick in the animal's ribs, and we certainly weren't on friendly enough terms for a swat on the rear end, then how to get us going? Everyone knows how stubborn mules can be. Should I then sit and wait for a mood change? That might take all night. Should I then get off and push or pull, but then who's to say I'd be allowed back on. Uncertain what to do, I leaned forward close to the ear stump. "Home, boy." Not too loud. "Take us home, Half Ear."

Off we trotted into the night with the other two mules in pursuit. As the click-banging of the windmill faded away, I regretted not having the presence of mind to take a last drink.

28

A Land That Never Got Rain

R<small>IDING BAREBACK ON</small> a half-starved mule the size of a Shetland pony proved anything but inactive. Bushes that didn't appear until the last second snagged my foot and tried to drag me off. I kept lifting one leg or the other or both at once to avoid them. Added to that, Half Ear's sharp backbone ridge underneath its wet fur worked like a blunt ax chopping me in half, forcing me to shift from side to side.

After we'd gone so far in the desert that there'd be no chance of me ever walking back to that windmill again, if I could even find it, Half Ear stopped. The other two mules did also. We stood three abreast, walled in by solid night. I hoped this only amounted to a breather or else a bathroom break. Still too timid to kick Half Ear in the ribs, I rocked back and forth whispering, "Giddy up," but I might as well have been on one of those coin-operated horses in front of the market. Finally, I decided it couldn't hurt to give Half Ear's rump a gentle tap.

The next thing I knew, I hit the ground backward. Half Ear squatted just long enough for me to tumble feet over head. The mule trotted off into the night. What'd I do wrong? A little tap on the rump? Football players do it all the time. What now? Even had I known the way back to the windmill, at night with no water and already thirsty, there'd be no chance.

I thought about chasing Half Ear, except the other two mules stayed behind. It seemed odd the three would split up. By the time I got back on my feet and had dusted off, one of the other mules stepped closer and pushed against me. Now what? Was I supposed to *pet it*? Or maybe a so-long hug before leaving me stranded in the desert? Before that, I'd...

What happened next brought me around like a slap on the cheek. The animal knelt down on its front knees in a sort of stepping stool posture, making it no more difficult to step aboard than to lift one leg. I sat on an even bonier back. As we resumed our journey, I fell on the mule's neck and stroked the fur, wet from my tears. "I didn't know!" I kissed its smelly, matted coat. "I didn't understand!"

Hot tears prevented me seeing the bushes coming, so I kept my legs locked straight over the mule's shoulders. At one point, I caught a watery glimpse of Half-Ear plodding beside and cried even harder. If only there was some way to apologize. How could I not know what a tiring load I must've been? Through the night, we changed mounts often.

At first light, a lone mountain stood above a lacy haze hovering along the surface of the desert. No longer sitting, I now lay atop Half Ear's back, trying to absorb the animal's warmth in the freezing night air. Houses appeared at the base of foothills. Except that it might frighten the mules, I'd have thrown my arms and legs out and hallooed a war whoop. The houses multiplied into a village, but before reaching town, we detoured to a corral.

The mules walked right up to the fence and put their necks over the top rail as if they'd done so a thousand times. After I slid off, my knees wouldn't unlock and, holding onto Half Ear's short mane, I lifted one leg at a time to work out the kinks. My jeans, inside my thighs, had so much gray hair glued on by sweat, how was it possible the animals had any left?

A pack of yapping dogs charged us. The mules wheeled around to face them, shoving me into the rail fence. I quickly climbed to the top rail, and would've stayed treed too but for an old man shouting. He leaned on a homemade crutch, hollering in Spanish from a tiny porch attached to a house about the size of the shack Hect and I burned down. The dogs tucked their tails and trotted off a ways.

The crippled man pointed with his gnarly crutch at the corral gate. After a wary look at the pack of mutts, I climbed down and opened it. The mules filed in one at a time as I hugged each ones neck, unable to recall feeling such strong emotion at parting from anyone before.

The man turned on his crutch and waved at me to follow. I stayed close to the fence as the dogs trotted along parallel, their tongues dangling over pointy teeth. At the last post, I dashed for the house with the pack chasing after, barking.

Once safely inside, I did a double take. The tiny kitchen had a table and two chairs in the center. The stove, sink, and four walls could almost be touched without rising from the table. The old man, whose ears looked clownishly large, greeted me with nods and a handshake. Neither he nor his short, barrel-shaped wife spoke English. She handed me a glass of water, which I gulped in one swallow practically. After several refills, she served scrambled eggs along with cold chicken, fried tortillas with butter, black beans, and a bottle of Coke, plus Oreo cookies, which seemed oddly American.

The couple watched me eat, him seated and her cooking. Judging by their grins, the more food I shoveled in, the more it pleased them. In the meantime, the dogs got inside, some wrestled under the table, others barked and yelped, and still others chased chickens through the house. Not until my third helping did I look around at the bare furnishings and realize what a sacrifice the meals meant.

The crippled farmer then led me through the house to a closet that, from its unfinished looks, had been added on recently. The walls had been waxed with a thick paste of some type, and a drain in the floor clued me to the room's purpose. Showering consisted of pouring a paint bucket full of cold water over my head—one to soap up and two to rinse—but a hot-and-cold shower at home never felt that good. After I dried off, the man handed me a robe so tattered and holey my mom would've cut it up for rags. He then gave me a cup of vinegar, indicating I should rub it over my sunburn, and did it ever ease the sting.

I slept most of the day until a rooster perched on my bed rail and let out a piercing "Cock-a-doodle-doo!" He got a pillow hurled at him for his trouble.

My clean clothes had been folded neatly on a chair, fresh with that outdoor-clothesline smell. Once dressed, I felt like a new person. That evening, we played volleyball with neighbor kids, while the old people sat under a tree and talked in Spanish. I had to admit, they entertained one another just fine without the modern gadgets of radio or phonograph. After volleyball, I pet the dogs and listened to the voices in the night. During the conversation, I understood that the crippled rancher, Bernardo, along with his wife, Maria, had suffered some kind of tragedy lately, as neighborhood women cried with both of them.

The next morning, everyone dressed for church, which surprised me, as I'd lost track of days in the desert. Maria gave me a string tie to wear and started calling me *desierto niño*, which I suspected meant something along the lines of "desert boy." I didn't mind, especially as the name brought tears to her eyes whenever she said it.

Across town, in a tiny, airless, stuffy room big enough to seat ten people, thirty crammed inside. I endured the entire church service without so much as a fan, squished between bodies on a hard wood bench, unable to scoot down in my usual slouch as my knees touched the backsides of those in front. Despite the discomfort, the church members seemed to have the times of their lives, but who could understand why. What reason did they have to be happy? Had they no idea how poor they were? How deprived? Or maybe they didn't know because no one was rich, and so they thought owning next to nothing normal?

After church, the members lunched together outside where the air moved a little at least. I sat next to the pastor who spoke English so well he hardly had an accent. Come to find out, he'd grown up in Yuma, Arizona. He'd already heard, no doubt from Bernardo, how I'd come out of the desert on the mules, and asked if I'd tell everyone at the table about it. I did, with the pastor translating, as the people sighed and nodded to each other. I credited God for everything, mainly because in such a religious setting it would be expected, even though deep down, I really hadn't made up my mind about all that.

Once the dishes had been cleared off, wet clothes were passed around to cool sweaty faces and necks. Seeing everyone so talkative and enjoying each other, an urge came over me. Why not tell about my promise to God to return home, confess my crimes and take whatever punishment? That would cause a sensation, wouldn't it? Wouldn't that put me back into the limelight? At the last moment, though, my nerve failed. Crestfallen, I knew what that meant. When the time came, I wouldn't have the courage to follow through.

Afterward, the pastor caught up to me. "Everyone is so happy, except you. Is something wrong?"

"No. I mean, well, yes. What I'm trying to say is there's something I have to do, but I don't want to, or can't, only I've got to, or…at least, I should."

"I see. Yes, that's a problem. Do you believe in God?"

How could he ask? Didn't he know that after hearing about my rescue, his own church members took me for practically a saint? "Well, sure."

"Yes, I see you do—in a God who rescues, but is that all? Do you also believe in a God you can count on? You can trust? Or is it just when you're in trouble and need help?"

"There's a difference?"

"When I lived in Arizona, I felt sad for the poor people in Mexico, but not to help, not to suffer with them. In America, I'd live better, own more stuff, provide for my family, and not deal with so much government corruption, but God promised to take care of me. So, I had to decide—do I trust Him? I admit, the decision was not easy, but I made up my mind, and I'm glad I did. Most people never get to know God beyond a rescuer. Would you like to?"

All at once feeling uneasy, I'd just gotten used to the notion of there even being a God, and now this? It seemed a good time to change the subject. "Right now, my main concern is to get across the border."

"Oh, that's easy," he said. "Bernardo, he will borrow Victor's truck. For the moment, it is broken, but they will, they will…how you say…

repair. Ah, yes, they will repair it. Sorry, the longer I live here, the more English words I lose—no one to talk with, you understand. Anyway, we have one other truck in town, but it's away because of getting supplies for the store. Don't worry, you'll be home by night."

"*Tonight?* As in, 'today?' I mean, so soon?" I faked a half laugh. "That fast, really?"

"Pardon my asking, but I have the feeling you're troubled. We have a saying around here: 'If you're pushing while pulling, don't strain.' You seem to be straining. Can I help?"

Why not? Who would he tell way out here in the middle of nowhere? Besides, I was sick to death of pretending. "Once back across the border in Texas, I'll have to go to jail."

He didn't say anything for a moment. "Live here, with us. Bernardo has no one to help with the farm. He was most delighted when you brought his mules back. The pay would not be much, but you will eat and be safe. In time, you will learn our language and feel at home."

"If only I could."

"You can. Bernardo and I talked about this last night while you played ball. He told me he wished for you to stay and help work his place. He says you're a good boy, he can tell, because the mules like you."

We laughed.

"You will be doing a good thing," he said, becoming serious. "His son disappeared. One day, he went into the desert and never came out. We looked but never found him. Bernardo, with his broken hip, needs help." He shook a gnarled finger to make a point. "Why go to jail? Policia will forget you. They have too many *mala hombres* to occupy them. This way, Bernardo will not lose his place one day. It's better for you to work than sit in a cage. We'll make a real caballero out of you—that's a 'cowboy,' for your beginning lesson in Spanish."

I thought about it. He'd told the truth. The authorities would forget one day. I could work, learn Spanish, live on the ranch, and maybe go home after however many years. At least I'd be free. Besides, what good would my going to jail do the poor hobo who burned up in the shack?

"You make Bernardo happy and stay, OK? This will be a good thing."

"There's only one problem." I thought I'd better get it all out. "I may have killed a man."

"You—?"

"But I'm not sure." I spoke hurriedly. "I may have, but then again, maybe not. I'd been seeing strange things that day so maybe I imagined it, I'm not sure."

"More reason to stay," he said, sounding relieved. "You must have time to rest and settle your mind and pray. God will guide you what to do."

"Speaking of that." I took a deep breath. The more we talked, the better I felt. It was as though all the turmoil and confusion I'd kept bottled up began to clear. "You see, in the desert, I made this promise to God. I swore if I ever got out alive, I'd go back and take my punishment."

I fully expected him, as the good pastor, to say something along the lines of God loves you and wouldn't want you to suffer among low-life criminals. No, you should do good deeds, attend church, and be happy.

"I see," the pastor said, a note of sorrow in his voice. "In that case, you must keep your word. That is honorable. I cannot argue."

Before I could gather my thoughts enough to backpedal, he called the church members to return to the table. After speaking to them in Spanish, they gathered around me, put their hands on my head and shoulders, and murmured. Their prayer lasted a long time without my saying a word, which, from my view, I'd said too much already.

☙∽❧

BERNARDO HOBBLED ON his crutch alongside me across a town square that looked much like something out of a Wild West movie. We headed for the tallest structure around—a tree with real leaves, no less. Half the tree appeared dead, and the rest went from pale green to yellow. Still, it reminded me of the Elm I used to climb as a kid, so big and roomy and strong. I hadn't seen one even close to that size since New Mexico. Within the tree's shadow, a man's legs stuck out from under the raised hood of an old pickup.

By midmorning, the temperature was already hot enough to be afternoon. Shade under the tree felt as cool as walking beneath a rain-cloud. Bernardo leaned on the fender next to the man's legs. After a while, they both emerged. Much younger than Bernardo, the man held up greasy palms to show why he couldn't shake hands.

"Victor," he said, wiping his palms on his shirt.

For an instant, I thought he'd declared 'success,' as in fixing the truck, but then realized he'd introduced himself. "I'm Tim!" I waved. "So, you got it running, I take it?"

The man glanced at Bernardo with a puzzled expression, showing that'd been too many words to handle in one burst, so I shortened it. "Just, Tim."

"Ah, Justin. Bueno, Justin."

I started to correct him, but then why bother? I'd been known as "desierto niño" up until now, why not "Justin" as well?

After tying the hood down with an extension cord, the three of us drove a short distance across town to a house with a high fence topped by barbwire. We parked next to a red, fifty-five-gallon barrel as a pregnant woman lumbered out of the house, smoking a long narrow stogie. She spit on the ash end and stuck the butt in her black hair over one ear. No sooner had she taken the lid off the barrel than gasoline fumes about gagged me. With a plastic pail, she dipped liquid out and funneled it into the truck's tank. The two men teased her, and all three laughed, not the least concerned about a live spark being left in that cigar ash. It reminded me of the last time fumes cut my wind, just before we threw the Molotov cocktail and set the shack on fire. I felt about as far away from their carefree fun as anyone could get.

The road through the desert appeared in dots and dashes of hard-packed dirt in the loose sand. Pot holes bucked us into the air so often I kept one hand braced against the roof. Now and then, we descended into a dry channel, crossed over a rocky bed from flood runoffs, climbed out, and then traveled through sand drifts so vast

Victor could only know the way by memory. On top of that, we had a flat tire that took up the rest the morning.

A sure sign of civilization appeared at last—a brown haze over Juarez, no doubt caused by everyone burning trash and all the open air cooking fires. The man-made cloud looked as big as an incoming sandstorm, only smoky yellow and flat on top.

A joy rose inside me that I'd escaped the desert at last, followed in the next moment by a dread of what lay ahead. How long of a prison term would I get? For burning an old shack, a slap on the wrist, but for taking a human life, even accidently, long enough to be old when I got out. The idea turned my stomach. All because of a last-minute promise. Who wouldn't make such a bargain when facing so horrible a death? Surely, God wouldn't consider such a pledge binding. Then again, what if there was another way? What if I hitchhiked to, oh, say, Alaska? Would that be breaking my vow, or just 'putting off' deciding for now? At least I'd be free. Not in jail.

Houses appeared at the base of the mountain. Once we reached Juarez, it'd be too late to change my mind and go live with Bernardo on his ranch. Time was almost gone. "OK, OK." I clutched Bernardo's arm, who flinched. "You talked me into it. I'll go back and live with you. Forget crossing the border. You're right—who needs arrest and prison? Not me. Only take me back with you. I'll work and learn and be safe."

The old man frowned. Victor glanced over with a puzzled squint. Of course, neither had understood a word and a good thing, too. How could I go back to live at the village? After my confession to the preacher and everyone praying for me, the whole town would know. Whoever met me on the street would see a coward who couldn't keep his word. No, that would never do. Forcing a smile, I pointed at Juarez as if that'd been the cause of the excitement.

Both men smiled and nodded.

As we drove around the city's outskirts, I watched for those over-sized tire prints, hoping to find the route we'd taken after escaping jail. At one point, we drove over a pair of grooves—big ones—but they went by so fast. Still, I made a mental note of the landmarks.

A long line of salt cedars marked where the Rio Grande ran along the Texas border. We parked atop a sandy ridge. Down below by the river, two wiry men dressed in chaps, spurs, and sombreros sat on horseback. They dismounted and untied a skiff floating on brown waters. From out of nearby bushes, a man, woman, and two kids lined up, waiting to cross. The family wished to bypass the inspection stations on the bridge, same as me.

I helped Bernardo down the embankment on his crutch. He spoke Spanish to one of the ferrymen, and some coins clinked. More sacrifices. Would I do the same for a stranger, especially a foreigner? Before I could figure the answer to that, the rancher came over and put his hands on my shoulders. "Vaya con Dios, amigo."

I looked into his face. His thick bronze skin, dark eyes, and those enormous ears—if only there was a way to tell him. He couldn't afford this, I knew. His and Maria's gifts only made their circumstances that much worse. But I'd pay them back…somehow. Oh, what's the use? Instead, I gave him a bear hug. He squeezed me back.

We both ended up with tears in our eyes as we struggled back up the sandy hill together. At the pickup, he reached inside and handed me a sack, a lunch made by Maria. Overwhelmed, I had to make him understand. "I'll pay you back, honest. You may not think so, and it may not look like it now, but I will. I swear!"

He shook his head agreeably, even though he couldn't have understood. I ran down the hill without looking back.

Seven of us ferried across the river, including the two men rowing. Once we got to the other side, I hurried up the bank, intending to throw a final wave at Bernardo, but the salt cedar stood too high. The brush grew so impossibly thick along the river bank that a few steps into it, and there'd be no way to tell which direction led to El Paso.

None of this deterred the family I'd ridden with as they plowed into the brush. I hurried after them. The smallest child had a hard time keeping up, so I carried her on my shoulders.

Salt cedar didn't last long, but next came sand hills, then towering crags and ravines so deep we had to slide down on our rears. I would've never found the way, and with the steamy heat off the river, just getting enough air meant panting twice as hard. When it seemed I couldn't keep up, especially with the little girl, the family stopped. They shared jars of water while I split Maria's lunch—lukewarm fried chicken, hardboiled eggs, and tortillas enough for all.

A truck down-geared in the distance, and my hopes sprang to life. Highway 80 couldn't be all that far away. Sure enough, over a rise and around a bend, cars shot past, speeding both directions. The family and I said good-bye. The little girl I'd carried most of the way motioned for me to bend down and kissed my cheek.

They waved the whole way headed back toward the city. What would become of them? Something made them cross the border—jobs or family or both. After they got out of sight, I surveyed an all-too-familiar desert. The wide, empty expanse no longer appeared such a scary place where everything either stung, stuck, bit, pricked, poked, or poisoned. Now it just looked like a land that never got rain.

The problem became which side of the highway to stand on. Across the blacktop led west to California and then north to Alaska. This side of the road meant home, arrest, and prison. How could that be a hard choice? Thirty feet amounted to two very separate and different lives—one, a new start, new identity, a buried past; the other shame, misery, and punishment. Little did I know that as I stood there debating the toughest decision of my life, directly across Highway 80 someone watched me.

29

An Odd Coincidence

TIRES SCREECHED, AND I looked across Highway 80 in time to see a car leap headlong into traffic, U-turn across two opposing lanes, and fishtail with its rear tires smoking. A speeding bus and a dump truck, going opposite directions, dodged into each other's lanes, barely missing one another. The car that almost caused the head-on collision swerved to the shoulder and parked in a cloud of dust. I couldn't have been more speechless had some lunatic valet pulled up.

Idling next to me, according to the dealer plate inside the front windshield, was a 1954 Studebaker Commander, with the loudest lime-green color I'd ever seen. No factory paint job, for sure, but who on earth would be dumb enough to repaint a brand-new car? I should've been glad maybe, but the second before the Studebaker pulled up, I'd already made up my mind to cross over the highway and head to Alaska.

"Hey!" The voice came through the open passenger window. "Which way, bucko?"

My head snapped around. Impossible! No, chance! Not that odd of a coincidence! I let go a sigh, realizing that everyone in these parts must call each other that.

Just the same, I approached the car cautiously and leaned over, putting my hands on my knees. Because of the low roof, the driver remained in the shadows. Unsure I wanted to get in, it seemed best to find out some information. "How far you going?"

"Webb Air Force Base."

I breathed easier. An airman, must be. For a second there, I had this off-the-wall idea that it might be Eli from the Pines Diner, but such a racy car didn't fit the cowboy's image at all. Still on edge, though, I had to ask. "Webb Air Force Base near Midland?"

"Forty miles t'other side in Big Spring."

I knew the place. Even though smaller than Midland, we'd played them in school sports every year.

"How come you to mention Midland, bucko? You headed there?"

Each time he called me that, I winced and, frankly, wished he'd find another nickname. "Not hardly. Anywhere but."

"My little brother's stationed at Webb. Come on. Hop in. We'll bypass Midland and go up through Kermit."

"Say, this's some car." I stepped back for one last look at the racy Studebaker. The roof came to my chest, and I'd not seen white walls so wide where they covered the entire tire. Once inside, I sat on pinstriped upholstery and admired a curved dashboard of shiny vinyl and round gauges edged in chrome. Had my luck changed? How often did a guy get such a ride? Anyhow, what harm would a little side trip do? Once we reached Big Springs, there'd be plenty of time to go whichever direction from there would take me to Alaska. "She smells brand new." I stroked the polished dash. "Bet she's fast."

"Yep, she is. Where to, bucko—not *west* again, I hope."

My head whipped around so fast my neck crackled. No longer wearing a cowboy hat, long sleeves, and padded vest, he now sported a baseball cap, Hawaiian shirt, and cutoff jeans. Except for calling me "bucko," I'd never recognized him. I grabbed the door handle.

"Hold on, bucko. Where you off to?"

"I...I...I..." My mind raced for an excuse. "I forgot, I'm going the other way."

"Calm down and shut the door. Geez, what's wrong with you?"

I did what he said, reluctantly. "I, ugh, well...you're not mad at me?"

"Why? Cause you run off from the diner and left me shorthanded? Naw, not no more. At first, maybe. Oh, I'd'a skin't you up some, especially when I had to wash dishes, but that's over."

I still couldn't believe it. He acted so different. "Eli?"

"Crazy, ain't it?" He laughed. "I was gassing up at the truck stop yonder." He pointed at lines of eighteen-wheelers parked row after row that I hadn't even noticed.

"You said you was headed to El Paso at the diner," he continued, "so I come this way and been looking high and low for you. I asked at the bus stop, and the gal remembered you, said she thought you went to Mexico. I've probably asked a dozen hitchhikers if they'd seen hide nor hair of you and was about to give up, when, glory be, there you was standing like you'd been waiting the whole time."

So, it hadn't been such a coincidence after all. He'd been searching for me, but for what reason? Because of the food I took before leaving? That made no sense. Why chase me all this way for a hunk of ham and a bottle of milk? Nothing added up. "Where's your pickup, Eli?"

"Repo'ed. I got behind, and them sneaking snakes snuck up one night and taken it back, so I brought this here spank new one. Painted her myself. They won't find it so easy next time."

"What about the Pines Diner?"

"Left it. Too much work, not enough moolah. Let the bank take it back. I ain't slaving for nothing."

"Your ranch?"

"Gone. Mortgage payments about did me in. And you're forever having to cut weeds and prop up fences and the like. 'T'warn't no life for me."

"Snowball?"

"Hist'ry. She was messing with my nerves anyhow. Always nagging about my drinking and partying out late. If it don't suit me to come home till dawn, so what? No one appreciates nothing I do for them."

I felt a twinge inside, thinking he might have me on that list. "Sorry for leaving the diner in a rush like that, after you were nice enough to give me a job and a place to stay. If it wasn't for you, I don't know where I'd ended up."

"'Bout time someone noticed. Anyhow, I got tired of the diner. Durn health department had shut me down three times already and was about to the fourth when, one morning after an all-nighter, I lit out. Didn't take time to pack. Borrowed what I got on from an old gal's hubby, but I hate it for my Stetson. He got him a dang good hat."

I envied how little Eli cared about giving his word. It certainly wouldn't bother him to break a promise to God, or anyone else for that matter. He may have absolutely nothing in his character to admire, but he wasn't burdened by feeling obligated either.

"So, bucko, like I was saying, I got me a plan. I'm on my way to pick up my brother after talking him into going AWOL from the air force. I figure me and him, and now you too, can form up a gang. You and him can be my followers."

He didn't say it like a joke either. So that was why he'd been looking for me. He must've seen in me something that would make a good soldier for him to general around.

For the next several hundred miles, I found out exactly what he'd meant by "follower." Roll down the window, bucko, roll it up, back down, and so on; switch radio stations, bucko, switch back, switch again; push your side mirror out, bucko, back in, back out, in-out, adjust the rearview mirror on the dash even though he could reach it just as easily. On and on the orders went until he hadn't meant a "follower" at all but a slave.

On the outskirts of Big Spring, we stopped to fill up. While the gas station attendant cleaned the windshield, Eli and I went inside. As soon as we got past the front door, he leaned over the counter, opened the cash register, stole a twenty, and stuck it in *my* pocket. Snickering, he ambled to the restroom while I stifled an urge to scream bloody murder. Now I really saw what a "follower" meant—someone to do his dirty work.

On the other side of the front window, the attendant bent over to check the tire pressure and, thankfully, hadn't seen us. Unable to think what else to do, I tossed the twenty behind the counter, hoping the gas station guy would think it'd fallen out of the register, and then hurried outside where he could see me.

I knew Eli had only begun. He meant trouble, big trouble, and I needed to escape before his brother got in the mix. But how far could I run in broad daylight? In a one-horse town like Big Spring, there'd be little chance of finding a place to hide. Not only that—what excuse could I give Eli for where the stolen twenty went?

A highway patrol car pulled into the station. The black and white cruiser parked on the other side of the gas pump from the Studebaker. The attendant went over and started talking in the driver-side window. Unable to move, I felt trapped.

Was this another odd coincidence? Maybe, but in my mind a highway patrol showing up at that moment meant only one thing—I had a choice to make. Like the time Blacky and I faced each other, the question came down to now or never. As the attendant put gas in the tank, I took a deep breath and let it out slow; then walked over to the black and white car. An officer shuffled papers behind the steering wheel. He looked up with the steeliest gray eyes ever. I exhaled long and slow again. "Good morning, Officer."

He frowned. "It's afternoon."

"Afternoon, then." My words came out fast. "Can I talk to you?"

The man had a red welt across his forehead and a sweat ring pressed into his short brown hair from the cowboy hat sitting on the seat next to him. "That's what we're doing, right?"

"Yes, it is. I'm wrong again." He sure wasn't making this any easier. "May I get in?"

"You can tell me what you want from there, can't you?"

"I guess I can, sorry." I never remembered being so nervous. "Well, sir, you see, that is, well…" Might as well blurt it out. "I'm wanted."

"Wanted?" His eyes turned even steelier. "In that case, come to think of it, maybe you better have a seat." He stepped out, holding a clipboard and pen ready. "Are there any warrants out on you, son?"

"Probably."

"Probably?" he repeated, sounding as if he hadn't cared for that answer. He scribbled something down. "So, you're not sure, but you did commit a crime?"

"Probably." I really hadn't meant to say that a second time, but at that moment, Eli came out of the station. His eyes got big, his chin dropped, and he made a beeline for the Studebaker. At the sound of squealing tires, the trooper looked up as the sleek car sped out of the station. He turned back to me. "Did you just say 'probably' again?"

"Well, sir, I'm not sure, but I think so. It's all very confusing."

"What the devil kind of crime are you not sure you might or might not have committed?"

"Well...I think...maybe hurting, or, no, killing someone by accident, or maybe not."

He dropped his clipboard to his side and put his pen in his front pocket. "Now look, son, let's not play games. Seems to me you either did it or you didn't. Which is it?"

"I didn't mean to—if I did, that is. Can I tell you from the beginning?"

"After I clamp the cuffs on you and put you in the backseat. I may end up hauling you across the highway to the bug farm if you don't start making better sense."

I glanced at a complex of red brick buildings surrounded by old elm trees. He meant Big Springs State Mental Hospital. The place had a reputation around West Texas for keeping penned up the worst criminal madmen. The sight gave me the willies. After he bent my arms behind my back and snapped cuffs on my wrists, I took a seat in the back of the patrol car.

I told my story without stopping except for when, unable to hold it longer, I asked to go to the restroom. He undid the cuffs and, while I went inside the station, moved the car into the shade. When I came out, he didn't cuff me this time.

I finished my confession, leaving out the part about Eli. The officer rubbed his hand over his short-cropped flattop. "Well, that's one for the books, I'll grant you." He paused. "You know, for little of nothing, I'd haul you out to that junkyard myself. You got me curious, but it's not my jurisdiction. Too bad, I'd like to see how everything ends up, but I've got no choice. You'll have to remain at the Big Spring

Courthouse until they come over from Midland. Sorry, son, you look like a decent enough sort."

It took maybe five minutes to drive across town to a two-story courthouse. Out back, a concrete block structure had barred windows. Barely bigger than a garage, I shivered at seeing such a tiny jail, but then, how bad could it be after Juarez? At least it had a roof, probably a bed and a toilet too.

The sheriff went inside the courthouse, leaving me in the car. Two squirrels ran around the lawn, looking so playfully free and light-hearted. I thought about Hect. Right then, I'd have given anything to swap places with him. Or, come to think of it, would I? That depended on what went on at the "camp," as Ju called it, whatever that was. One thing, though, I wished we'd been able to stay together. It never seemed half so bad to face troubles with him along.

I didn't have to wait in the jail after all. The Big Spring sheriff's secretary said to seat me on a bench outside her office until they came from Midland. I sat there without handcuffs and eavesdropped on her and the highway patrolman. The Big Spring sheriff had been called out on an emergency. Seems a farmer overturned a tractor, barely avoiding being crushed, and ended up trapped underneath the heavy machine with gasoline spilling. Afraid the hot motor might ignite the fuel, the sheriff rushed "out'a here like a house afire."

Oh, pity the poor farmer, but not again. Please, not yet another version of someone being burned alive. What became of troubles like drowning or falling off heights or armed robberies? Must everyone in the world burn up just to make me feel guilty?

The secretary sat behind a large, black typewriter that hid all her head except for a bun of gray hair like a bird nest atop the black carriage. On his way out the door, the highway patrolman said good-bye and even patted my shoulder, meaning either "good luck" or "too bad"—I wasn't sure which.

I eyed the door he closed. Outrunning the secretary would be a snap, if she even got out of her chair in time to see me go. It seemed too easy, as though they'd left me by the door to see if I'd try it. They needn't have bothered. I'd already run once and knew how that turned out. Sure, I'd maybe avoid a trial, the shame, prison, but hitchhiking up through New Mexico, escaping the Juarez jail, barely missing being mashed by a truck, surviving the Mexican desert, nearly dying under a scorching sun, and then being saved by mules and Bernardo and Maria—it'd all be for nothing. I'd end up right back where I started. No, I'd made up my mind.

∽∽∂∾∞∾

ONE LOOK OUT the courthouse window ended any thoughts of escape. A white Ford pulled to the curb, the same one that'd parked that night in the desert ravine. The sheriff couldn't drive the forty miles from Midland that fast unless he'd either been over here already or else out on Highway 80. So that was why they hadn't put me in jail. Had I gone ahead and bolted out the door, the sheriff would've been right there, waiting.

All at once I felt old, as if waking up after dreaming about being young, like Rip Van Wrinkle. Then again, maybe those happy-go-lucky times ended when Hect and I set the shack on fire.

A shuffling sound of boots climbing the wooden staircase outside made my heart pound. The brass doorknob turned as, along with it, my insides twisted into knots. The wooden plank started inward but stopped half-open. More torture.

The last time I'd heard that voice, now making small talk with a second man outside, the sheriff had been calling, "Mauler! Mauler!" which added yet another worry. What would happen when he found out I was to blame for his dog being killed on Highway 80? How mad would he get then? Would I even make it back to Midland? The sheriff and the other man laughed. How could they find anything funny while I waited inside, suffering?

A tall, rectangle of a man with a star on his chest, a large gun on his hip, and pant legs stuffed into his boot tops, stepped inside. As he removed his cowboy hat, we traded looks. I shrank under the gaze, wanting to slide off the bench and crawl underneath. He, on the other hand, lifted one side of a crooked smile, reminding me of the smirking disapproval the moon wore that night on the back of the truck. Everyone's a critic.

Without so much as a hello, he walked into the secretary's office. From the sounds, he and the woman must've been pals. Once again, I listened to an account of the accident involving the man on the tractor and the sheriff leaving like a "house 'a' fire."

Oh, please, won't someone take pity on me? One measly kind word, was that too much to ask? Or, maybe a friendly smile? Did no one care that I tried to do the right thing and turn myself in?

When the sheriff came back out, he jerked his thumb in a get-up motion. I expected to be put in the backseat of the Ford, but he opened the front door instead, making me feel a little less a convict. A radio on the floorboard squawked in between bursts of static.

The entire trip, the sheriff said not one word, while I repeated my confession. I reached the end as a cluster of buildings poked up out of the mesquite. The tall skyline of oil companies made Midland seem a much larger city than it was. That's the reason my hometown had earned the nickname "Tall City," even though not really a city at all.

"Let me get this straight," the sheriff said at last as we passed under those power lines that cut diagonally across Highway 80, the same ones that'd served as landmarks that night in crossing the desert. "You and this buddy of yours—Hect, you say his name is?"

I couldn't believe it. Unthinkingly, I'd mentioned Hect's name. Dumb me; that's exactly what I'd intended *not* to do. Why bring him into it? That hadn't been the plan at all. As if I didn't feel low enough already, here I'd gone and stabbed my best pal in the back. Well, nothing could be done about it now. "Yes, sir."

"OK, so the two of you started that fire east of town in that old, fallen-down office at the junkyard. Now I got it. But tell me this, did either of you have anything to do with the crime that went on out there?"

That stumped me. Had he heard a word I'd said? I felt like saying, "What do you think the whole point of my confession was?" But instead bit my tongue. "Yes, sir, we did."

The sheriff slowed the Ford down for a rickety pickup loaded with workers riding in the back bed. The pickup followed a three-axle, oilfield work-over rig. Part equipment, part trailer house, part derrick, the work-over rig had layers of dirt, grease, and grime coating it, which may have been all that held it together. I half expected either vehicle to fall to pieces any second.

"How exactly?" the sheriff asked after a moment. "I mean, in what way were you two involved in the crime?"

Talk about weird. How could I make it any clearer? "Like I told you, sir, the man died, or, at least, he must've of in that fire, after we threw the Molotov cocktail, although like I said, we didn't mean it."

"How do you mean *died?* Who're you talking about now?"

That left me blank as could be. I didn't know what to say.

"Who died, I mean?" he asked again. "What's that about?"

If it was this hard to confess, how did bad guys ever get caught, was what I'd like to know. How many times must I say so? "The man in the window, sir, like I told you. He was inside the shack and burned up with the fire. I saw him, or at least I think I did. Like I said before, there were a lot of flames and smoke and such. I couldn't see clearly."

The sheriff half turned, looking at me instead of the road, while I glanced to the front, worried the driver of the pickup might slow down suddenly and we'd rear-end him. "So, that's what this is all about." He turned back to the front. "There's been a killing, you say, and you're itching to take the blame for it."

That was a strange way of putting it, to say the least, but something else occurred to me. "You found his body, didn't you, sir?"

"Not actually, no."

"But you looked through the ashes of the shack, right?"

"Sure we did." The engine moaned in acceleration and we swung out around both trucks at once. Angling back into the right lane, he slowed down. "Not carefully enough, apparently."

"So then…" I never guessed admitting guilt would be this difficult. "So then, whoever the poor fellow was, he's still *out there?*"

The sheriff pulled to the side of the road and parked. He put his arm along the seat back and stared me in the eye. "This is mighty serious, son. It's not a game, you understand?" The two oilfield trucks passed us. "I want you to think carefully about what you're saying."

I wondered if all criminals had this hard a time going to jail. "But I gave up on my own, voluntarily, I mean." I felt it important to remind him. "Doesn't that count for something?"

"Oh, everything, you kidding? No one's reported a killing or, for that matter, even filed a missing persons report. All we got for evidence is your testimony. The prosecutor will call you as his star witness." He pulled the Ford back onto Highway 80. Cars lined up behind us, no doubt afraid to pass. "I just want you to know beforehand, you better not be trying to make a fool out of me. I wouldn't care for that."

"Me! You mean, *me?*"

"Shoot, yeah, we get phony confessors all the time in my line— guilt-ridden old boys who admit to crimes they hadn't no more committed than a jackrabbit. Who knows what drives them? Maybe the notion they ain't been punished enough by their folks, so they make stuff up. It wastes lots of our time."

We passed those same two oil trucks again. This time, the workers waved.

What the sheriff said never entered my mind before now. It put things in a different light altogether. Maybe what I saw really had been an illusion. He made guilt and the tricks it plays on the mind sound so common like it happened all the time. If true, that explained everything, but there was only one way to find out for sure. "Sir, can we drive out there? It's not far. I'm not sure how to go exactly, but the place is right outside of town."

"I know the way. Who you think investigated the fire?"

"Then can we go?"

"There's only one problem, and maybe something you might think about. Should we find a body, I'll have to take you in on the spot."

Why worry about that? I didn't. Not anymore. Everything had been cleared up. What other explanation could there be? The whole incident had been solved—the phantom, the fiery image in the window, my guilt over not being punished—I'd made the entire fantasy up in my mind. After all I'd been through, worried about, fretted over, who wouldn't want to go out there and uncover the truth? To get this burden off my shoulders, why, I could hardly wait. "No, sir, I'm not afraid."

"It's up to you, sonny." The sheriff gave me a sideways look. "But don't say I didn't warn you."

I didn't like the sound of that. Did he know something? Had I been too hasty? What if we actually found human ashes? It wouldn't be the first time I'd acted impulsively lately. I should've left well enough alone. Why jump to conclusions like that? Wouldn't it have been better to come out by myself later and found out the truth? Now it was too late. Changing my mind at this point would look suspicious. An image came to mind of buzzards swarming through the shack's debris, struggling over pieces of cooked meat in the rubble. What then? Bracing myself for the worst, I had no idea what to expect.

We turned off Highway 80 onto a narrow, two-tire-rut trail through the mesquite. Thorns clawed the sides of the Ford. Once we got past the brush and into a clearing, the junkyard looked the same as I remembered—cars stacked two high, others lying on their sides, others wrecked, others upside-down or stripped to bare rusty frames. Nothing had changed. I hoped the sheriff hadn't noticed all the bullet holes that'd spider-webbed car windows.

The shack, on the other hand, didn't appear at all as I expected. The burned ruins had been sorted into neat stacks—charred lumber placed in order of lengths; strips of metal and electric wiring arranged in a tangled clump; plumbing fixtures, such as pipes and hydrants piled in a heap—and then any large, partly burned pieces like a chunk of shingled roof and part of a wall had been set off from the rest.

One look and it was obvious what it all meant. A crime scene! What else? The parts so tidily separated and sorted by type could only amount to one thing. The reason I'd insisted on coming out had been to prove no crime happened, but it turned out just the opposite. Once again, everything backfired on me. I hadn't imagined any hallucination. There really had been someone in that window, and whoever had burned up died a horrible death.

And yet, hold on one second. How come the sheriff acted like they hadn't found anyone? With only a halfhearted try, they must have come across human remains. A body doesn't burn up to nothing and vanish in smoke. What possible purpose could it serve to act like there'd been no crime? He didn't seem the type who'd taunt somebody or play a cruel practical joke, but what other explanation could there be?

As we drove closer, I noticed a blackened ball off to one side that looked different from the other piles. The peculiar heap didn't seem to belong to any part of a house. To call the sight odd would've been an understatement. A melted, plastic-like glob the size of a boulder had fur clumps, shreds of shiny fabrics, satiny cloths, sparkly material, and strips of silk hanging off in tatters, but compared to what else jutted out of the tar globe, the clothing was hardly noticeable. Legs, feet, arms, hands on wrists, and round objects that had to be skulls poked up out of that molten clump like spikes on a giant cocklebur.

"One hobo, my hind foot!" The sheriff gasped, slamming on the brakes. A cloud of dust swept past us. "Sonny, you burnt up a whole bum village!"

I stared ahead, speechless. Sure enough, less than a stone's throw away, what looked like hot lava had hardened, trapping everyone inside it. I tore my eyes away from the gruesome sight to glance at the sheriff, then back to the ball of body parts, then back to the sheriff, then back to the massacre, and finally back to the sheriff. The lawman collapsed onto the steering wheel in laughter, then jerked backward in his seat, hallowing.

I thought he would never stop. He dragged out his handkerchief and wiped tears from his eyes and drool off his chin. "There's…your… crime…sonny," he managed. "Burned…the lot, you…you…" He fell apart again. "Burnt…every…last one, you…coldhearted butcher."

I'd been the butt of jokes before at the gag shop, but for the life of me, I couldn't figure out this one.

"Dummy!"

That seemed a little over the top and, frankly, beneath the dignity of a sheriff to rub it in like that.

"All of them—dummies."

I waited for the punch line.

"Don't you get it, sonny? *Mannequins.*"

One more look at the black globe of body parts and the fog began to clear even though, at the same time, nothing made sense.

"The shack was full of them," the sheriff went on. "In the whirl-wind of heat off that fire, one of them figures rolled up on casters in front of the window. That's who you seen ablaze. If you'd stayed a little longer, you'd watched the dummy melt and drape over the window ledge, bubbling like a skillet full of hot oil. We found the puddle. Not only was the shack full of them, but also a goodly amount of women's expensive clothes. That's them all melted together."

"You mean, or, what you're telling me…there're *no warrants*?"

"None." He chuckled. "At least not on you. Oh, the look on your face—priceless! Maybe I let the joke run on a bit too long, but I figured it wouldn't do any harm for you to learn a lesson you're not likely to forget. Maybe you'll think twice next time before pulling anymore mischief, eh?" He smiled as if pleased. "No, there're no warrants out on you, son."

"So, a while ago, when you acted like you didn't know anything, you were just, well, pulling my leg?"

"Not altogether." The smile left his face. "I also wanted to see if you'd developed some character along the way. I got to admit, you have. Otherwise, when I gave you a chance to back out and forget about everything, you'd have jumped on it."

Before I let myself feel too relieved, I wanted to make sure there'd be no surprises later on. "But, the fire? I mean, we did burn the place down."

"And solved a crime. Because of that fire, we caught us a crook, a fraud, and a tax cheat all at once. A while ago, a dress shop here in town burned to the ground. The insurance money would've kept the lady who owned it from bankruptcy. According to her story, a thief broke into her store one night, stole all her merchandise, and set the place afire. It seemed a little too handy for me, so I went to the insurance company and got the payment delayed. Only, I couldn't come up with any real proof. Might never have, except you set that shack ablaze. The firemen come across her stash, and it was easy to find out she owned title to this junkyard. Case solved, thanks to the luckiest pair of juvenile delinquents to ever dodge justice. Before we nabbed her, though, she skipped and is hiding out in France, last I heard."

I looked back at the crime scene. "So that ball's nothing but clothes and dummies?"

"Which reminds me, if you'll help me load that baby in the trunk, we'll take it back with us. We've got pictures and all, but it ought to be inside the evidence warehouse in case she ever comes back to Texas. My useless deputy should have done that already."

I sat back, trying to process it all. "You mean, I'm free? I really am free?"

"That's about the size of it, sonny boy."

I still could hardly believe it. "So, there's no crime at all?"

"Nope."

"And all this has all been for nothing?"

"Not exactly. For uncovering the fraud and saving the insurance company from having to pay for the store's merchandise, there's a reward. Something in the neighborhood of a couple of thousand, last I heard."

"*Dollars!*"

"You'll have to claim it, but I'll verify everything."

"Well, can you beat that?" I still couldn't grasp it all. "Of course, I'll split it with my friend, Hect."

"Oh, your buddy, that's right. Where'd he end up?"

"Lost out in the desert somewhere on the backside of Old Mexico. He doesn't know he's innocent or about the reward or anything."

"I can't wait to hear about that."

"If you don't mind, I'll tell you later."

About the Author

WH Buzzard is not only the author's pen name, it's also a nickname given to him in high school. The joke in those days was that he was so skinny, he couldn't be seen when he turned sideways. All the teasing was offered in good fun, though, and one day fortune smiled from a most unlikely source.

His speech teacher, a normally cranky older lady, must have thought the shy boy in back of her room who was so reticent when called upon to give a speech, needed encouragement. Whatever her reasoning, she informed her students that, after reading a paper written by him, she saw writing talent. She even read the homework assignment to all her classes. Although the compliment was never forgotten, it was years later when it finally bore fruit. During an especially lonely time in life, he started writing. It became a godsend. His personality changed as he wrote and told stories to anyone who would listen. His greatest joy came from making other people laugh. That's still true today.

However, having done below average in school, his worst marks coming in English, he had to learn the craft of writing from scratch. He taught himself by reading every book he could find. He read with a novel, usually a classic, in one hand and a dictionary in the other (Boy, would a Kindle have come in handy then). Some stories he not only read, but then analyzed, dissected and reconstructed to see how authors, such as Mark Twain, did it. In fact, *There is a Generation,* draws a subtle comparison between Missouri in the mid 1800s to West Texas in the mid 1900s. Like Twain's classics, the story is a boyhood adventure that satirizes society. Thus, the sub-title 'Kids of the Greatest Generation.'

Although he'll forever be a West Texan at heart, he now lives in Central Texas with his wife, who is one of his most ardent and particular editors. If he's not working on the sequel to his first book, *There is a Generation II,* due out in the fall of 2015, he'll either be at the pool swimming laps, reading, taking walks or attending church.

In summary, WH Buzzard spent half his life living this action/adventure tale, with its troubles, fiascos, adventures, humor, hardships, and ended up finding out how to be grateful and glad for them all. Then he spent the second half of his life writing this book.

There is a Generation is his debut novel.

If you enjoyed reading the book or have a suggestion, please leave a review. For advance notice of publication on further adventures of Tim and Hect, leave your email address with the title "Sequel" at whbuzzard@gmail.com. I take your privacy seriously and will not sell your email or contact you in anyway except to notify you of the exact date the sequel will be available.

Made in the USA
Columbia, SC
05 June 2021